Palgrave Shakespeare Studies

General Editors: **Michael Dobson** and **Dympna Callaghan**

Co-founding Editor: **Gail Kern Paster**

Editorial Advisory Board: **Michael Neill**, University of Auckland; **David Schalkwyk**, Folger Shakespeare Library; **Lois D. Potter**, University of Delaware; **Margreta de Grazia**, University of Pennsylvania; **Peter Holland**, University of Notre Dame

Palgrave Shakespeare Studies takes Shakespeare as its focus but strives to understand the significance of his oeuvre in relation to his contemporaries, subsequent writers and historical and political contexts. By extending the scope of Shakespeare and English Renaissance Studies the series will open up the field to examinations of previously neglected aspects or sources in the period's art and thought. Titles in the *Palgrave Shakespeare Studies* series seek to understand anew both where the literary achievements of the English Renaissance came from and where they have brought us.

Titles include:

Pascale Aebischer, Edward J. Esche and Nigel Wheale (*editors*)
REMAKING SHAKESPEARE
Performance across Media, Genres and Cultures

James P. Bednarz
SHAKESPEARE AND THE TRUTH OF LOVE
The Mystery of 'The Phoenix and Turtle'

Silvia Bigliazzi and Lisanna Calvi (*editors*)
REVISITING THE TEMPEST
The Capacity to Signify

Mark Thornton Burnett
FILMING SHAKESPEARE IN THE GLOBAL MARKETPLACE

Carla Dente and Sara Soncini (*editors*)
SHAKESPEARE AND CONFLICT
A European Perspective

Cary DiPietro and Hugh Grady (*editors*)
SHAKESPEARE AND THE URGENCY OF NOW
Criticism and Theory in the 21st Century

Darlene Farabee
SHAKESPEARE'S STAGED SPACES AND PLAYGOERS' PERCEPTIONS

Kate Flaherty, Penny Gay and L. E. Semler (*editors*)
TEACHING SHAKESPEARE BEYOND THE CENTRE
Australasian Perspectives

Lowell Gallagher and Shankar Raman (*editors*)
KNOWING SHAKESPEARE
Senses, Embodiment and Cognition

Daniel Juan Gil
SHAKESPEARE'S ANTI-POLITICS
Sovereign Power and the Life of the Flesh

Stefan Herbrechter and Ivan Callus (*editors*)
POSTHUMANIST SHAKESPEARES

David Hillman
SHAKESPEARE'S ENTRAILS
Belief, Scepticism and the Interior of the Body

Anna Kamaralli
SHAKESPEARE AND THE SHREW
Performing the Defiant Female Voice

Jane Kingsley-Smith
SHAKESPEARE'S DRAMA OF EXILE

Katie Knowles
SHAKESPEARE'S BOYS
A Cultural History

Lori Leigh
SHAKESPEARE AND THE EMBODIED HEROINE
Staging Female Characters in the Late Plays and Early Adaptations

Rory Loughnane and Edel Semple (*editors*)
STAGED TRANSGRESSION IN SHAKESPEARE'S ENGLAND

Stephen Purcell
POPULAR SHAKESPEARE
Simulation and Subversion on the Modern Stage

Erica Sheen
SHAKESPEARE AND THE INSTITUTION OF THEATRE

Kay Stanton
SHAKESPEARE'S 'WHORES'
Erotics, Politics and Poetics

Alfred Thomas
SHAKESPEARE, DISSENT AND THE COLD WAR

Deanne Williams
SHAKESPEARE AND THE PERFORMANCE OF GIRLHOOD

Paul Yachnin and Jessica Slights
SHAKESPEARE AND CHARACTER
Theory, History, Performance, and Theatrical Persons

Palgrave Shakespeare Studies
Series Standing Order ISBN 978–1–403–91164–3 (hardback)
978–1–403–91165–0 (paperback)
(*outside North America only*)

You can receive future titles in this series as they are published by placing a standing order. Please contact your bookseller or, in case of difficulty, write to us at the address below with your name and address, the title of the series and the ISBN quoted above.

Customer Services Department, Macmillan Distribution Ltd, Houndmills, Basingstoke, Hampshire RG21 6XS, England

Shakespeare's Staged Spaces and Playgoers' Perceptions

Darlene Farabee
Associate Professor of English, University of South Dakota, USA

© Darlene Farabee 2014
Softcover reprint of the hardcover 1st edition 2014 978-1-137-42714-4

All rights reserved. No reproduction, copy or transmission of this publication may be made without written permission.

No portion of this publication may be reproduced, copied or transmitted save with written permission or in accordance with the provisions of the Copyright, Designs and Patents Act 1988, or under the terms of any licence permitting limited copying issued by the Copyright Licensing Agency, Saffron House, 6–10 Kirby Street, London EC1N 8TS.

Any person who does any unauthorized act in relation to this publication may be liable to criminal prosecution and civil claims for damages.

The author has asserted her right to be identified as the author of this work in accordance with the Copyright, Designs and Patents Act 1988.

First published 2014 by
PALGRAVE MACMILLAN

Palgrave Macmillan in the UK is an imprint of Macmillan Publishers Limited, registered in England, company number 785998, of Houndmills, Basingstoke, Hampshire RG21 6XS.

Palgrave Macmillan in the US is a division of St Martin's Press LLC, 175 Fifth Avenue, New York, NY 10010.

Palgrave Macmillan is the global academic imprint of the above companies and has companies and representatives throughout the world.

Palgrave® and Macmillan® are registered trademarks in the United States, the United Kingdom, Europe and other countries.

ISBN 978-1-349-49103-2   ISBN 978-1-137-42715-1 (eBook)
DOI 10.1057/9781137427151

This book is printed on paper suitable for recycling and made from fully managed and sustained forest sources. Logging, pulping and manufacturing processes are expected to conform to the environmental regulations of the country of origin.

A catalogue record for this book is available from the British Library.

Library of Congress Cataloging-in-Publication Data

Farabee, Darlene, author.
Shakespeare's Staged Spaces and Playgoers' Perceptions / Darlene Farabee.

pages cm. — (Palgrave Shakespeare Studies)

Includes bibliographical references and index.

1. Shakespeare, William, 1564–1616—Dramatic production.   2. Shakespeare, William, 1564–1616—Criticism and interpretation.   I. Title.
PR3091.F37 2014
792.9'5—dc23   2014022915

Typeset by MPS Limited, Chennai, India.

for Paul

Contents

List of Figures viii

Acknowledgments ix

Note on Texts xi

Introduction 1

1 Perceptions and Possibility in *A Midsummer Night's Dream*: "To leave the figure or disfigure it" 15

2 Grounded Action and Making Space in *Richard II*: "How comest thou hither?" 42

3 Narrative and Spatial Movement in *Hamlet*: "To find his way" 70

4 Place, Perception, and Disorientation in *Macbeth*: "A walking shadow" 98

5 Direction and Space in *The Tempest*: "Through forth-rights and meanders" 126

Conclusion: Movements of Genre and Other Directions: "As strange a maze" 155

Bibliography 169

Index 177

List of Figures

5.1   The scenes of *The Tempest*   130

Acknowledgments

In some important ways, this book has arisen from questions raised in conversations about Shakespeare's plays and my subsequent attempts to offer answers to the questions that most interested me. Those conversations occurred in many different places with many different people and undoubtedly I am forgetting in these acknowledgements some willingly incurred debts.

A university research grant funded a stay at the Folger, where I had many interesting conversations and, when meant to be reading other materials, I became interested in how early modern culture understood vision to function. The College of Arts and Sciences and the English Department at the University of South Dakota generously supported my participation in Shakespeare Association of America meetings, where I received invaluable feedback on several pieces of material that became parts of this book. Support to attend the Blackfriars Conference in Staunton, Virginia also provided me opportunities for conversations about these materials. I am grateful to the following people for their interest in and support for the project: Joshua Calhoun, Ralph Alan Cohen, Brett Gamboa, Heidi Brayman Hackel, Peter Hyland, Peter Kanelos, Phillipa Kelly, Rosalyn Knutson, Tom Leitch, Jillian Linster, Jeremy Lopez, Genevieve Love, Shannon Miller, Mark Netzloff, Kevin Petersen, Bradley D. Ryner, Andrea Stevens, Stephanie Tschetter, Ann Thompson, Barbara Traister, Evelyn Tribble, Travis Williams, and Julian Yates.

In addition to those concurrent with the Blackfriars Conferences, I have had the good fortune to attend many productions at the Blackfriars Playhouse, and I thank all the playhouse actors, especially Benjamin Curns, Sarah Fallon, Allison Glenzer, John Harrell, Chris Johnston, James Keegan, Gregory Jon Phelps, and René Thornton, Jr., for hours of thought-provoking pleasure and entertainment.

My colleagues in the English department faculty writing group, over the course of the past few years, read a good portion of this book in various forms, and I thank them for their willingness to engage with these questions: Jason Berger, John Dudley, Emily Haddad, Sarah Townsend, and Skip Willman. I particularly want to thank those friends and colleagues who attend the playreadings, especially Ed Allen, Robert Haddad, Leroy Meyer, and Susan Wolfe. I owe thanks to my students and specifically the members of the graduate seminar on early modern perceptions. I would also like to thank the series editors Michael Dobson and Dympna Callaghan with especial appreciation for Dympna Callaghan's encouragement to submit the manuscript.

My dear friends Lisa Gleysteen Dill, Marie-France Guigue, James Kirby, Josephine McCormack, and William Keyse Rudolph can never be repaid for their generosity, understanding, and support. My parents, Dale Farabee and Marlene Battelle, have always managed to support me in my endeavors without swerving my direction. I thank my mother, Marlene Battelle, and Tom Hummell; their generosity has been unlimited. My mother deserves more thanks than I can offer, for her kindness as I finished it. As an example of engaged curiosity and enjoyment of life, I could not have a better example than my father.

Much of this book is infused with the enjoyment I have found in attending productions of early modern plays; much of that pleasure has been encouraged and enhanced by the intellectual generosity, kindness, and friendship of Lois Potter. Attending performances with Lois and discussing productions either she or I have seen has enriched my understanding of the plays and, more broadly, my life.

Paul Trachtman deserves and has my thanks for the poetry, images, conversation, and careful reading that have done so much to sustain and feed this project. To him, I dedicate this book as poor repayment for the friendship that means so much to me.

Note on Texts

Quotations from Shakespeare, unless otherwise noted, are from *The Riverside Shakespeare*, ed. G. Blakemore Evans, 2nd edition (Boston: Houghton Mifflin, 1997); the square brackets in Evans' text are silently removed.

When quoting from *Mr. William Shakespeares Comedies, Histories, & Tragedies* (London: Jaggard and Blount, 1623), these First Folio quotations are taken from the Norton Facsimile, prepared by Charlton Hinman (New York: Norton, 1968), using the through-line-numbers (TLN) of that edition.

In quotations from early modern printings of texts, i/j and u/v are silently modernized. Additions, for ease of reading, appear in square brackets. In bibliographic listings of early modern printings, dates or emendations in square brackets are taken from the *English Short Title Catalog*. Citations of the *Oxford English Dictionary* refer to the updated online version (Oxford: Oxford University Press, 2010).

Portions of the *Macbeth* chapter have appeared in different form in the Arden Shakespeare volume *Macbeth: The State of Play*, edited by Ann Thompson (London: Methuen, 2014).

Introduction

This study of text and performance brings together questions of stagecraft and close readings of locations in Shakespeare's plays. Often masked by the force of his language, Shakespeare's development of locations through stagecraft is a key to how playgoers find meaning in the plays. It is a commonplace of Shakespeare's time to speak of being transported by a play, and we still say, more metaphorically, that literature transports us. Early modern plays commonly claim the ability to move playgoers in ways that have clearer connections to actual transport. For example, in *Henry V*, the chorus directly addresses playgoers at the beginning of the second act, setting out the necessity for imagined movement and using language tied to the actualities of travel:

> The King is set from London, and the scene
> Is now transported, gentles, to Southampton;
> There is the playhouse now, there must you sit,
> And thence to France shall we convey you safe,
> And bring you back, charming the Narrow Seas
> To give you gentle pass; for if we may,
> We'll not offend one stomach with our play.[1]

Obviously, the chorus does not propose to bodily transport the playgoers, rather "there must you sit." At the same time, the concern for the "gentle" passage to "not offend one stomach" slyly offers a reassurance against seasickness as well as against offending playgoers' taste. We are meant to be transported, and we are reminded of the possibilities of that movement through descriptions dependent on the language of travel.

When we attend a play, we accept the vantage points that are offered and developed by the play, and through these perspectives we are moved by the narrative from place to place. In many ways, we are encouraged to understand the changes in location as similar to what happens when we actually travel. Plausibility, the apt translation of experience, matters in early modern drama. By linking our literary transport to literal travel, plays offer us ways to understand the imagined movement we are meant to experience with the characters. This conceit is common enough that, in 1598 when he introduces his prose narrative of travel in France, Robert Dallington reverses the terms. Dallington assumes that readers already understand how locations in plays work, and he relies on that knowledge to explain how to read his travel book. In the prefatory letter to *A Method for Travell*, he says, "When you come to a play, you imagine the Scene to be far of[f], at Rome, or at Rhodes, according to the subject presented you on the stage: so must you here conceit."[2] In his example, understanding plays' locations will help us understand his travel narrative. Dallington's phrase, "according to the subject presented you on the stage," refers to those parts of the play that tell us, as playgoers, where we are. In 1598, Dallington assumes for his travel book a readership who may well understand stage movement better than travel.

In some cases, *how* we know where we are is obvious: characters tell us directly. "This is Illyria, lady," the sea captain tells the shipwrecked Viola in *Twelfth Night* (1.2.2). "This is call'd Pentapolis," the fisherman explains to the shipwrecked Pericles (2.1.99–100). These are both instances of characters who experience mishaps of travel; the information provided to the characters by other characters helps us as playgoers to know where we are meant to be. But where we imagine ourselves to be is not merely a case of being able, like eighteenth-century editors, to put a location note at the beginning of the scene. The plays continually control our vantage point in a multitude of ways: Which characters do we see? What information do we hear? What are we told happens or has happened? What do we see happen? These varied vantage points give us the illusion of being in the action of the play. The plays – their frameworks and constructions – produce their effects through the perceptions of playgoers. Because theater must have playgoers to move plays beyond the stage of rehearsal, we can consider how Shakespeare counted on the perceptions of playgoers to help produce meaning.

When we read a play or attend a performance, we are caught up in the emotions and anticipations of the characters. We forget ourselves and see into the world of the play through the window of the narrative. Any production or engaged reading manages, to some degree, what Coleridge called "stage-illusion." He explained, "The true stage-illusion in this and in all other things consists – not in the mind's judging it to be a forest, but, in its remission of the judgment that it is not a forest."[3] Noticeably, Coleridge's example in this instance of a "stage-illusion" refers to a setting, a location. In these matters, more than many others, we must simultaneously see what we immediately perceive – "it is a stage" – and understand what stagecraft builds for us – "it is a forest." We might be tempted to dismiss the stage mechanics that allow these concurrent understandings as simply being a matter of the generic conventions of dramatic presentation. But these connections, which are so important to stage-illusion, are more complicated and more thoroughly embedded both in the texts and in playgoers' experiences than previously has been allowed.

The connections between what we immediately perceive and the stage-illusion arise through Shakespeare's stagecraft. Even in instances when we might think we are simply told the location, as in the example of the fisherman offering Pericles a place name, other elements of stagecraft help to develop and produce that knowledge. In the first act of *Pericles*, we have already seen travel, treachery, and Pericles' delivering relief to the people of Tharsus. At the beginning of the second act, Gower, acting as chorus, tells us that Pericles, traveling to escape a murderous plot against him, encounters a storm so violent "that the ship / Should house him safe is wrack'd and split" (2.0.31–2). Gower ends his speech, not by telling us where the shipwrecked Pericles lands, but only that "Fortune, tir'd with doing bad, / Threw him ashore" (2.0.37–8). Unlike the information about locations offered by the Chorus in *Henry V*, we experience with Pericles the confusion about place as he lands from the shipwreck.

Multiple stagecraft elements are at work before we are able to put a name to the place Pericles lands. After the stage direction, "*Enter* PERICLES *wet*," his short, despairing soliloquy at the beginning of 2.1 engages us with his perspective. Then we overhear, as does Pericles, the conversation of the fishermen, and we have the advantage of

Pericles' commentary in asides to us. When Pericles hears the name of the king mentioned, he repeats it, ensuring that we remember that name. When he finally begins the conversation with the fishermen, after listening to them for about forty lines, Pericles continues to speak mostly in verse despite the fishermen's prose. Thus, the fishermen recognize him as of a different class than themselves, and the rhetorical difference also maintains for us the distance between Pericles and the other characters on stage. After another forty lines of dialogue, the following exchange occurs:

1st Fisherman: Hark you, sir; do you know where ye are?
Pericles: Not well.
1st Fisherman: Why, I'll tell you. This is call'd Pentapolis, and our king the good Simonides. (2.1.96–100)

We are given the name of the place in conjunction with the repetition of the king's name. We know where we are, but as important as the place name are the ways the scene has established that awareness. Through the delay in knowing the name, we experience Pericles' lack of interest in knowing; in fact, he does not ask where he has landed. As his interest reawakens, two more fishermen arrive bearing the armor they have drawn up in their nets. In succession, the soliloquy, the entrances of the fishermen, the asides from Pericles, Pericles' verse, the dawning interest in local events, all lead us away from Pericles' idea in the opening soliloquy, "Here to have death in peace," to his assertion at the end of the scene, "This day I'll rise" (2.1.11, 166). There are many stagecraft elements at work here, and they produce much of our understanding of where we are and how we should concern ourselves about that location.

Although this book discusses plays in the Shakespeare canon, these elements of stagecraft are not confined to Shakespeare's plays. Some of them are, however, aspects specifically of early modern drama. Many of the elements of stagecraft I discuss depend on the language and methods of thought that were available, and sometimes newly available, for describing and understanding location. Recent scholarly research has expanded our knowledge of early modern scientific and philosophical thought, which in turn has changed some of the ways we can approach early modern drama. Henry S. Turner, in his compelling book *The English Renaissance Stage*, has shown that, simultaneous with developments in philosophical thought, "a fundamental shift towards the mechanical and mathematical systems of thought [...] was also occurring in the field of early seventeenth-century literary discourse, and [...] this shift derived from the growing popularity and epistemological authority of the spatial arts in everyday early-modern life."[4] As Turner makes clear in his discussion of plays by a number of different playwrights, these systems of thought were part of the wider dramatic discourse of the period. Despite the broader use of these elements of thought, I have focused my discussion of stagecraft in this book to rely primarily on plays in the Shakespeare canon, including collaborative works such as *Pericles*.[5] In the conclusion of this book, I return to the appearance of these stagecraft elements in other early modern dramatists' works.

I use stagecraft very broadly in this book to include those less examined frames of drama that allow us to understand the play and that produce the meaning of the play through our experience of it. As playgoers, we are in an active position. We experience the narrative differently from the characters; we see and hear different things than they do. These perspectives depend on stagecraft to produce dramatic irony, sympathy, or distance. In an intrinsic way, these elements of stagecraft connect to questions of location. In what position do we find ourselves as playgoers? One important aspect of stagecraft is the control of stage space through entrances and exits and the anticipation of the arrival of other characters. In 2.2 of *Henry V*, for example, Exeter, Bedford, and Westmerland, three men loyal to Henry, enter and have eleven lines of discussion before the entrance of Henry with the traitorous men, Scroop, Cambridge, and Grey. We already anticipate the revelation of the treason, since the chorus' speech opening act two describes the treason and gives the traitors' names. As we await the king's entrance, our anticipation is increased by the loyal men's discussion of the traitorous actions and, furthermore, that "The King hath note of all that they intend / By interception which they dream not of" (2.2.6–7). The eleven lines before Henry's entrance pass quickly in performance, but the focus remains on the king, leading up to his entrance with the traitors. We, like the loyal men, understand the test of mercy Henry offers before the accusations are levied. The delay in Henry's entrance establishes playgoers' understanding of events in ways not available to traitorous Scroop, Cambridge, and Grey. We are on the king's side, with loyal Exeter, Bedford, and Westmerland, partly because of their speeches before the king's entrance.

Staged activities before another character's entrance can have quite different effects. After the Venetian excitements and difficulties of act one of *Othello*, in act two the play shifts to Cyprus. As playgoers, we arrive in Cyprus and are already with those in residence in Cyprus before the major characters of the play arrive from Venice. Because the scene delays the entrance of Othello and sets up that entrance in interesting ways, it is useful to remember the exact order of the entrances and exits in the scene. The scene opens with the governor of Cyprus and a pair of gentlemen discussing the sailing conditions and the arrival of the ship that carries Cassio. Cassio then arrives after a brief description offered by a third gentleman. We hear cries of "A sail, a sail, a sail!" and a messenger arrives with news of sightings of Othello's ship (2.1.51). A man is sent out to check on the information and returns quite quickly (within six lines) with the news that Iago, rather than Othello, has landed. Then, about fifteen lines later, Desdemona, Iago, Roderigo, and Emilia arrive together. After more cries of "a sail," Cassio sends a man out to check on the news (2.1.93). Finally, about a hundred lines later, Othello and attendants enter. The bulk of this hundred-line time is consumed with lengthy, witty word-play between Iago and Desdemona, not anticipatory, tension-building discussions of Othello. In fact, no one returns to supply Cassio with more information about the offstage cries. As playgoers, we are established with the Cypriots, then the staggered arrival of the other characters develops the sense of dispersed control of the space. We settle into the rhetoric and discussion in this foreign place before Othello arrives. Much of this effect, of being elsewhere before the entrance of Desdemona, arises from the emphatic descriptions of the ships, pilots, dangerous storms, and of Desdemona herself as "riches of the ship [...] come ashore" (2.1.83). Simultaneously, the verbal effects work in concert with the stage mechanics to develop playgoers' sense of Othello as an outsider. Othello's delayed entrance divides us from his experience. These aspects of Shakespeare's plays arise not only from the specific rhetoric employed by the characters but also through the controlled entrances into the space of the stage.

In a different register, we can see how an initially controlled stage space becomes disordered in the opening scene of *1 Henry VI*, when the solemn funeral of Henry V enters accompanied by a dead march.

As the first thirty lines of the scene offer elegiac praise to the dead king, all seems appropriate and consonant, until Gloucester questions the Church's support for Henry. The Bishop of Winchester quickly speaks up with a quibble about the Protector's power, until Bedford attempts to return them all to their mourning duties. Then the members of the nobility seem to resume the activities the scene initially sets up: a ceremonious and royal funeral. But within ten lines these obsequies are interrupted by the first of three messengers, all three of whom bear unwelcome, disruptive news. The control of the stage space in this opening scene embodies the power struggles that become the major conflicts in the remainder of the play. Despite the articulated desire to maintain the ceremonious order of the funeral and court, the nobles begin the fracturing of power that events – delivered here by messengers as news – continue to develop throughout the play. If we pay attention to the control of stage space, we can see more clearly the craft of the playwright.

Soliloquies are one of the more frequently examined aspects of stagecraft in Shakespeare's plays, for several reasons. In soliloquy, characters often have long, rhetorically complicated speeches that excite attention, both from playgoers and scholars. Also, soliloquies offer playgoers what appear to be moments of unmediated access to the thoughts and often the feelings of characters. Frequently soliloquies can directly address playgoers, particularly in productions interested in maintaining early modern playing conditions. Asides can also be directed to playgoers. In these instances, playgoers are granted an access denied the other present characters. In soliloquies, direct address engages us in those revelations and decisions by a character alone on stage. In performance, this connection is heightened by both our shared temporal experience of the moment with the character and, if we do not already know the play, our inability to predict how long we will have that access.

By convention, in early modern plays characters speaking in soliloquy tell the truth. In the only soliloquy from a main character to open a Shakespeare play, a great deal of the power of the opening of *Richard III* rests on Richard's soliloquy,. However, some of the power of that opening subsequently increases because of the canny use of soliloquy throughout that scene and the scene immediately following it. We believe Richard when he tells us, "I am determined to prove a villain" (1.1.30). As soon as Clarence enters in Brakenbury's custody,

Richard demonstrates his perfidy. After the exit of Brakenbury and Clarence, although we can hardly have misunderstood Richard's actions, he is left alone on stage for a short five-line clarifying commentary. Hastings then enters and delivers more fodder for Richard's machinations. Hastings' exit leaves Richard alone and in control of the stage space for another soliloquy of over twenty lines, which introduces his plan to "marry Warwick's youngest daughter. / What, though I kill'd her husband and her father?" (1.1.153–4). The strength of his opening soliloquy reverberates and then increases from the later uses of soliloquy and the absolute control over the stage space that Richard maintains throughout the scene.

While this first scene of *Richard III* establishes the effect, the differences in the next scene retroactively exacerbate it. Lady Anne enters with guard, attendants, and the corpse of Henry VI. On the page, the speech has the appearance of soliloquy, since she is the only speaker for the first thirty lines of the scene and this monologue is only broken after the entrance of Richard. However, the opening of the scene is the antithesis of soliloquy. Anne enters with other characters, she gives orders to the bearers of the corpse, and in multiple instances she directly addresses, using the second person familiar pronoun, the corpse of Henry VI, describing herself as made "wretched by the death of thee" (1.2.18). She provides us with a great deal of information and we understand her situation the better for it, but the scene does not allow her the immediate access to playgoers that Richard has in the previous scene. Richard's access in the first scene becomes more compelling through this immediately antithetical display. Noticeably, in the second scene, the first person to break into Anne's monologue is Richard himself, when he arrives thirty-three lines into the scene. His first line when he enters demonstrates his physical control over the stage space as he orders, "Stay, you that bear the corse, and set it down" (1.2.33). If we do not find the wooing of Anne compelling enough to convince us of his power, Richard still has, at the end of the scene, another soliloquy of thirty-eight lines. Obviously, the opening soliloquy of the play has a great deal of rhetorical power; however, some of its power, as it relates to the play as a whole, depends on the way soliloquy is handled in the remainder of that opening scene and in the scene following.

Part of the pleasure of attending a play depends on the experience of having live actors performing in front of us. David McInnis has pointed out that "the player is ultimately beholden to his audience for the success or failure of theatrical illusion, and the imaginative effort must be shared."[6] Not only do we take in the choices that actors and directors have made for that particular production, but the realities of our own perceptions become necessary to the experience. We may strain to hear and see; we may miss bits of stage action if our attention wanders to another place on the stage. The time and plot move inexorably toward the interval (if there is one) and then toward the end of the play. We are aware of other playgoers, sometimes more aware than we might wish. We see the stage as the playing space and we know that it is a stage. Simultaneously, we are willing to see the stage as forest, in the stage-illusion world of the play. In the auditory play world, characters talk to and about one another, expose events in the pre-play past, conjecture about their futures, and develop the realities of the worlds in which the characters live. And, of course, they perform and experience actions: move on and off stage, fight battles or individuals, travel to and from different places, move through different times in their lives, threaten and are threatened by one another, fall in and out of love, trick and are tricked by one another, live and sometimes die.

This world of the play only exists within the frameworks established by stage mechanics. And these stage mechanics depend on the perceptions of playgoers, as mediated and manipulated by the characters and setting. We may not consciously notice the delayed entrance of Othello in Cyprus, but these kinds of effects rely on the mechanics built into the play. For example, in the Porter scene in *Macbeth*, we playgoers cannot see who knocks, but we hear the knocking as the Porter delays in answering. Part of the oddly developing sense of suspense depends on playgoers *not* seeing those who knock. Caught up in the narrative of the performance, we may not register these particular aspects, but they are dependent on control of the playgoers' perceptions. We know what has just happened and the porter does not; we have a strange sense in the opening of this scene that the Porter's response to the knocking is not *right*. The point surely in this scene is that the Porter's response would not be right for us; we know too much. The response is perfectly right for the Porter himself. As playgoers we cannot see who knocks, and this physical circumstance helps to develop our response to what happens on stage. In the stage-illusion world of the play, we have just experienced the immediate aftermath of the extraordinary murder of Duncan; in this scene, we are returned with a thump to the ordinary world of the complaining, drunken servant. And yet, we know that the unseen knocker probably belongs to the extraordinary world of Duncan's death. Many of the effects of the scene depend on disconnects between the different spheres within the world of the play. At the same time, the effects also depend on playgoers' experiences: What do playgoers see or hear? What do we *not* see or *not* hear?

A lively critical debate has developed around the questions of whether early modern playgoers "saw" plays or "heard" plays.[7] In this book, I am interested in the question of what playgoers see and hear, but not in trying to determine which of these descriptions was prevalent in early modern theatergoing. As most playgoers notice, both means of apprehension are important when attending a performance. Interestingly, a correlative reality of attendance at a performance includes the moments of *not* seeing and *not* hearing. In the Porter scene in *Macbeth*, not seeing those who knock helps to produce part of the effect of hearing the knocking. J.L. Styan asserted that:

> The contrasts and emphases of [Shakespeare's] visual effects – in form and movement, mime and gestic expression – are as powerful an agent as the aural skills of his craft. The existence of these in such abundance throughout his plays suggests that he rarely forgot his audience. For stage contrasts are created only on the assumption that an audience will deduce meaning from them.[8]

Not only did Shakespeare not forget, but he also conscientiously uses his control over what playgoers perceive. Part of the project of this book is to extend, through a more concerted attention to playgoers' perceptions, the work Styan began in *Shakespeare's Stagecraft*. Because of these kinds of experiential elements in the plays, I have decided to use the word "playgoers" rather than "audience" or "spectators." Using the term "playgoer" helps to keep in the forefront of my discussion the fact that this book considers how particular elements of Shakespeare's plays produce particular effects as they were written for the theater. In some instances, I discuss verbal or auditory effects and visual or spectacular effects, and I have reserved "audience" and "spectators" to refer to experiences of these specific instances.

Generally I assume that early modern plays were written to be performed in spaces similar to the reconstructions of Shakespeare's Globe Theatre in London or Blackfriars Playhouse in Staunton, Virginia. In other words, playgoers and players are similarly lit, roles can be doubled, the stage space includes at least two if not three doors, and a playing space exists above the main stage. These spaces offer many different kinds of vantage points; playgoers can be on three sides of the thrust portion of the playing space and, in some cases, seated on the edges of the stage itself or in the above playing space. In some instances, playgoers are in extremely close proximity to the actors allowing detailed observation. The wide variety of spaces for the playgoers means that sightlines and vantage points are different for different playgoers even at the same performance. Theaters less interested in early modern playing conditions have the possibilities of altered or mobile playing spaces and often have absolute control over lighting. Leaving an audience in the dark, and having control over which parts of the playing space are lit, offers its own challenges and possibilities. In Parker Reed's 2010 production of *Romeo and Juliet*, the entire theater went dark after the Nurse found Juliet's body.[9] The lamentations of the various characters were wailed out in the darkness, lines mingling and spoken on top of one another. In this instance, the production decided to highlight the verbal elements of the scene while removing the possibility of visual effects. These choices worked in several interesting ways for this production. The darkness made visual the way Juliet provided the "light." The darkness was also disconcerting, because it made it more difficult to separate out the voices of the various characters speaking over the top of one another. Here, the absence of the visual muffled the verbal. In the text, one of the jolting effects of the scene rests on the fact that playgoers know about the Friar's concoction and its purported effects. Thus, we see the shocked reactions and hear the lamentations of characters for a dead Juliet who we think we know is not dead. The distancing of dramatic irony cannot be eliminated from the scene. Reed's production worked through this distancing in a different fashion than would have been possible in an early modern theater space. In Reed's production, that distancing was altered and in some ways enhanced by the disconcerting darkness. So, although I assume that the plays were written for early modern playing spaces, productions in other kinds of theaters have a great deal to show us about how the mechanics of stagecraft function.

In what follows, I include instances from a variety of types of productions when those examples are especially useful. In general, I assume that the theatrical choices involved in any production offer a specific reading. In other words, productions are always "thesis-presenting;" they are a live argument for a particular reading of a play. Often we call "thesis-driven" those productions that are focused to illuminate a director's particular concept. But, planned or unplanned, directorially driven or actor driven, particular readings of the texts emerge from any performance. The instances from performance that I include offer examples of specific readings rather than offering a performance history of these plays. The performance moments to which I refer come from a variety of types of productions; their common elements are that they offer interesting staging options or illuminating choices. I have not used the differences between professional, amateur, and university productions as criteria for inclusion in or exclusion from the discussion, and many of the productions to which I refer are university productions. Critical approaches to the plays often neglect university productions. However, as Andrew James Hartley compellingly argues, they deserve to be paid more attention because they are driven by artistic development and expression rather than the box office.[10] Moreover, as Hartley explains, these productions often have more resources, more support (dramaturges, dedicated rehearsal space, fixed rehearsal schedules) than many professional productions.

This book offers close readings of what are usually considered implicit elements of Shakespeare's stagecraft: location development, stage-illusion, position of the playgoers, entrances and exits, activities preceding character entrances, character control over stage space, and elements that disorder stage space. Consideration of these elements in conjunction with the more explicitly rhetorical parts of the play develops a better understanding of the workings of early modern drama. Each of the following chapters focuses on an individual play to explore how stage mechanics and stage-illusion interact to produce effects for playgoers and readers. The first and last chapters both depend on specifically early modern ways of apprehending the world. In the first chapter, early modern notions of how vision functions illuminate many aspects of how *A Midsummer Night's Dream* produces effects on playgoers. The final chapter uses early modern ideas of movement and travel to elucidate aspects of *The Tempest*. In these two plays, many aspects of stage-illusion arise through strict understandings of the locations of events and actions within the world of the play. For this book, these two plays make appropriate beginnings and endings of the discussions of stage space and early modern space, partly because they emphasize the ways these concerns continue to interest Shakespeare over the course of his work. One central question for me is what happens to playgoers' perceptions as places are presented in the confined spaces of the early modern stage.

This book does not attempt to theorize early modern space; instead, I have chosen to explore how stagecraft, character experiences, and playgoers' apprehensions are a means of production of space. The second chapter approaches *Richard II* to examine some of the ways that the spaces of the play produce history. Although firmly embedded in the generic questions of making history, *Richard II* has other formal and stagecraft elements that distinguish it from Shakespeare's other history plays: the consistent use of dramatic verse, the near absence of soliloquy, the emphasis on verbal efficacy, the frequent comment on the physical production of words, and the possible reversals of empathy for Richard's widely varying situations.

The third and fourth chapters use *Hamlet* and *Macbeth* to approach similar questions of how effects are produced on playgoers. Both of these chapters focus on questions of location and dislocation in both the stage space and the world of the play. Both *Hamlet* and *Macbeth* depend on the inexorable momentum of tragedy combined with the temporal realities of performance, but the effects for playgoers differ between the plays in significant ways. The stage spaces of *Hamlet*, I suggest, essentially trap playgoers into a play world defined through Hamlet's location. The fixity of Hamlet's own location at the end of the play draws all of the other characters toward him in ways that are simultaneously literal and metaphorical. *Macbeth* entices us into a play world where our own perceptions are as tricked as Macbeth's. As playgoers, we become more enmeshed in Macbeth's confusion, and we are encouraged to experience Macbeth's dislocation in ways that are singularly filtered through our understanding of his perceptions. The fifth chapter of the book uses *The Tempest* to examine how the experiences of the stage space and characters' perceptions are diffused through multiple characters embodying a variety of notions of how travel and location function.

These differences, between the diffuse experiences in *The Tempest* and the more individual-focused tragedies, arise in some ways from the differences in genre; tragedy often emphasizes the singularity of purpose or experience, while romance or tragicomedy tends to produce effects of resolution and reconciliation. As playgoers experiencing *The Tempest*, we are engaged with a variety of understandings of location from many different characters. That range of perspectives helps produce an ending that reconciles those differences. Although grounded in historical understandings of perception and stagecraft, one goal of this project is to understand how these plays still continue to work as dramatic narratives. If we take seriously the notion that without playgoers or imaginative readers there is no performance, we must assume that Shakespeare was aware of playgoers' perceptions as he constructed his plays. Attention to Shakespeare's stagecraft amplifies what we hear and magnifies what we see in early modern plays.

Notes

1. These lines appear in *Henry V* at 2.0.34–40. All subsequent quotations from Shakespeare appear as in-text citations.
2. Robert Dallington, *A Method for Travell. Shewed by taking the view of France. As it stoode in the yeare of our Lord 1598*, (London: Thomas Creede, [1603]), STC 6203. This quotation comes from the Folger copy 3; it appears on A1^v.
3. Samuel Taylor Coleridge, *Lectures and Notes on Shakspere and Other English Poets*, T. Ashe, ed. (London: George Bell, 1897), 207.
4. Henry S. Turner, *The English Renaissance Stage: Geometry, Poetics, and the Practical Spatial Arts 1580–1630* (Oxford: Oxford University Press, 2004), 278.
5. Suzanne Gossett, in her Arden edition of *Pericles* (London: Thomson, 2004), summarizes the evidence for collaboration: "A survey of the cumulative evidence strongly supports the view that *Pericles* was a collaboration by Shakespeare and Wilkins, and that the division of labour in the play was broadly between Acts 1 and 2 and the last three acts. However, uncertainty remains about the details" (68).
6. David McInnis, *Mind-Travelling and Voyage Drama in Early Modern England* (Basingstoke: Palgrave Macmillan, 2013), 44. McInnis' book focuses on voyage drama, which offers fully articulated examples of many of the implicit types of movements I explore in this book.
7. For example, see Gabriel Egan, "Hearing or Seeing a Play?: Evidence of Early Modern Theatrical Terminology," *Ben Jonson Journal* 8 (2001), 327–47.
8. J. L. Styan, *Shakespeare's Stagecraft* (Cambridge: Cambridge University Press, 1967), 196.
9. I reviewed this production: "*Antony and Cleopatra* and *Romeo and Juliet*," *Shakespeare Bulletin* 29.2 (2011), 196–204.
10. Andrew James Hartley, "A Dream of Campus," *Shakespeare Survey* 65 (2013), 194–210.

1
Perceptions and Possibility in *A Midsummer Night's Dream*
"To leave the figure or disfigure it"

A Midsummer Night's Dream uses early modern notions of vision to alter and confound the ways playgoers see the play. The initial conflict arises from Hermia's insistence that she cannot possibly "choose love by another's eyes" (1.1.140). Like many of the characters in *A Midsummer Night's Dream*, she insists that her own visual perceptions are trustworthy and immutable. In this play, the frequent mention of the word "eyes," the importance of the visual tricks, and the characters' misperceptions of other characters' actions belong to a world made of different ways of seeing.[1] I shall take up sight in the play specifically as it relates to the ways early modern playgoers understood vision to function and then explore how characters see: see events, see themselves, see other characters, and "see" in the more abstracted sense of understand. This exploration opens the possibility of examining afresh what playgoers see when watching the play; it also offers an answer to the question, how do these framings of characters' sensory experiences alter or even produce playgoers' understanding of the play? Obviously, not all playgoers react in the same fashion, experience the play similarly from their respective vantage points, or necessarily visually comprehend the play in the terms that I set out here. However, this reading outlines a system of visual markers that exists within the narrative organization of the play and that intrinsically connects to early modern notions of sight.

In the early modern era, multiple concurrent and irreconcilable descriptions of vision offered explanations for sight and attempted to bolster belief in the certainty of vision. Pre-Keplerian notions of vision depend heavily on the idea of objects being visible through representational impressions on the eye, hence the common descriptions of representational figuring, marking, stamping, or impressing on the mind or memory. In Richard Banister's *Breviary of the Eye* (1622), he explains initially that 'seeing beames come from the Eye."[2] Banister goes on to explain how those beams function: "Three things are required for sight: That the beames associate the Ayre. That seeing spirits slide not out. That the visible spirits be united with the Ayre. A certaine alteration, and not a substance is cast into the Eye."[3] A wide variety of descriptions of the mechanics of that impressing and the role of imagination in perception complicates matters.

Andreas du Laurens (translated into English by Richard Suphlet in 1599) explains that the philosophers agree on the parts of the eye and the necessary elements for vision to occur. But once the philosophers go on to "shew the maner of this action [...] they jarre among themselves and cannot agree."[4] Laurens describes the two general approaches:

> Some of them would have that there should issue out of the eye bright beames or a certaine light which should reach unto the object, and thereby cause us to see it: other some would have it, that the object commeth unto the eye, and that nothing goeth out of the eye: the first doe hold that we see by emission or having something going forth of the eye, the latter by reception or receiving of the object into the eye.[5]

Both of these versions of seeing, "emission" and "reception" in Laurens" terms, theorize that vision depends on some type of representational impression.[6] Stuart Clark argues that the "representational model of vision" collapsed between the early fifteenth and the late seventeenth century "under the weight of the anomalies counting increasingly against it."[7] Clark points particularly to the increasing number of what he terms visual paradoxes: "situations where appearances that were supposed to be true proved difficult, perhaps impossible, to distinguish from appearances that were deemed to be false."[8] It was not only a matter of ghosts, spirits, or visionary seeings; new methods of measurement made ever more clear that the visual perception of distances could often be tricked simply by the circumstances of sight. The Renaissance "rediscovery" of linear perspective, as Samuel Edgerton describes it, allowed representational art to develop visual verisimilitude, but it also encouraged the development of perspective paintings that tricked the viewer's eye.[9] While the early modern era struggled with both the desire for visual veracity and the awareness of the breakdowns of that model, the drama of the period – and particularly *A Midsummer Night's Dream* – depends on contemporary playgoers who can understand these disparities through their own experiences.

In *A Midsummer Night's Dream*, the play's frequent questioning of visual accuracy changes the ways playgoers understand their experience of the play. This effect, I think, was greater for early modern playgoers who had rather different and disparate ideas of how vision worked. However, any Shakespeare production reminds us of our roles and labors as playgoers. In *The Defence of Poesy* Sidney might disparage the conventions that both mark and shift locations on stage, but his description makes clear that these conventions are easily understood:

> Now you shall have three ladies walk to gather flowers: and then we must believe the stage to be a garden. By and by we hear news of shipwreck in the same place: and then we are to blame if we accept it not for a rock. Upon the back of that comes out a hideous monster with fire and smoke: and then the miserable beholders are bound to take it for a cave. While in the meantime two armies fly in, represented with four swords and bucklers: and then what hard heart will not receive it for a pitched field?[10]

Sidney's description points out several tasks early modern playgoers apparently perform without difficulty, and it is worth taking a moment to think about how these tasks require of any playgoers different imaginative actions. We are meant to be able to fix locations and shift them quickly; not only must we imagine the stage a garden, we must quickly shift to seeing the same place as a seaside rock. The other two examples Sidney offers require that playgoers fix locations through recognition of the characters and actions we see performed. In the first instances, the locations appear through exposition ("we hear news"), in the cases of the monster and the soldiers through actions (entrances with "fire and smoke" or "swords and bucklers"). The shifting settings require certain self-conscious imaginative work of the playgoers. Brent M. Cohen has pointed out how the "Elizabethan theatre includes us in the action without permitting our total absorption or abandonment of self-consciousness."[11] In *A Midsummer Night's Dream*, the question of visual veracity can engage that self-consciousness of the playgoers and alter the perception of events presented on stage.

Two moments in the opening scene of the play, Egeus' complaint against Lysander and Theseus' description of Hermia's duty, use the language of forms and impressions in ways that are not immediately visual, but clearly relate to Hermia's understanding of the root of her love for Lysander. Pressure and the resulting impressions appear in Theseus' description of the role Hermia ought to play:

> To you your father should be as a god;
> One that compos'd your beauties; yea, and one
> To whom you are but as a form in wax,
> By him imprinted, and within his power,
> To leave the figure, or disfigure it. (1.1.47–51)

Theseus emphasizes the strength of control and formative power her father has over her, but his reference to "imprinting" refers to the thoughts and impressions in her mind as well as the unpleasant suggestion of physical violence. This paternal control extends so far as remaking the mental images, the figures, and can extend to the visible alteration, disfiguration. Egeus accuses Lysander of having "stol'n the impression of [Hermia's] fantasy" (1.1.32). G. Blakemore Evans glosses this line as "stealthily stamped your image on her imagination, i.e. made her fall in love with you" and thus asserts that Lysander is guilty of imprinting his own desires onto Hermia's notions. Peter Holland glosses the line as "stamped his image on her imagination by secret trickery" or "captured her imagination by making a secret impression on it."[12] Both of Holland's readings show Lysander as the maker of the impression. However, there is also the possibility that Hermia's fantasy has itself exuded a force for impressing, and Lysander is guilty of the theft of that resulting impression. This line exhibits difficulties endemic in the concurrent notions of how eyesight functioned. The fallibility of perceptions is the fearful possibility raised by Egeus' description of the possible trickery Lysander has performed. Shakespeare establishes an exchange here that depends on playgoers who can entertain contradictory notions of how vision worked.

Singularity of vision

The continual questioning of visual veracity is paired with a certainty of the singularity of the visual experience in the play. Hermia asserts the individuality of visual impressions when she responds to Theseus, "I would my father look'd but with my eyes" (1.1.56). This impossibility forms a central question of the drama: what would it mean to look with another's eyes? The question becomes not simply a desire for another to see from exactly the same vantage point, but a larger existential question of inhabiting the senses of another to begin to feel what another feels. Ralph Berry points out that "the 'eye' in this comedy is a channel of passion as well as an organ of perception."[13] The "channel of passion" implies the possibility of fully experiencing another person's perspective. The *Oxford English Dictionary* notes 1605 as the first use of "perspective" to denote, "The relation or proportion in which the parts of a subject are viewed by the mind; the aspect of a subject or matter, as perceived from a particular mental point of view," while the senses of the word relating to "light, vision, and visualization" were the more common early modern uses.[14] Clearly, when Hermia asks that her father inhabit her visual perspective, the connection she draws depends on the possibility of both the visual aspect and the shift to a particular mental understanding, to look with someone else's eyes. Helena begs Hermia for a lesson in just this kind of sense swapping: "O, teach me how you look, and with what art/ You sway the motion of Demetrius' heart" (1.1.192–3). Helena, fixated on Hermia's eyes, continually compares herself to the ways Hermia appears, the way Hermia looks, and the way Hermia sees. Part of Helena's conviction that Hermia's eyes are the cause of the difficulties depends on period descriptions that credit the eyes with an amazing array of actions. For example, Helkiah Crooke's anatomy manual *Mikrokosmographia* (1615) describes how,

> these Eyes doe burne and shine, they twinckle, they winke, they are sorrowfull, they laugh, they admire, they love, they lust, they flatter, and in one word they decipher and paint the image of the Mind with so artificiall a pencill, that they seeme to be a second soule.[15]

In Crooke's description the eyes perform multiple actions, but the culmination of the actions appears in the verb "decipher" – if we take seriously Crooke's "in one word." Ciphers refer usually to puzzling writings, and deciphering intimates a relationship, figurative or literal, to writing. Crooke makes explicit this figurative connection with his description of "so artificiall a pencill" and suggests that a viewer might understand the eyes of another person as a second soul since the eyes have written in them these various actions. Helena's complaints about the strength of Hermia's eyes depend on these encyclopedic attributions of visual action. Interestingly, Helena and Hermia, so focused on both the manner of appearance and on the ways each sees through her own eyes, go through the entirety of the play with their vision intact.

Despite Egeus' accusation that Hermia's vision is wrong or tricked, her vision is not tricked through magical means: Puck does not alter her vision with the love potion. However, her own senses are untrustworthy once Lysander's vision is altered. When she originally departs from Lysander, she describes the sight of him as a visual sustenance: "we must starve our sight/ From lover's food till morrow deep midnight" (1.1.222–3). After the misplaced potion has its effect on Lysander, Hermia wanders alone in the woods, finds the other characters, and notes her confusion in relation to the altered abilities of her senses:

> Dark night, that from the eye his function takes,
> The ear more quick of apprehension makes;
> Wherein it doth impair the seeing sense,
> It pays the hearing double recompense.
> Thou art not by mine eye, Lysander, found;
> Mine ear, I thank it, brought me to thy sound. (3.2.177–82)

Hermia finds herself in the dark, literally; playgoers realize she is in the dark metaphorically as well. She describes her sense of hearing as more quickly grasping signs of Lysander's existence. "Apprehension" in this period means a variety of types of acquisition: "physical seizure," "the action of laying hold of with the senses; conscious perception," and emotional "sensitiveness or sensibility to."[16] In these varied uses, the central notion of acquiring has the double possibility of taking from outside the body or of the body being altered within. Hermia has not yet realized the sea-change that has taken place in Lysander's affections, but her description of her dark-induced blindness prefigures Lysander's response. He adopts Hermia's notice of darkness and claims that it is "Fair Helena! who more engilds the night/ Than all yon fiery oes and eyes of light" (3.2.187–8). Lysander conflates the stars, the "oes," themselves with "eyes of light" that are less bright than Helena. Helena herself becomes the source of illumination in his description. Appropriately, Lysander does not question the validity of his own visual perceptions here, the potion has changed his vision. Lysander's altered vision undermines the usefulness of Hermia's perceptions. Her functioning senses – her ears – provide her with accurate information, but validity does not ensure value.

Helena, whose eyes are also unaffected by the love potion, frames her difficulties over the course of the play through problems of visual fascination. Helena complains that Demetrius "errs, doting on Hermia's eyes" (1.1.230). In a play with very few soliloquies, Helena's speech when left alone on stage at the end of act one also carries through this controlling function in the play, the idea that sight and vision powerfully alter understanding and possibly alter the physical realities of the viewed. She asserts:

> Things base and vile, holding no quantity,
> Love can transpose to form and dignity.
> Love looks not with the eyes but with the mind;
> And therefore is wing'd Cupid painted blind.
> Nor hath Love's mind of any judgment taste;
> Wings, and no eyes, figure unheedy haste;
> And therefore is Love said to be a child,
> Because in choice he is so oft beguil'd. (1.1.232–9)

Her description of Cupid as a blind child using the mind's eye to alter the perception of the love object is hardly an uncommon notion in poetic rhetoric. But we might profitably consider other ways of thinking about Helena's lines here.

In her especially compelling presentation of these lines in the 2011 Lantern Theatre production, actor Lee Ann Etzold made clear that Helena was working out these relationships between vision and reality through the soliloquy.[17] Particularly in that production, Helena was not a young woman setting out the commonplace poetic notions of Cupid, but a confused late-adolescent character attempting to sort out how reality could be so altered by an individual perspective. In Etzold's delivery, each "therefore" marked a realization on the part of Helena rather than a recapitulation of a standard poetic trope. The framing of this soliloquy determines much of how the remainder of a production will handle Helena's awareness. Regardless of production decisions, Helena's speech emphasizes the possibilities for alteration through certain types of perspectives. As Helena describes physical changes in that which is viewed, she comes to realizations about how that viewing functions. Helena's correlation between "Wings, and no eyes" and the subsequent "unheedy haste" imagine that the lack of vision results in unheeding choice. The play, in larger terms, undermines her assumption here that visual accuracy would lead to more heedful decisions. And yet she still describes sight as a means of contact and affection. She hopes, by telling Demetrius of the others' escape plan, to "have his sight thither and back again" (1.1.251). On one level, she seems to understand the difficulties of trusting to the "love vision" of Cupid, yet the possibility of loving sight shifting from one object of affection to another, in fact, is borne out in the play.

Despite Helena's realizations about Cupid's vision, she continually returns to the same frustrations and misunderstandings about vision. When she wanders in the wood alone, she complains, "Happy is Hermia, wheresoe'er she lies, / For she hath blessed and attractive eyes" (2.2.90-1). Helena's fixation on Hermia's eyes leads her to question, "How came her eyes so bright? Not with salt tears; / If so, my eyes are oft'ner wash'd than hers" (2.2.92–3). Finally she wonders, "What wicked and dissembling glass of mine / Made me compare with Hermia's sphery eyne!" (2.2.98–9). Through all of these comparisons, Helena continually returns to the possibility of altering her own eyes and switching her visual perspective with Hermia. Even when berating her own chances, Helena describes affection in terms of sight, saying that she "did never […] / Deserve a sweet look from Demetrius" eye" (2.2.126–7). Convinced the two men are mocking her when they do woo her, she describes the experience as one "To conjure tears up in a poor maid's eyes" (3.2.158). Although Hermia recognizes, when events become too confusing for her, that she is unable to see because of darkness, Helena frames nearly all of her experiences in terms of vision. Rarely does Helena question how well her own vision functions. These differences between the two young women are in reverse correlation with their own certainties about being beloved. Hermia questions her own abilities to see, but does not question whether the two men remain in love with her. Despite her constant focus on how love proceeds through vision, Helena does not believe in the veracity of the love declared by the two men once they are affected by the love potion.

Lysander and Demetrius have the circumstance of being affected by the love potion to explain their altered vision. Lysander's shift in affections is Puck's later rectified error; for Demetrius, the spell that rekindles his pre-play affection for Helena remains in place through the end of the play and presumably into their post-play marriage. Like Helena and Hermia, both young men trust in the legibility of visual markers. Lysander's first criticism of Demetrius, as a "spotted and inconstant man" (1.1.110), claims that Demetrius, at least metaphorically, is visually marked with inconstancy. Once under the spell of Puck's potion, Lysander reveals that his understanding of her emotions is linked to his vision: "Transparent Helena, nature shows art, / That through thy bosom makes me see thy heart" (2.2.104–5). His notion here is that Helena's own body becomes transparent and the revelation allows him to see her emotions that are both lodged and visible in her heart. Obviously, his reading of Helena's emotions mistakes her feelings, but his certitude rests in a figuring of love as perceptible by sight. He explains his realization in terms that link his new vision with being capable of "deciphering": "Reason becomes the marshall to my will, / And leads me to your eyes, where I o'erlook / Love's stories written in Love's richest book" (2.2.120–2). In many ways, his description reinforces the images of emotion written in the eyes and embodies Crooke's description of eyes that "decipher and paint the image of the Mind with so artificiall a pencill, that they seeme to be a second soule." We might dismiss as purely poetic rhetorical questioning Demetrius' exclamation, "To what, my love, shall I compare thine eyne?" (3.2.138), except that so many of the characters in the play are so fixated on eyes, sight, and seeing that these instances take on extra resonance.

Despite the obvious divisions of the various strands of the plot and groups of characters, the emphasis on vision permeates the entirety of the play. Oberon's original intentions with the vision-altering love potion refer mainly to Titania, but Oberon's miscarried order to Puck to find the "disdainful youth" and "anoint his eyes" furthers the confusions amongst the four young lovers (2.1.261). Puck's errors are in fact visual errors; Puck anoints the wrong man's eyes because of two misreadings. Initially, he identifies his recipient of the potion by the "Weeds of Athens he doth wear" (2.2.71), and more convincing to him, Puck sees the distance between the sleeping maid Hermia and the Athenian Lysander as an indication of his lack of affection for her. Hermia insists on the distance between them as a propriety arising from love; Puck sees the distance as proof of disdain. When Oberon describes to Puck the process for reversing the potion, he links the effects to visions in a dream:

> Then crush this herb into Lysander's eye;
> Whose liquor hath this virtuous property,
> To take from thence all error with his might,
> And make his eyeballs roll with wonted sight.
> When next they wake, all this derision
> Shall seem a dream and fruitless vision. (3.2.366–71)

This description frames a sleeping sight, a dream or vision, in terms that are strangely metaphorical and actual at the same moment. Oberon notes the particular physical effect of the removal of the error and asserts that the "wonted sight" can be restored. This effect is truly a part of the magical world, since this is not a forgetting but instead an alteration and restoration of previous vision. Lysander's sight will be regained, and he will take "True delight / In the sight / Of thy former lady's eye" (3.2455–7). For Demetrius' sight, he remains attached to Helena as she wishes. As he puts it, "the object and the pleasure of mine eye, / Is only Helena" (4.1.169–70). At the end of the visual confusions, Demetrius, whose spell has not been removed, describes his awakening as if his perception had been physically altered: "These things seem small and undistinguishable, / Like far-off mountains turned into clouds" (4.1.187–8).

Hermia responds to their awakening in a way that also questions the process of sight, "Methinks I see these things with parted eye, / When everything seems double" (4.1.189–90). The possibility of tricking one's own vision to see double almost reassures Hermia that her misperceptions could have been a matter of her own doing.[18] One 2006 production (with many interesting staging decisions) apparently took this description of doubleness as a literal direction and cast two actors each in the roles of Helena and

Hermia.[19] Each of the two characters was portrayed by two actors in matching costumes; these actors were on stage together only during the scenes in the forest. The lines for these two characters were divided amongst the four actors. Although the splitting of the lines confused matters in places, this casting choice visually emphasized for playgoers the otherwise interior changes the characters experience. Even without an actual doubling of the two female characters into four actors, playgoers understand Hermia's comment about the splitting or doubling of the events. In another instance of performance doubling, Bob Hall's 2011 production added three male actors as "henchmen" to accompany Puck. Partly this addition served to aid some necessary stage business in the outdoor production; more importantly, it served to emphasize and expand the regularity in duplication of characters.[20] In the Hall production, the choice provided matching male "henchmen" attendant on Oberon to duplicate the female fairies attendant on Titania. The doubleness Hermia remarks on in her own experience encourages playgoers' awareness of the pairings in the play, an awareness I explore later in this chapter.

Titania, the originally proposed victim of the potion, confirms the visual basis of the experience when the effects are reversed. When the spell is removed from Titania, her first comment reveals her impression of the events, "My Oberon, what visions have I seen!" (4.1.76). It is worth taking a moment with this use of "visions," which correlates with the first usage offered in the *Oxford English Dictionary*: "something which is apparently seen otherwise than by ordinary sight; *esp.* an appearance of a prophetic or mystical character, or having the nature of a revelation, supernaturally presented to the mind either in sleep or in an abnormal state."[21] Titania accurately assesses her experience, it was both "seen otherwise than by ordinary sight" and supernaturally caused by the love potion and Puck's cranial trickery. She does not, however, claim that perhaps she dreamt the events as Bottom claims. Nor does Titania attempt to reconcile her memory by asserting that her eyes were tricked, which of course would be true for Titania in ways it is not for either Hermia or Helena. She recognizes the change in her perceptions, "O, how mine eyes do loathe his visage now!" (4.1.79), but she does not question what might have been wrong with her sight.

Bottom's memory of his experience rejects the events that he, without the aid of eye potions, experienced:

> Methought I was, and methought I had – but man is but a patch'd fool, if he will offer to say what methought I had. The eye of man hath not heard, the ear of man hath not seen, man's hand is not able to taste, his tongue to conceive, nor his heart to report, what my dream was. (4.1.208-14)

Bottom's suggestion that he might be "a patch'd fool" is usually glossed as referring to the patchwork motley of a fool.[22] He might also refer to a man with a patch covering an eye as described in George Chapman's *Blind Beggar of Alexandria*, when Irus obligingly tells the fortune – sees into the future – of Elimine and describes a man she will see when she looks out of her father's tower:

> And if he woe [woo], you chuse him from the world,
> Though he seem humorous and want an eye,
> Wearing a velvet patch upon the same,
> Chuse him your husband, and be blest in him[.][23]

Irus has his own deceptive plan underway here, but the patch is an aspect of the vision Irus provides in a contemperaneous play also heavily dependent on visual trickery. Bottom's description of a "patch'd fool" may refer to his sight having been hindered. In Bottom's description, the mixing of the senses and their proper actions does more than rotate the various means of apprehension and the sense organs. The initial confounding of sight and sound switches the role of the eye and the ear as sense organs. However, if we attempt to reorient the other sense organs to their more accustomed means of apprehension (tongue with "taste" or tongue with "report"), we are still left with the heart and hand as sense organs in Bottom's description.[24] Peter Holland suggests that this "garbling may be taken, of course, as the complex synaesthetic experience of the mystic who sees visions but it is more likely to be the kind of mistake to which Bottom and his fellow-workers are prone."[25] In the context of so many other characters' experiences of misapprehension, the confusion connects, I think, to the widespread concerns in the play about functional and dysfunctional sense organs.

Seeing the play

The characters in *A Midsummer Night's Dream* all rely heavily on sight even while questioning its accuracy. Yet, on the whole, the characters are a particularly uninformed batch of individuals. None of these characters has a grasp of the activities of the others in the play. Bottom interacts with all of the other groups of characters, but this access does little to offer him a complete picture of events. Oberon seems to know quite a lot about the events in the wood, and he and Titania knowledgably discuss the upcoming wedding between Theseus and Hippolyta. However, Oberon and Titania have no knowledge of Egeus' complaint against his daughter, which precipitates the lovers' flight into the wood. In many of Shakespeare's plays at least one character is a lot more aware of what is happening than is any character in *A Midsummer Night's Dream*.[26] Yet, in this play, playgoers have a fairly complete view of the events. No last-minute revelations surprise the playgoers with a long-lost family member; no sudden recovery from assumed death presents a missing character; no removal of disguise effects an untangling of narrative knots. Unlike the characters, the playgoers have in hand all of the strands of the plot.

The experience of this play offers playgoers different types of confusions. It is a commonplace to remark on the "chaos of the first four acts" of the play and to assert that the performance of the play-within-the-play functions as a separate piece tagged on to the end of the plot and action of the play.[27] However, the chaos effected by the love potion occurs in just over a third of the entire play.[28] Playgoers' confusion is more likely to arise from other constructs in the play's narrative structure. Despite the fact that we have nearly complete knowledge of the series of events, the opening moments of the play raise questions about how we might perceive those events. Theseus and Hippolyta offer conflicting descriptions of the passage of time, and this disparity emphasizes the ways that perception alters individual experiences of events. While Theseus complains at "how slow / This old moon wanes," Hippolyta observes that "Four days will quickly steep themselves in night" (1.1.3–4, 8). The assertion of the multiplicity of experiences of the same events (or here the passage of the same amount of time) establishes immediately that characters will see things differently from other characters who experience the same happenings. As playgoers, we can reconcile these differences by separating ourselves from the ways the characters perceive events. In other words, we already know we will not be watching the performance over a period of four days, and it is a small step to noting that the experiences on stage differ between the characters.

Part of how we, as playgoers, process discontinuities in a play depends particularly on which of the playgoers' sensibilities the discontinuities disrupt. Shakespearean play texts establish and disrupt continuities for playgoers in several ways. Recent work on early modern staging has revealed ways that conditions of particular theaters alter the staging possibilities.[29] Plays written with early modern stages in mind clearly depend on the physical apparatus available to the theaters of the period. I am interested in the ways these early modern conditions of staging, represented in the texts, permeate the construction of the narrative. Janette Dillon has explained, "The design of Elizabethan playhouses, like the writing habits of their dramatists, encouraged attention to symmetry and balance in the blocking of scenes."[30] In most cases, these factors in the narratives are, I think, still apparent in more recent productions regardless of the playing space. For example, regardless of the number of exits available on a modern stage, Shakespeare's plays rely on characters moving on and off stage in ways that create spatial meaning for the playgoers. Oftentimes these requirements in the text create difficulties for modern productions that do not have the physical apparatus; and canny staging can often produce similar effects without the staging conditions that would have been available in the early modern era. For example, in an open space completely lacking in clearly delineated exits, Bob Hall's 2011 outdoor production of *A Midsummer Night's Dream* had additional henchmen characters in 3.2 hold opposite ends of long swaths of material to effect the exits of Lysander and Demetrius by swooping the fabric over them. Not only do the characters need to be baffled here in this scene, but the playgoers need to have the characters hidden from sight to emphasize the bafflement that allows Puck to tire Lysander and Demetrius into forgetting their argument with one another. In scenes such as this one, where multiple, quick entrances and exits form an integral part of the narrative, early modern theater architecture clearly inflects the play text.[31]

Control of the stage space likewise contributes to the narrative. Playgoers can recognize entrances of royalty, often accompanied by heraldic sounds, and the roles of the other characters are often established by the relative physical position of a monarch The opening First Folio stage direction of *A Midsummer Night's Dream* reads, "Enter Theseus, Hippolita, with others" (TLN 3). Theseus' relative importance becomes immediately clear and generally the blocking of the scene leaves Theseus in the position upstage holding the power as Egeus enters with his daughter and the two young men seeking the adjudication the ruler can provide. The dialogue tells us that Egeus must abide by Theseus' decision. Importantly, the organization of the space and the control of it which Theseus has, prior to Egeus' entrance, also support and bolster these power structures. When a character remains onstage after a scene with many characters, we assume that the character is still in the same location, but generally the character's solitary situation is heightened. I have already mentioned Helena's soliloquy at the end of 1.1, and it is worth noticing that Helena is twice-removed from the powers of decision making. The adjudicating scene finishes, leaving Hermia and Lysander onstage to make their plans when Helena arrives to complain of Demetrius' treatment of her. After Hermia and Lysander tell her of their plans, they exit, leaving Helena alone on stage for her soliloquy. This double-remove from the allegedly binding decisions of the first part of the scene and the slightly more proximate remove from Hermia and Lysander's decision emphasize how far Helena is from being able to realize her desires. We, as playgoers, know of her existence before her entrance since Lysander has described Demetrius' shabby treatment of her; Theseus in that moment, seems unlikely to take up the situation in any meaningful manner. No one acts on behalf of Helena in the first scene, and her delayed and removed entrance reinforces these structures.

   Being left alone on the stage is the opportunity for a soliloquy (although there are instances when certain aside speeches could be considered soliloquies and occasionally there is a possibility of soliloquy being overheard).[32] The accepted convention – which functions perfectly well through early modern drama – is that characters speaking in soliloquy tell truth. Or at least the truth as it appears to them at the time. In *Two Gentlemen of Verona*, we may not believe Proteus' descriptions in 2.6, but we believe that *he* believes in his dilemma over Valentine, Silvia, and Julia. Likewise, we might not believe in the logic of love's blindness that Helena sets out in her soliloquy, but we do believe that *she* believes it. Because we as playgoers accept the convention, solitary appearances on stage are weighted with a truth value and form a connection between those soliloquizing characters and playgoers not quite possible for characters who do not have those interactions. In *A Midsummer Night's Dream*, Helena is the only character who has a soliloquy in the most common circumstance of being left alone on stage after interacting with the other characters. When Theseus enters alone in 3.2, he only has three lines before Puck enters bearing the news Theseus wants. In the other two instances of characters left alone on stage, both are characters awakening and imagining they are not alone. Hermia wakes from her dream in 2.2 and frantically seeks the already absent (and potion-affected) Lysander; Bottom awakes in 4.1 worried about the performance of *Pyramus and Thisbe*; he calls out his instructions, "When my cue comes, call me and I will answer" (ll. 200–201). In the soliloquy that follows, we learn that Bottom understands his experiences to have been a dream.

These three soliloquies from these three different characters all function in different ways to move the narrative. In the first scene, we are given to understand how Helena sees her love situation, but we are not provided with a later chance in soliloquy that could encourage us to continue to see events from her perspective. Hermia's soliloquy functions not so much as a soliloquy for the playgoers as for an absent Lysander, and we are in fact more separated from her experience through the dramatic irony of already knowing the reason for his absence. Bottom's soliloquy does occur as he is left alone onstage, but he has not been interacting with the scene immediately preceding his awakening. In some productions, his awakening surprises some playgoers who have forgotten he remains on stage. Noticeably, *A Midsummer Night's Dream* does not allow the playgoers' sympathies to be aligned with any particular character's difficulties. Through Bottom's soliloquy, we may understand his perspective on the events he experienced, but since we saw what he did experience even if he does not believe it, dramatic irony again separates us from his perspective. Soliloquies in many of Shakespeare's plays encourage playgoers to shift perspectives, but the soliloquies in *A Midsummer Night's Dream* do not take advantage of this possibility and instead more carefully maintain the separations between the characters and the playgoers.

Another way playgoers orient themselves in relation to the actions on stage is reliance on a particular character as a "normalizing" character. These are characters the playgoers depend on to verify particular events, often supernatural. I mentioned above that, in many plays, at least one character has more awareness of the entirety of the narrative than any one of the characters in *A Midsummer Night's Dream*. Often knowledgeable characters act as "normalizing" characters, providing playgoers with a perspective from a trustworthy character. Kent in *King Lear* shows us the folly of Lear's early actions by enduring the king's wrath for the chance to speak what we assume to be the truth. Banquo's presence with Macbeth, when both encounter the witches, ensures that playgoers see that the witches' exist outside Macbeth's imagination. In *A Midsummer Night's Dream*, we do not have a "normalizing" character to assure us of the experiences of the characters. However, we do know of the potion in advance of its use, we see Puck follow Bottom off stage before he returns "translated," we hear Puck's description of the events, and we know before Puck of the error he made in anointing Lysander's eyes. In other words, the machinery of the magical or supernatural elements of the narrative is revealed to us as the events occur or even before they occur. In a correlative fashion, the literal for the characters becomes metaphorical for the playgoers in a manner not always the case in Shakespeare plays. Part of our awareness of the narrative extends to understanding metaphorical aspects the characters cannot discern, as when Hermia finds herself in the dark and we realize she is in the dark metaphorically. Ralph Berry has pointed out that, although "'eye' is easily the main motif," analyses of Shakespeare's metaphors and imagery often pass by the eye motif, "because the word is normally a part of the literal text and not a metaphor at all."[33] Yet, as playgoers, we do in some instances experience these literal uses as metaphorical. These literal uses that shade into the metaphorical have some correlations with articulated metaphors. We might consider the storm in *King Lear* an articulated metaphor that realizes the storm and upheaval of Lear's turbulent mind; the characters in the play experience the metaphorical implications.[34] The pervasive use of eyes and the visual, in *A Midsummer Night's Dream*, functions literally for the characters and metaphorically for the playgoers.

In many of Shakespeare's plays, there are multiple time frames at work simultaneously; this play disrupts the time frame slightly but maintains locations in unusually strict ways. Although four days pass between the trial scene at the beginning and the wedding celebrated by the production of *Pyramus and Thisbe* at the end, playgoers see the characters experience only one night. The locations of the series of scenes make a clear pattern: the beginning in the court, the casting scene with the mechanicals, five scenes in the woods, return to a short scene with the mechanicals, and finally the return to court. The center-most of the five scenes in the woods is 3.1 when Bottom's metamorphosis takes place. J.L. Styan reminds us "it is a modern habit to query the place of the action," and he claims that Shakespeare wrote drama that "created its own atmosphere and identified its own locality, if it needed to."[35] But locational markers in a play do establish relationships between the places where events occur, even if a specific locality might not be clear. So while some characters offer clear statements, "so this is Tyre, and this the court" (*Cymbeline* 1.3.1), in many more instances, the events of the narrative establish locations. *A Midsummer Night's Dream* depends heavily on the magical atmosphere of the woods, but despite the importance of fantastical events, the locations in the play are stable. We know we are seeing the court: the nobility have entered with attendants and a citizen arrives seeking adjudication. We know we are seeing characters in the woods, because we know of the plan (and the reason) to meet "in the palace wood, a mile without the town, [...] for if we meet in the city, we shall be dogg'd with company" (1.2.102–4). Likewise, we hear Lysander and Hermia's plan to meet "in the wood, a league without the town" (1.1.165). The play offers firm locational markers for playgoers, even for upcoming spaces.

In the middle section of the play, the portion with the most visual confusions, the structure of the scenes includes another way of absolutely fixing the location for the playgoers. In the only such instance in the First Folio, stage directions clearly note that characters remain on stage (asleep, but remaining) through act breaks. Titania falls asleep during act two and is awakened by Bottom's singing in the third act. In 3.2, Puck leads Demetrius and Lysander astray from one another to keep them from fighting and essentially to deposit them, asleep, in full view on the stage. The Folio stage directions are more explicit than usual about the actions and include an "*Exit*" for Puck, a note of '*shifting places*," and the imperative "*lye down*" (TLN 1446, 1460, 1462). Once all four of the young lovers are asleep on the stage, the scene (and act) ends with the note that "*They sleepe all the Act*" (TLN 1506). This textual imperative contradicts the usual notions of act or scene breaks, which most commonly occur when characters have cleared the stage. As playgoers, we may not realize that an act break occurs at this moment, but the oddity of it in the text is noticeable. A central effect of these continuations through the act breaks is playgoers' certainty that the location has not shifted. While we may not know the exact location in the wood, these matters of stagecraft establish the stage as stable space. Importantly, in this play so fixated on vision, the playgoers establish the location visually, so other discrepancies (in time, for example) matter less.[36]

Given the connections between sleep and not seeing, it is interesting that, in this instance of anchoring the space of the stage, we depend visually on bodies that themselves are unseeing. In his aphoristic manner, Richard Banister in the *Breviary of the Eye* says, "sleep is caused by the retraction of the spirits, into their secret places."[37] In *A Midsummer Night's Dream*, sleeping characters are removed to secret places and the instances of waking alone show us where they have gone in their dreams: Hermia dreams of a serpent; Bottom reorients himself to understand his experiences as a dream. Helkiah Crooke goes into the question of sleep and perception at greater length. In the marginal gloss on the following passages, he notes, with certainty, "The poets say sleepe is the brother of death. Disproved." Crooke explains,

> then those which sleepe with open eies should also see because the colour doth alter the Organ. In like manner a sound might be heard, odours smelt; and any tactile quality might be felt by us; seeing that the Organ is altred by the Object, and yet when wee are asleepe we neither do see, nor heare, nor *Perceyve* with anie other Sense except the Objects be verie vehement. Have therefore the Poets truly faigned that sleepe is the brother of death, because it dooth deprive us of all our sense, yea of our verie Touch; insomuch that it seemeth to extinguish the creature & bereave it not of Sense onely but of life also? Or else do we *perceyve* while we sleepe, and know not that we have Sense? The first cannot be, for although sleepe have a great corrrespondencie and affinitie with death, yet it doth not deprive the creature of sense. For these things do concurre unto Sense: a convenient object, an organ fitly disposed, the alteration of the same organ and a sensitive Facultie, al[l] which things we have even when we sleepe.
>
> [...]

> Seeing therefore in sleepe we have the object actuallie prepared unto sensation, seeing also the organ fitly disposed is not wanting, and the judging Faculty at hande, and that nothing more is required unto perfect sense; it is not to be doubted but that Sensation may be absolved in the organ and judgement also given of the object even when we have no sense at all, but because we know not that we have Sense.[38]

I quote Crooke at length here because his ways of setting out the question of whether the poets are right to connect sleep and death are particularly useful when thinking about the perspectives on sleep that appear in *A Midsummer Night's Dream*. Sleeping and dreaming are obviously important to both thematic and narrative framings of the play, and we are invited as playgoers to view more sleeping bodies together on stage in this play than in any other of Shakespeare's plays. We are reminded that the sleepers are still capable of perception as they are sleeping, but what they perceive has little to do with their surroundings and everything to do with their sleeping visions or dreams. We do not have characters awakened with an awareness of some "vehement" interruption, instead the characters, while sleeping, "know not that [they] have 'sense.'" In the same ways that characters do not read their own sensory abilities as metaphorical, characters do not attain more awareness through their sleep. Garrett Sullivan has clarified that, in epic and romance in the period, "On the one hand, then, sleep is a *binding* of the senses. On the other, sleep encodes an *overindulgence* of the senses. This seeming contradiction certainly speaks to a slippage between sleep's narrow medical definition and its broader conceptual resonances."[39] The characters in *A Midsummer Night's Dream* have their senses bound by sleep; we as playgoers are encouraged to take the other position here and see the possibility of dreaming as an overindulgence.

Crooke's description catalogs the possible actions of the body that sleeps; as playgoers we have a different perspective on the sleeping bodies on the stage. The resonances in the theater between a sleeping body and a dead body are encouraged by the conventions of onstage deaths. Juliet's sleep that passes for death, Imogen's accidentally feigned death, Henry IV's sleep, and Falstaff's counterfeit death all make clear the possibility of sleeping bodies being mistaken for dead bodies. *A Midsummer Night's Dream*'s stage filled with vulnerable, unmoving, unsensing bodies might cause playgoers to recall other, similarly filled, stages of tragedies. One sign that an early modern tragedy nears its end is a disregard for removal of the dead. This visually tragic possibility – a stage filled with sleeping bodies – contributes to the feeling in *A Midsummer Night's Dream* that once the characters regain their senses, then the play has run its course. This awakening may account for the tendency to read the play as mainly and essentially over once the lovers awaken and are reintegrated into the waking society of Theseus and Hippolyta. Ralph Berry seems to point to these convergences in generic images when he says, "The tragedies were always present in the comedies; and they were always going to be written. The conclusions implied, but not stated in the comedies, were one day to be pursued."[40] Possibly the connection between the end of a play and seeing the reanimation of sleeping or dead bodies was a clearer correlation for early modern playgoers, if they were more accustomed to seeing the actors at the end of a tragedy rise for post-play activities. Some of Shakespeare's tragedies (*Hamlet* and *Antony and Cleopatra*, for instance) have removal of the bodies built into the mechanics of the final scenes. In other cases, we cannot be certain about post-play activities or the methods employed to clear the stage. Even if dead characters are removed rather than reanimating at the end of the play, the end of a tragedy is the usual moment for the stage image of multiple inanimate bodies in the playing space.

However, the final act of the play insists, in several ways, that playgoers question or at least confront the reliability of their own visual perceptions. The mechanicals make a strong point of how Moonshine will illuminate the proceedings:

> Sweet Moon, I thank thee for thy sunny beams;
> I thank thee, Moon, for shining now so bright;
> For by thy gravious, golden, glittering gleams,
> I trust to take of truest Thisby sight. (5.1.273–5)

Pyramus makes so much of how his vision depends on the light from the moon that when he says, "Moon, take thy flight" (5.1.305), Hippolyta inquires, "How chance Moonshine is gone before Thisby comes back and finds her lover?" (5.1.310–11). Theseus, apparently more accustomed to the theatrical conventions, assures her, "she will find him by starlight" (5.1.315). Pyramus has sufficient light to see the mantle "stain'd with blood" (5.1.283), but like so many characters in this play, he mistakes the meaning in what he sees. Thisby still has sufficient light to see the dead Pyramus, whether by starlight or by the illumination of the end of the play. When Theseus refuses the epilogue, he claims that they "this night have overwatch'd" the play" (5.1.366). Evans notes that "overwatch'd" here means "stayed up too late," which may well be the case, but the emphasis on the visual aspects are noticeable. In Hall's 2011 production, these aspects of the final act were accentuated by the after-intermission electric lighting, which replaced the natural evening lighting of the first half. In the American Shakespeare Center 2009 production, universal lighting at the Blackfriars Playhouse emphasized that the concerns about lighting for the play-within-a-play were unmentioned worries in the play itself.[41]

The fact that playgoers know a good deal more about the narrative of the play than any of the characters encourages us to imagine that our knowledge extends farther than it might. Particularly in the final act of the play, we see characters offered what might be considered choices while we imagine these as already decided. When Theseus asks, "say, what abridgement have you for this evening,/ What masque? what music?" (5.1.39–40), there seems to be little question about what entertainment will be chosen. As playgoers we have seen Bottom and the mechanicals rehearsing and must be fairly certain that their performance will be the one we will see. Despite what seems a foregone conclusion here, other entertainments are offered.[42] H.R. Coursen notes that Richard Sewell's 1982 production took advantage of this opening in the play where "Lysander mimed a desire for the keen satire that Theseus dismisses."[43] As playgoers we cannot take seriously the other possibilities on offer. Even without knowing the play, our narrative certainty makes us smugly aware that we will see the "tedious brief scene of young Pyramus/ And his love Thisby; very tragical mirth" (5.1.56–7). The fulfillment of this expectation adds to playgoers' impressions of accurate perception and awareness.

This perception by playgoers – that we can understand the play better than any of the characters in it – might contribute to the multiplicity of ways of producing the play and the fact that many of those productions rely heavily on visual spectacle. Jeremy Lopez has noted that the proliferation of productions of this very popular play actually increase the multiplicity of approaches to it; he continues,

"But, also due to the proliferation of productions, the strikingly varied performance styles and concepts have a persistent underlying similarity, namely the self-conscious insistence upon their own novelty or ingenuity."[44] The structures of novel visions, which form so much of the construction of the play's narrative, may contribute to the desire for novelty on the part of productions.

The ending of the play insists that playgoers confront the reliability of their own visual perceptions. Oberon frames his blessing "to the best bride-bed" (5.1.403) in terms of guarding against the existence of visible marks of imperfection on the off-spring:

> And the issue, there create,
> Ever shall be fortunate.
> So shall all the couples three
> Ever true in loving be;
> And the blots of Nature's hand
> Shall not in their issue stand;
> Never mole, hare-lip, nor scar,
> Nor mark prodigious, such as are
> Despised in nativity,
> Shall upon their children be. (5.1.405–9)

Oberon's blessing on the bride-bed sounds as both a warning and a reiteration of the entire narrative's insistence on the primacy of a completely fallible sense – vision. More pointedly, Puck's immediate direct address to us as playgoers, the imperative to think "That you have but slumb'red here/ While these visions did appear," encourages us to question our own notions about the "weak and idle theme" that may be "but a dream" (5.1.425–6, 427, 428). The play presents a narrative that constantly placates us with much more information than the characters have, while simultaneously reminding playgoers that we receive the information through the very sense shown to be capable of gross misperceptions.

Notes

1. These ways of seeing are related to what Harold Brooks terms, in his introduction to the second-series Arden edition of the play (London: Thomson, 1974), "love-sight, true and false, a principal motif [that] belongs to the wide-ranging subject of appearance and reality" (xcii).

2. Richard Banister, *Banister's Breviary of the Eyes*, in Jacques Gillemeau, *A treatise of one hundred and thirteene diseases of the eyes, and eye-liddes. The second time published, with some profitable additions of certaine principles and experiments*, by Richard Banister (London: Felix Kynston for Thomas Man, 1622), STC 12499.5, Folger Call Number STC1362. This quotation appears on b1^r.
3. Ibid.
4. Andreas du Laurens, *A Discourse of the Preservation of the Sight: of Melancholike Diseases; of Rheumes, and of Old Age*, trans. Richard Surphlet (London: Felix Kingston for Ralph Jacson, 1599), STC 7304. This quotation appears on G3^r.
5. Ibid.
6. In his anatomy manual, *Mikrokosmographia: A Description of the Body of Man. Together with the Controversies Thereto Belonging* (London: William Jaggard, 1615), STC 6062, Helkiah Crooke sets out the standard descriptions answering the question of "Whether sight be made by Emission or Reception" (Lll3^v). Although he claims "the nature of the sight is accurately explained," he sets out a variety of opinions and finally supports reception with Galen as his main source (Lll3^v–Lll4^v).
7. Stuart Clark, *Vanities of the Eye: Vision in Early Modern European Culture* (Oxford: Oxford University Press, 2007), 20.
8. Ibid.
9. Samuel Y. Edgerton, *The Mirror, the Window, and the Telescope: How Renaissance Linear Perspective Changed Our Vision of the Universe* (New York: Cornell University Press, 2008). See also Kristen Poole, *Supernatural Environments in Shakespeare's England: Spaces of Demonism, Divinity, and Drama* (Cambridge: Cambridge University Press, 2011), where she reads *Othello* in the context of visual representations on the stage (58–94).
10. Sir Philip Sidney, *The Defence of Poesy*, in *The Oxford Authors: Sir Philip Sidney*, ed. Katherine Duncan-Jones (Oxford: Oxford University Press, 1989), 212–250, 243.
11. Brent M. Cohen, "'What is it you would see?' Hamlet and the Conscience of the Theatre," *ELH* 44.2 (1977), 226. Cohen's argument reads *Hamlet* to contend that the specific conditions of Elizabethan theatre produced an audience experience that (contrary to Romantic notions of identification or subjectivity) raised questions about "the implications of producing plays for entertainment" (223).
12. In Peter Holland's edition of the play (Oxford: Oxford University Press, 1994), the quoted line appears at 1.1.31.
13. Ralph Berry, *Shakespeare's Comedies: Explorations in Form* (Princeton, NJ: Princeton University Press, 1972), 91.
14. The 1605 example from the *Oxford English Dictionary* is from Francis Bacon's *Advancement of Learning*: "We haue endeauoured in these our Partitions to observe a kind of perspectiue, that one part may cast light vpon another" (II: Hh3). The question of "perspective" arises also in *Richard II*; see Chapter 2.

15. Crooke, *Mikrokosmographia*, Kkk2^{r-v}.
16. The *Oxford English Dictionary* uses this example from *A Midsummer Night's Dream* as illustrative of *n*.5: "The action of laying hold of with the senses; conscious perception."
17. *A Midsummer Night's Dream*, by William Shakespeare, directed by Charles McMahon, Lantern Theater, Philadelphia PA, March 10–April 17, 2011. Etzold discussed her interpretation of these lines in a theater-sponsored event on March 21, 2011.
18. In her revelatory reading of *A Midsummer Night's Dream* in *Shakespeare From the Margins: Language, Culture, Context* (Chicago: University of Chicago Press, 1996), Patricia Parker connects these lines to the joinery she traces through the plays: "the disjunctions and parodic deformations committed by characters dismissed by their superiors as rude mechanicals opens this play's own ending to the seaming as well as seeming of the 'parted eye / When everything seems double' (IV.i.189–90), exposing its more conventional joinings as the *exercise* of closure, the mechanical production whose 'rule' brings about its sanctioned matrimonial end" (107).
19. *A Midsummer Night's Dream*, by William Shakespeare, directed by Mark Lord, Goodhart Theater, Bryn Mawr PA, November 10–18, 2006. This production by the Bi-College Theater Program of Bryn Mawr and Haverford Colleges emphasized the connections to sleeping and dreaming with a stage space constricted by an enormous bed as the main set piece; the mechanicals initially appeared perched on the footboard downstage.
20. *A Midsummer Night's Dream*, by William Shakespeare, directed by Bob Hall, Flatwater Shakespeare at Lincoln Foundation Garden, Lincoln NE, June 15–26, 2011. For a more complete description of the stage business and the effects of these added roles, see my review: "*A Midsummer Night's Dream* and *Othello*," *Shakespeare Bulletin* 30.2 (2012), 181–188.
21. The *Oxford English Dictionary* lists an instance from 1290 as a first use; the uses continue through the nineteenth century, with several examples from the sixteenth century.
22. See Holland, *Midsummer*, 4.1.207fn.
23. See the *Oxford English Dictionary* "patch, n.1.I.d" where a portion of this passage from the *Blind Beggar* appears as an early example. George Chapman, *Blind Beggar of Alexandria* (London: William Jones, 1598) STC 4965. This passage appears on B1^v.
24. For a clear discussion of Bottom's reliance on 1 Corinthians 2:9–10, see Peter Holland's introduction to the Oxford edition of the play.
25. Holland, "Introduction," 83.
26. For example: Kent in *Lear*, Horatio in *Hamlet*, Prospero in *The Tempest*, Rosalind (arguably) in *As You Like It*, Friar Lawrence in *Romeo and Juliet*, Leonato in *Much Ado About Nothing*, the Duke in *Measure for Measure*, Helena in *All's Well That Ends Well*.
27. See R. W. Dent for both a note of the "chaos of the first four acts" and an attempt to better integrate a reading of the performance by the mechanicals; "Imagination in *A Midsummer Night's Dream*," *Shakespeare Quarterly*

15.2 (1964), 104. Patricia Parker's more recent reading of the play in *Shakespeare from the Margins* centers on the role of the mechanicals and thus emphasizes the last act of the play.
28. The love potion has its effects in the last fifty lines of 2.2 and is resolved within the first forty-five lines of 4.1. The confusion then includes the entirety of 3.1 (approximately 213 lines) and all of 3.2 (approximately 519 lines). If the total number of lines in the play is 2,328, the love potion is mistakenly in force for approximately 35 percent of the entirety. Other Shakespeare plays often maintain these confused identities through more of the narrative; for example, Viola in *Twelfth Night*, and Rosalind in *As You Like It*.
29. Alan Dessen and Leslie Thomson's *A Dictionary of Stage Directions in English Drama 1580–1642* (Cambridge: Cambridge University Press, 2001) proves an invaluable reference for comparing the use of particular stage directions. Tim Fitzpatrick's *Playwright, Space and Place in Early Modern Performance: Shakespeare and Company* (Aldershot: Ashgate, 2011) convincingly traces a number of textual markers that frame and determine early modern staging possibilities.
30. Janette Dillon, *Shakespeare and the Staging of History*, (Oxford: Oxford University Press, 2012), 31.
31. See Mariko Ichikawa, *Shakespearean Entrances* (London: Palgrave, 2002) for a systematic tracing of meaning making through entrances and exits.
32. For example, Leontes' asides in *The Winter's Tale* or the possibility of Hamlet being overheard. In *Themes and Conventions of Elizabethan Tragedy* (Cambridge: Cambridge University Press, 1935), Muriel Bradbrook pointed out that, "The aside is the bridge between dialogue and soliloquy in the Elizabethan drama. Some asides are so lengthy that they are practically soliloquies" (121). See also Jeremy Lopez' more recent work on the aside in *Theatrical Convention and Audience Response in Early Modern Drama* (Cambridge: Cambridge University Press, 2003).
33. Berry, *Shakespeare's Comedies*, 95–96.
34. Henry Turner has described the importance of what he calls "a *topographic* approach to theatrical representation," particularly in relation to locations in *King Lear*. Turner, *The English Renaissance Stage* (New York: Oxford University Press, 2006) 165.
35. J.L. Styan, *Shakespeare's Stagecraft* (Cambridge: Cambridge University Press, 1971), 29.
36. I depend on J.L. Styan's descriptions and terminology in *Shakespeare's Stagecraft*. On the ways meaningful patterns are formed by the necessities of the stage, see Emrys Jones, *Scenic Form in Shakespeare* (Oxford: Oxford University Press, 1971).
37. Banister, *Breviary of the Eye*, B1^v.
38. Crooke, *Mikrokosmographia*, Kkk6^r.
39. Garrett Sullivan's *Sleep, Romance and Human Embodiment* (Cambridge: Cambridge University Press, 2012) uses sleep to examine epic and romance, within the context of Aristotelian notions of the tripartite

soul, and he convincingly argues that we need to attend more closely to the modes of humanness revealed in these genres. The quotation in the text appears on page 18. His examination of *1 Henry IV*, *2 Henry IV*, and *Henry V* reveals that sleep "represents the ground for biological being—that which binds man to animal—and the condition that must be transcended to be fully, monarchically human" (95).
40. Berry, *Shakespeare's Comedies*, 23.
41. *A Midsummer Night's Dream*, by William Shakespeare, directed by the Repertory Company of the Actors' Renaissance Season, Blackfriars Playhouse, Staunton VA, Jan–Mar 2009.
42. The First Folio assigns reading the descriptions to Lysander; Brooks offers a note justifying the use of Q1 assignment of the lines to Theseus (Brooks, *Midsummer*, 5.1.43 fn). Evans likewise assigns the lines to Theseus.
43. Coursen remarks on the appropriateness of the action in that production: "a nice bit of action for a Lysander imaged as a young Tennyson." Coursen also describes, in the same Richard Sewell 1982 production, that: "Kim Gordon's Helena recognized, however inarticulately, the relationship between 'Pyramus and Thisby' and the lovers' experience in the woods. No one else, of course, paid Helena any attention. I later asked Director Sewell whether I had read Helena's reaction aright. 'Yes,' he said, 'but we didn't think it would play that way.'" H.R. Coursen, "Shakespeare in the Sticks," *Shakespeare Quarterly* 36.5 (1985): 644–647, 647.
44. Jeremy Lopez, "*Dream*: The Performance History," in *A Midsummer Night's Dream: A Critical Guide*, ed. Regina Buccola (London: Continuum, 2010), 44–73, 53.

2
Grounded Action and Making Space in *Richard II*
"How comest thou hither?"

In the previous chapter, I concentrated on the repeated use of "eyes" and sight in *A Midsummer Night's Dream* as a way of understanding how playgoers are exposed to a variety of notions of how sight functions, both within the frame of the play and for the playgoers themselves. While *Richard II* is not so obviously dependent on the motif of vision, the visual has important reverberations in the moments when characters are left alone on stage. The noticeable dearth of soliloquies in *A Midsummer Night's Dream* is also the case in *Richard II*. In *Richard II*, only two characters have soliloquies: Salisbury in 2.4 and Richard in 5.6.[1] I think it worthwhile in the first of these to tease out some of the connections to vision in order to pave the way for some of the larger concerns of this chapter.[2] Salisbury remains on stage after the departure of a Welsh Captain in the very short 2.4. Salisbury's soliloquy before departure is a brief seven lines, but effectively connects the truth-telling aspects of a soliloquy to many of the recurrent images in the play. Noticeably, Salisbury draws attention to his vision of Richard through the "eyes of heavy mind" (2.4.18). He even more emphatically notes the metaphoric nature of his vision by providing the linking "like" when he says, "I see thy glory like a shooting star / Fall to the base earth from the firmament" (2.4.19–20). The emphasis on the cosmic realms of shooting stars is immediately linked to the "base earth," an important recurrent motif in the play. The remaining four lines present visually metaphoric images of the decline of Richard's power:

> Thy sun sets weeping in the lowly west,
> Witnessing storms to come, woe, and unrest.

Thy friends are fled to wait upon thy foes,
And crossly to thy good all fortune goes. (2.4.21–4)

Salisbury's use of the sun, storms, fleeing friends, and the possibly-personified fortune all connect to recurrent image patterns in the play. Seeing these images through the "eyes of heavy mind" reminds the playgoers of the visual nature of the images and also compresses many of the concerns of the play into the only soliloquy before Richard appears alone in 5.6.

In the play's most obvious example of a visual conceit, Bushy tries in 2.2 to convince the queen that her sorrow changes her manner of vision so thoroughly that those things upon which she looks are seen as if they were complicated perspective pictures.[3] In his complex imagery, he seems to suggest that her attempts to see the king's departure have perceived "shapes of grief" rather than the realities of the situation. Bushy says the queen must be mistaken about her grief,

> For sorrow's eyes, glazed with blinding tears,
> Divides one thing entire to many objects,
> Like perspectives, which rightly gaz'd upon
> Show nothing but confusion; ey'd awry
> Distinguish form; so your sweet Majesty,
> Looking awry upon your lord's departure,
> Find shapes of grief, more than himself, to wail,
> Which, look'd on as it is, is nought but shadows
> Of what it is not; (2.2.16–24)

Scott McMillan has shown some of the difficulties in this passage and says that Bushy's figure of speech "seems to outrun his intention."[4] More to the point for this chapter, Jeremy Lopez suggests that the moment serves to align Bushy with the playgoers, since Bushy tries to work out the same questions that trouble those of us watching the play.[5] Bushy's description encourages us to attempt to work through a visual metaphor that has everything to do with how vision functions and, as it turns out, very little to do with the remaining action of the play (since, of course, the queen is right to worry). The fascination with sight does not pervade *Richard II* the way it does *A Midsummer Night's Dream*, but characters in *Richard II* experience some of the same confused perceptions.

In ways related to those at work in *A Midsummer Night's Dream*, *Richard II* also encourages playgoers to rethink their interpretations of the visual presentations of events. Written at close to the same time as *A Midsummer Night's Dream* (and *Romeo and Juliet*), *Richard II* plays with the difficulties of visual representation using rather different means than *A Midsummer Night's Dream*. In this chapter, I shall take up two of the predominant motifs in the play, the emphasis on "ground" and what Charles Forker has called "the matrix of references to language itself" to explore how these related spatial and verbal motifs alter the ways playgoers understand the play.[6] The play and particularly these motifs encourage playgoers to reconcile disparate visual and verbal imagery to understand the play's functions as history play and tragedy simultaneously. Brian Walsh has explored some of the ways the play works on those who experience it in the theater. Walsh suggests that the most noticeable feature of the play is its verse, which

> introduces and then only partially or inconsistently releases tension in the bodies of those taking it in as they exert themselves to hear a rhyme that doesn't come after a pattern of them has emerged, as they feel the surprising sensation of a rhyme they did not anticipate, or as they fidget through an uncomfortable, uncertain pause. All of these responses add up to a general feeling of being put out of sorts at the theater[.][7]

While I focus on the ways playgoers experience the play, my approach differs significantly from Walsh's by considering a connection between the metaphorical patterning and the spatial frame of the stage. Critical discussions of the imagery of earth, land, and ground in the play have often focused on the way these images connect to nationalistic, historic, or patriotic questions.[8] If we examine these images as instances of spatial description that aid playgoers in fixing location, we can understand some of the ways the play constructs a narrative dependent on physical boundaries. The continual and pervasive reiterations of "tongue," "mouth," and references to speech itself both link themselves to those physical possibilities and, at the same time, undermine those physical possibilities. This chapter, in some ways, returns to a question that E.M.W. Tillyard raised, "namely, why did Shakespeare in *Richard II* make the ceremonial or ritual form of writing, found in differing quantities in the *Henry VI* plays and in *Richard III*, not merely one of the principal means of expression but the very essence of the play?"[9] I think Tillyard's question here a valid one, and one we can still take seriously, insofar as it raises the issues of the ceremonial aspects of the play's language and encourages us to think about how that language functions. Tillyard argued for reading the play as an epic depiction of English medievalism, but we might think of his question in conjunction with the spaces available on the early modern stage to lead to a better understanding of the ways the play constructs dramatic meaning. I am interested in tracing the ways the play continually embeds itself in an idea of "land" and "ground," while concurrently connecting and undermining those images through speech acts that depend on simultaneous notions of geographical space and stage space.

Seeing Richard

The decline of Richard's power over the course of the play has frequently been remarked, but it proves useful to chart this decline through the ways the scenes establish spatial power. The opening of the play establishes Richard's power as monarch as he enters with a train and then, much like the adjudication in the opening of *A Midsummer Night's Dream*, he hears Bullingbrook and Mowbray's complaints. Gaunt's departure, ten lines before the end of the scene, shows the beginnings of the cracks in Richard's facade of power. The First Folio stage direction *"Exit Gaunt"* functions to ease the opening of the next scene, where Gaunt appears with the Duchess of Gloucester (TLN 205). This early exit gives the exiting actor time for an immediate re-entry and also allows the playgoers to understand that we are now seeing a different place when the next scene opens. The difficulty of Gaunt's exit without any dismissal from Richard has been read mainly as a textual problem, but particularly in performance it importantly serves to undermine Richard's control over the space of the first scene.[10] In 1.3, Richard appears after the Lord Marshal and Aumerle have announced his approach, which is a common framing for the entrance of a king.

However, the exit of Richard and his train in 1.3 leave Gaunt and Bullingbrook in control of the space and facilitates Bullingbrook's description of the impossibility of alterations through imagination alone.[11] In many ways, Bullingbrook asserts the opposite of Helena's soliloquy and insists on the actuality of physical experiences: "O, who can hold a fire in his hand/ By thinking on the frosty Caucasus?" (1.3.294–5).[12] Richard's next entrance, with Green and Bagot in 1.4, and his conversation with Aumerle are devoid of the pomp of official appearances, but the scene serves to quickly show playgoers his interactions with these characters. Richard's appearance at Gaunt's deathbed shows Richard taking up another kind of power, rather than control of the spaces around him. Gaunt's description of England "leased out" depends on the idea that Richard has lost control over and care of the space of the country. The King's entrance immediately after that speech, into a space controlled by Gaunt, makes visually apparent that which becomes verbally apparent in the narrative after the news of Gaunt's death. Richard asserts, "Towards our assistance we do seize to us/ The plate, coin, revenues, and moveables/ Whereof our uncle Gaunt did stand possess'd" (2.1.160–1). It is only after York protests, and Richard reiterates the list of possessions, that Richard includes "lands." And then it comes last: "Think what you will, we seize into our hands/ His plate, his goods, his money, and his lands" (2.1.209–10). Richard's own connection with the land and ground has diminished as he has lost control of the stage space.

As playgoers, we do not see Richard's forays into Ireland. The play relentlessly maintains its hold on playgoers in England and Wales. When Richard does return, his relationship to the land and the space around him alters again. He, of course, does not return from Ireland until 3.2, at which point Bullingbrook has already returned and begun to muster support and take prisoners. When Richard enters in 3.2, he is accompanied but not with powerful trappings and ceremonies. Instead, we see him uncertain about his location, "Barkloughly castle call they this at hand?" (3.2.1). He wants, after receiving the news, to "sit upon the ground" (3.2.155). Phyllis Rackin has noted the precision of the question about Barkloughly castle and argues that the "vehicle of Richard's metaphor is a powerful poetic image, but the tenor is a factual error, and Shakespeare takes pains that his audience shall notice that fact."[13] I think the scene depends more heavily on the characters' constructs of space on the stage rather than on a geographical notion that points out an anomaly. It is not all that unusual to have traveling characters ask questions to establish with precision their locations; "How far is't call'd to Forres?" is one obvious example I explore in a later chapter (*Macbeth* 1.3.39). Importantly, Richard's statement opens the scene, and thus mirrors Bullingbrook's arrival in 2.3, which opens with him asking, "How far is it, my lord, to Berkeley now?" (2.3.1). The verbal echo is obvious. The usurper and the king are both unable to locate themselves in these instances of return from the unportrayed spaces abroad. Jonathan Baldo has read the non-appearance of Ireland in the play as exemplary of the play's forgetfulness, asserting

> The brief intervention in Ireland returns us to Richard's injunction to the combatants at the beginning of the play to "forget." The episode makes Richards of us all. As we struggle to hold Ireland in our memories, we witness Richard, immediately on returning from Ireland, forgetting himself. As always, it is Richard's dazzling, distracting theatricality that is the primary agent of oblivion.[14]

To some extent playgoers do experience forgetting with Richard. But, in important ways related to the staging of the events, playgoers cannot remember the unseen events. Forgetting implies that we had the knowledge or experience. The activity of remembering, with its reference to bodily completion of the missing "members," always returns to the bodily existence of memory.

Richard's embedded stage direction, "dear earth, I do salute thee with my hand" (2.3.6), ensures that we see Richard touching the stage in a manner to convince us of his own belief in the possibility of the land itself returning to him. The repetition of his actions, with "greet I thee, my earth, / And thee favors with my royal hands" (3.2.10–11), claims a reality for the experience of touching, an experience playgoers see. When Richard rebukes the lords, he figures the stones themselves as sentient and questions his own perceptions: "Mock not my senseless conjuration, lords, / This earth shall have a feeling, and these stones / Prove armed soldiers" (3.2.23-5). Richard uses "senseless" here partly to mean "foolish," but the phrase carries with it the possibility that his senses do not function as they ought and that the earth and stones might have gained the possibilities of perception. Scroop's news of Bullingbrook's forces "covering your fearful land" (3.2.110), combined with other emphases in his description of the actualities of the countryside, push Richard to seat himself as reassurance of the tactile reality of the earth.

Except for his final appearance, Richard's remaining entrances in the play show him entering an already occupied stage. These scenic enclosures of his presence serve to heighten the differences between Richard in the first scene and Richard after his return from Ireland. They also make even more apparent the distinctive entrance alone in his final scene. In 3.3, the physical relationships are redefined by Richard's entrance above, where the First Folio stage direction reads, "*Parle without, and answere within: then a Flourish. Enter on the Walls, Richard, Carlisle, Aumerle, Scroop, Salisbury*" (TLN 1646–8).[15] Richard's descent shows a capitulation of power in the scene, but the insistence in the stage direction also controls the space of the stage in unusual ways. When Richard enters below, to the space so thoroughly occupied by Bullingbrook, the earlier presence above means the playgoers perceive the now-vacated space as that which Richard previously had. Because the locations are delineated so carefully by Richard's entrance above, the playgoers must confront two spaces – one of which is now empty. Rarely do we have these kinds of separations of the stage space, especially in instances so focused on shifts of power.[16]

Richard's next appearance is the deposition scene (4.1), and the power dynamic here clearly rests with Bullingbrook, as if in completion of the reversals of 3.3. When Richard introduces vertical movement, that movement appears as a metaphor rather than the actual vertical movement shown in his previous appearance. It is a noticeable moment of stage imagery with embedded stage directions that ensure the actions: "Give me the crown. Here, cousin, seize the crown;/ Here cousin,/ On this side my hand, and on that side thine" (4.1.181–3). The unevenness of the meter (of what appear here as the second and third lines of Richard's speech) encourage an actor to alter the verbal presentation of the lines. While Evans sets out "Here cousin" as its own line, the Folio shows it as the beginning of one long line ending with "thine" (TLN 2104).[17] In either reading, the actor playing Richard must make some adjustment for the unevenness of the meter and the necessary pauses for the stage business at hand. Richard's metaphor includes vertical movement that does not appear in the stage image:

> Now is this gold crown like a deep well
> That owes two buckets, filling one another,

The emptier ever dancing in the air,
The other down, unseen, and full of water:
That bucket down and full of tears am I,
Drinking my griefs, whilst you mount on high. (4.1.183-9)

The metaphor has everything to do with the movement of the two buckets, but the stage image shows a static crown held as the opening of the well. Playgoers are confronted here with a spatial description never actualized and instead undermined by the static spatial reality of the crown as a stage property.

The visual disparity for the playgoers continues as Richard's engagement with the visual possibilities becomes more internal. When Northumberland again requests that Richard read over the articles, he responds,

Mine eyes are full of tears, I cannot see;
And yet salt water blinds them not so much
But they can see a sort of traitors here.
Nay, if I turn mine eyes upon myself,
I find myself a traitor with the rest; (4.1.244-8)

The action of turning "mine eyes upon myself" is exactly one missing from *A Midsummer Night's Dream*, where characters have little possibility of that kind of examination. Richard, thirty lines later, presents a stage image of someone doing this kind of self-examination in the mirror.[18] The playgoers are in an odd position at this moment in the play. Sightlines guarantee that playgoers will not be able to see, at the same time, both the face we have been seeing and the reflected image. Three staging circumstances are most obvious here: 1) Richard in profile faces himself in the mirror making it unlikely the playgoers can see the reflection or Richard's full face; 2) Richard continues to face the playgoers, in which case the mirror would possibly obscure part of his own face and definitely prohibit the audience from seeing the reflection; or (an unlikely) 3) Richard turns his back on the audience and allows a partial view of only the reflection. Richard's turning of his eyes upon himself appears in a way that thwarts the possibility of the playgoers engaging in the same actions, while offering a visual representation of an event unusual in Shakespeare's plays. In many ways, the scene returns to the difficulties of visual perceptions while building stage images that, by their nature, obscure spectators' sightlines.

Grounded space

Early in the play, Gaunt combines many of the play's motifs in ways that demonstrate the importance of their attendant difficulties for the playgoers. A discussion of "land" in the play must consider Gaunt's often-quoted description of the country and the finally delivered verb that shows it as "now leas'd out" (2.1.59). His speech is important in several ways for this discussion. His descriptors establish spatial boundaries for the playgoers imagining a larger space than the one in front of them. His speech depends on offering boundaries, within and without, and continually translates between smaller and larger frames. For example,

> This precious stone set in the silver sea,
> Which serves it in the office of a wall,
> Or as a moat defensive to a house. (2.1.45–7)

Despite the connections between stone and wall, it is the sea that is made a wall here; until the sea becomes a moat and the country a house. I point out these rather obvious separations between the country within and the exiled world without because the ending of the speech depends heavily on an abstraction: "is now bound in with shame" (2.1.63). Suddenly, being within no longer offers protection. For playgoers, the most obvious separations are onstage and offstage, which in this play translate to England onstage and "elsewhere" offstage. These images and descriptions have particular resonance because they appear after Bullingbrook's exile. As playgoers, we have these portrayals to remember as we hear of Gaunt's land being seized.

Gaunt raises the question of visual veracity when he speaks to Richard: "Now He that made me knows I see thee ill,/ Ill in myself to see, and in thee, seeing ill" (2.1.93–4). Despite the fact that "I see thee ill" can mean to have poor eyesight, Gaunt makes quite clear that the other two readings are those which apply: being made ill by the sights he experiences and noting the illness he perceives in Richard.

Gaunt's return to the within and without divisions of his descriptions becomes most apparent when he says:

> A thousand flatterers sit within thy crown,
> Whose compass is no bigger than thy head,
> And yet, incaged in so small a verge,
> The waste is no whit lesser than thy land. (2.1.100–103)

As playgoers we must continually shift between the physical reality of the "crown" that fits on the "head" with the reminder of 'small" and the larger perspective that frames the "crown" as the entirety of the monarchy and all its land. These aspects of expanding and telescoping measurement are emphasized through the language of measuring. "Compass" means "'diameter" here, but also calls to mind the tool of measurement. The "verge" is "limit" or edge, but also it is the "twelve-mile sphere of jurisdiction measurement around the king's court" or "a measure of land of some fifteen to thirty acres."[19] Waste is "useless expenditure or consumption, squandering," and simultaneously it is "uninhabited (or sparsely inhabited) and uncultivated country."[20] In each instance of Gaunt's punning, the playgoers are presented with descriptors moving back and forth between the smaller and the larger. The primary effect depends less immediately on these elements functioning metaphorically and more heavily on a continual alteration of the perspective of the playgoers. Because the shifts in perspective rest in an essentially visual size difference, the land, ground, and earth are connected to possibilities of measurement in the play.

It is Bullingbrook in 1.3 who initially raises these terms and connections. Gaunt picks up "verge" from Bullingbrook's earlier use and continues, in a more compressed form, the use of surveying terms that Bullingbrook introduces when he accuses Mowbray:

> Besides I say, and will in battle prove,
> Or here or elsewhere to the furthest verge
> That ever was surveyed by English eye
> That all the treasons for these eighteen years,
> Complotted and contrived in this land,
> Fetch from false Mowbray their first head and spring.
> Further I say, and further will maintain

Upon his bad life to make all this good,
That he did plot the Duke of Gloucester's death[.] (1.1.92–100)

Bullingbrooke's emphasis here rests in accusing Mowbray of "all the treasons," but there are two noticeable aspects of his description that depend heavily on the larger frames of "land" and the possibilities of moving over that land. The space in which Bullingbrook professes willingness to proclaim the treason uses "verge" as "limit" but immediately introduces the visual measuring term of a surveying "eye" and includes "complotted," a word with connotations of marking and mapping. The connections between "plot" and "plat" meaning "map" have been frequently discussed.[21] The phatic words Bullingbrook includes to move his speech forward are spatially resonant: "besides," "Further," "and further." It is not unusual in English for phatic words to include notions of movement, but Bullingbrook's repetition here emphasizes the connection. Richard introduces a similar connection between "moreover," a space-marking phatic word, and land in the opening lines of the play:

Tell me, moreover, hast thou sounded him,
If he appeal the Duke on ancient malice,
Or worthily, as a good subject should,
On some known ground of treachery in him? (1.1.8–11)

Richard raises the possibility of measurement, while he ends his question with a metaphoric use of "ground." Evans glosses "sounded" here as "questioned," but the word also resonates with measuring depths, as "soundings" are measurements taken of the depth to the seabed.[22] Many of these connections and repetitions between words offer playgoers the impression of movement, although the play, to some extent, thwarts that movement by maintaining the action in England. Bullingbrook refers to himself and Mowbray as, "like two men/ That vow a long and weary pilgrimage" (1.3.48–9), using the common image of death as a journey. After the trial halts, Bullingbrook returns to this notion of death, not only as a journey, but also as a banishment when he urges Mowbray to confess his sins. Bullingbrook claims, had the King allowed the continuance of the trial, "One of our souls had wand'red in the air,/ Banish'd this frail sepulchre of our flesh, / As now our flesh is banish'd from this land" (1.3.195–8). In this description, Bullingbrook calls the body itself (again, in a fairly common connection) a "sepulchre," but the description also connects the "land" to the sepulchre, which in itself is an embedded entombment place. Despite the characters' discussions of wanderings and movement, these rhetorical movements are not presented as staged movements.

Physicality of words

The obvious instances of exile affect both Mowbray and Bullingbrook early in the play. It is Mowbray's early description of exile that emphasizes the play's links between the sound possible in England and the silence of existence outside England. Since the play depends so heavily on the boundaries that establish the stage space as England and the offstage space as elsewhere, the division here extends to the sounds of the onstage space and the silence of offstage. In a complex description of the possible disruptions, Richard introduces the links between silence and peace in ways that establish a connection that becomes an important division for the rest of the characters in the play. In a rather extensive explanation of his own reasons, Richard describes how unrest would disturb the "kingdom's earth," how he wishes to avoid the sight of the unrest, and finally how the sounds of unrest would disrupt existence, specifically peace (1.3.125). He claims that envious thoughts drive Bullingbrook and Mowbray,

> To wake our peace, which in our country's cradle
> Draws the sweet infant breath of gentle sleep;
> Which so rous'd up with boist'rous untun'd drums,
> With harsh-resounding trumpets' dreadful bray,
> And grating shock of wrathful iron arms,
> Might from our quiet confines fright fair peace,
> And make us wade even in our kindred's blood,
> Therefore we banish you our territories. (1.3.132–9)

Richard's description compares the quiet of peace and the loud sounds of battle, while withholding the judgment until the final independent clause. The lengthy descriptions of noises connect the sounds and the hearing of sounds to the possibilities of what he does not explicitly name as wars. In the opening scene of the play, Bullingbrook describes how blood will cry out, "Even from the tongueless caverns of the earth" (1.1.105). Despite the lack of speech organ, this England is one capable of voicing the accusation against Mowbray. Much of the remainder of the play connects sounds to the staged space of England, while relegating silence to the offstage spaces.

The reiterations of "tongue" and "mouth" connect speech acts to the bodies that produce them, and this emphasis appears in the first scene of the play. When Richard describes them before their appearance, he calls Bullingbrook and Mowbray "full of ire, / In rage, deaf as the sea" (1.1.18–19). Despite the rage deafening them, both men find the means to speak, and they repeatedly remark on their own speech as that which issues from their bodies. Bullingbrook claims "what I speak / My body shall make good upon this earth" and says to Mowbray that "With a foul traitor's name stuff I thy throat:" and he reiterates that, "What my tongue speaks, my right drawn sword may prove" (1.1.36–7, 44, 46). The explicit connection between the spoken words and the corresponding actions makes the description of stuffing Mowbray's throat more than solely metaphorical. Bullingbrook claims a concrete existence for the words he wishes to force into Mowbray's mouth. Mowbray responds in a manner that takes the concrete notion of words and sets them in motion:

> First, the fair reverence of your Highness curbs me
> From giving reins and spurs to my free speech,
> Which else would post until it had return'd
> These terms of treason doubled down his throat. (1.1.54–7)

The image of words and speeches as horses to be ridden gives way to Mowbray's description of terms that could be forced back down Bullingbrook's throat. The "terms of treason doubled" would both unsay Bullingbrook's accusation and increase Mowbray's accusation. These concrete images of the words themselves as objects to be forced into mouths oddly conflate the bodily location of speech with the possibilities of ingestion. Mowbray wishes Richard could "bid his ears a little while be deaf" showing he has not completely conflated the sense organs (1.1.112). Bullingbrook however demands "Look what I speak," merging the possibilities of visual perception and hearing (1.1.87). The organ of speech gains importance in the play partly because of the number of times it is mentioned; "tongue" occurs more times in *Richard II* than in any other of Shakespeare's plays.[23]

To some extent, accusations are always verbal; however, this scene rests not only on the descriptions and accusations but also on the awareness of the sense organs that produce these accusations. Mowbray asserts to Bullingbrook that "Through the false passage of thy throat thou liest," and he orders Bullingbrook, "Now swallow down that lie" (1.1.125, 132). This repeated determination to make the other unsay by swallowing words relies on the notion of words as concrete objects that can be moved, removed, spoken, or swallowed. When he refuses to throw up his gage, Bullingbrook takes even farther the description of words as concrete objects and conflates words and tongue:

> Ere my tongue
> Shall wound my honor with such feeble wrong,
> Or sound so base a parley, my teeth shall tear
> The slavish motive of recanting fear,
> And spit it bleeding in his high disgrace,
> Where shame doth harbor, even in Mowbray's face. (1.1.190–5)

His tongue would be capable of giving voice to "base" words that could wound his honor; Bullingbrook's assertion that he would, with his own "teeth," tear out his tongue depends on the common and ancient notion of thwarting torturers desirous of information. However, his description merges together the tongue and the words it might voice and offers that voiced fear as an hypothetical object to spit at Mowbray. In this instance, biting out the tongue would prevent the construction of "feeble" and "base" words rather than revelations of truth, which is the more usual circumstance of the gesture.[24] Bullingbrook asserts control over his words and his tongue through the gruesome image toward the end of a scene that has consistently reiterated the corporeal reality of words and their production.

The physically static staging of the first scene of the play enhances the disparities between the staged action and the way words are thrown about on stage. Jeremy Lopez has remarked on the stasis of the opening scene of the play and notes that "the men's speeches could be performed in such a way as to suggest that they are deliberately echoing one another, throwing words back in one another's face."[25] Although there are ways to add more movement to the scene (through careful blocking and movement of the potential combatants), one important point of the scene is the physical stillness. And this disparity between active speech and halted action importantly foregrounds both the stasis and movement and the physical realities of words throughout the remainder of the play. Another important instance of halted action occurs in 1.3, when Richard stops the combatants and proclaims the banishment of both Bullingbrook and Mowbray. Richard describes Mowbray's sentence as something which "Breathe I against thee" and Mowbray also emphasizes the physical production of the words when he describes them as "all unlook'd for from your Highness" mouth" (1.3.150, 155). Bullingbrook's description of the lessening of his sentence marks the possibility of the breathed word carrying weight: "How long a time lies in one little word! / Four lagging winters and four wanton springs / End in a word: such is the breath of kings" (1.3.213–5). Gaunt reverses the possibilities and reminds Richard that Gaunt's own death cannot be halted by the word of a king: "Thy word is current with him for my death, / But dead, thy kingdom cannot buy my breath" (1.3.231–2). The scene's continual reiterations of "tongue" and the emphasis on words as spoken objects force playgoers to view the action as primarily performative utterances.

Mowbray describes his own exile in terms that reverse the normal boundaries of banishment and turn it into an enclosure. This reversal forms an important portion of the way the scene continually encourages playgoers to think of voiced, staged events in contrast to unembodied, offstage silences. Mowbray describes his banishment in terms of enclosure and silence:

> Within my mouth you have enjail'd my tongue,
> Doubly portcullis'd with my teeth and lips,
> And dull unfeeling barren ignorance
> Is made my jailer to attend on me.
> I am too old to fawn upon a nurse,
> Too far in years to be a pupil now.
> What is thy sentence then but speechless death,
> Which robs my tongue from breathing native breath. (1.3.166–73)

Imprisonment and jailing depend substantially on the confinement of a physical body; in this description the tongue becomes the entirety of the body to be contained. Mowbray describes his "speechless death" as that which occurs because his "tongue" cannot breath his "native breath." Not only does Mowbray set out his expulsion from the land as an odd type of containment, but he also conflates living breath with his tongue and speech. The speech gains resonance in this play from the earlier emphases on the connections between the voice and objects and Gaunt's later connection between words and life.

In 2.1 Gaunt relentlessly emphasizes the corporeal aspects of speech; he says to York, "Methinks I am a prophet new inspir'd, / And thus expiring do foretell" (2.1.31–2). York has already warned him that "'Tis breath thou lack'st, and that breath wilt thou lose" (2.1.30). Gaunt picks up the mention of breath and connects it through inhalation and exhalation to the inspiring, expiring of his own attempt to "foretell" the outcomes for the king. Of course the king does not hear this description of "this sceptred isle" (2.1.40), but he understands that what he hears when he does enter depends on "This tongue that runs so roundly in thy head" (2.1.22). Northumberland's news of Gaunt's death likewise emphasizes the physical aspects of speech:

KING RICHARD: What says he?
NORTHUMBERLAND: Nay, nothing, all is said.
His tongue is now a stringless instrument,
Words, life, and all, old Lancaster hath spent. (2.1.150)

It is the stoppage of speech that marks the end of life in Northumberland's description; noticeably, "Words" are the first of the three nouns describing the living Gaunt. Saying that "His tongue is now a stringless instrument" recalls Mowbray's description of his useless tongue as "an unstrung viol or a harp," "a cunning instrument cas'd up" (1.3.150, 162, 163). This silencing connects Gaunt's death back to the earlier banishment of Mowbray.

In *Romeo and Juliet*, a play composed near to the time of composition of *Richard II*, we see Romeo's reaction to and experience of his banishment. Despite his extended harangue on the horrors of banishment in 3.3, Romeo does not describe it as a prison. He calls it "purgatory, torture, hell itself," but he links that to death itself rather than imprisonment: "banish'd from the world,/ And world's exile is death" (*Romeo and Juliet* 3.3.18, 19–20). Staged space functions quite differently in these two plays and the establishment in *Richard II* of the internal speaking, staged England in contrast to the outside silenced elsewhere depends on these kinds of differences. Jane Kingsley-Smith has examined exile in Shakespeare's plays and points out that the exile in *Richard II* functions differently to the other instances of exile she examines. Kingsley-Smith persuasively argues that the true exile in this play is Richard himself, exiled by his inability to persuade through poetry, and that "a poetic subtext, created through literal acts of banishment, repeatedly identifies Richard as an exile."[26] Tangled descriptions and experiences of exile appear in other of Shakespeare's plays. In *King Lear*, Kent's banishment does not result in exile, since he does not actually leave. Kent reverses the terms of exile, but in a much different way than either Mowbray or Bullingbrook: "Fare thee well, King; sith thus thou wilt appear / Freedom lives hence, and banishment is here" (*King Lear* 1.1.180–1). In this instance, Kent describes "elsewhere" as the location of possible freedom. In *Richard II*, exile depends on the specific terms of space established by the surrounding events in the play. None of the descriptions of exile in the other plays is framed in the ways that Mowbray's and Bullingbrook's banishments are described.

Bullingbrook, early in 1.3, uses terms of bondage and captivity to describe the possible freedom of the upcoming battle with Mowbray:

> Never did captive with a freer heart
> Cast off his chains of bondage, and embrace
> His golden uncontroll'd enfranchisement,
> More than my dancing soul doth celebrate
> This feast of battle with mine adversary. (1.3.88–92)

The emphasis here rests in the possibility of his "dancing soul" having been set free from the bondage of indecision. But his choice of descriptors rings a bit oddly, since the more commonly used description of a soul set free from bondage is through the freedom death offers from the bondage of the body. Even in this odd moment, the shadowy unrealized corporeality of the body intrudes on the image Bullingbrook uses. When Bullingbrook faces the prospect of banishment, it is in terms that leave no doubt about his bodily perceptions of reality. Despite his assertion to Richard that his banishment would be gilded by the same "golden beams" from "That sun that warms" Richard, Bullingbrook cannot imagine his banishment in the terms Gaunt sets out (1.3.146, 145). The various metaphorical tropes Gaunt proffers are all refused and reread in lackluster terms. Gaunt's "travel that thou tak'st for pleasure" is turned to Bullingbrook's "enforced pilgrimage" (1.3.262, 264). Importantly, Bullingbrook and Gaunt are left in control of the stage space when they have this conversation, and these circumstances help to establish Bullingbrook's own physical control of the space and the realities of his own perceptions.

Michael Grene has discussed how 4.1 offers a "glimpse of a world elsewhere" when Carlisle describes Mowbray's crusading exploits while in exile.[27] As Grene points out:

> For Bullingbrook, Mowbray's Act 1 rival, banished at the same time as him, his is the path not taken. Both of them were sent out into the emptiness, the wilderness that was not-England. One repealed his own banishment, returned to overthrow his king and take the throne. The other turned his enforced exile into a glory and died at peace.[28]

The fact that the enforced exile turned to glory does not appear on stage means that playgoers accept the report of these events without visual affirmation. It may be a path not taken for Bullingbrook; it is also a path not shown to the playgoers. Instead of the silence Mowbray posits for his exile, Bullingbrook concentrates his descriptions on the bodily movement necessitated by banishment. He says, "every tedious stride I make/ Will but remember me what a deal of world/ I wander from the jewels that I love" (1.3.268–70). His description of "remember" connects this word again to the striding legs, the moving members of his body. His body is not imprisoned by the exile despite his banishment from "England's ground," the "sweet soil" (1.3.306). The path that Bullingbrook takes to return from his exile depends on his ability to circumvent this kind of imprisonment.

Sounds of history

Earlier, this chapter explored some of the visual and spatial implications of 4.1, but we may now revisit this deposition scene to see the intertwined resonances with verbal sounds as they are presented in this important and central scene. The opening repeats and redoubles the staged accusations and actions of 1.1. These scenic parallels are undoubtedly noticeable to playgoers. Much of the scene relies on the importance of spoken words – accusations in the case of the lords in the opening and Richard's refusal to read out the accusations against himself. Jeremy Lopez has pointed out the impossibility of the playgoers being able (with the knowledge of the staged events) to appropriately adjudicate the disagreement between Bagot and Aumerle.[29] Partly because we as playgoers have inadequate information, we must rely more heavily on what the lords say to one another and possibly take their accusations as they present them. This circumstance again weights heavily the spoken word in a scene filled with accusations. Bagot's accusation against Aumerle claims, "I know your daring tongue/ Scorns to unsay what once it hath delivered" (4.1.8–9). Charles Forker notes the importance in the play of the coinages and constructions of negation, noting this use of "unsay" as one example.[30] The most noticeable coined words of negation in the play have to do with speech and hearing; for example *"undeaf* his ear" and *"uncurse* their souls" (2.1.16; 3.2.137). In many ways, Richard's "undo myself" is performed through the spoken reversal of his ceremonial trappings (4.1.203). The incantatory repetitions of "With mine own" increase the ritualistic and performative elements of the scene, especially since Richard relinquishes his position saying, "With mine own tongue deny my sacred state,/ With mine own breath release all duteous oaths;/ All pomp and majesty I do forswear" (4.1.209–11). As Richard continues with his list, the instances of verbally potent actions multiply. These are performative utterances in so far as they perform the function through their verbal articulation; noticeably, these are all *un*doing earlier rituals.

The lords likewise emphasize the verbal and oral nature of their accusations and actions. Fitzwater claims, "I dare meet Surrey in a wilderness/ And spit upon him, whilst I say he lies/ And lies, and lies" (4.1.75–7). Another lord has already claimed that accusations will be "halloaed in thy treacherous ear" (4.1.55). Carlisle, attempting to support or protect the king, insists on the performative necessity of Richard's presence saying, "Thieves are not judged but they are by to hear" (4.1.124). His insistence that Richard must hear the accusations against him increases the importance of not only the spoken words but also the hearing of those words. Carlisle insists that it would be improper that the king "Be judg'd by subject and inferior breath" while "himself not present," thus linking the physical presence of the king and the breath-propelled words of his accusers (4.1.128, 130). By the time Richard enters in 4.1, the scene has established again the importance of the spoken word and the organs responsible for speech and hearing. Richard's initial complaints against the lords, and possibly the playgoers, rely on the already established mode of verbal existence when he asks, "did they not sometimes cry 'All hail!' to me?" and demands, "Will no man say amen?" (4.1.169, 172). His reliance on, and lack of, the verbally resonant cries of the lords makes the silence of the onlookers more important than they would otherwise be. His own sounds mark out the silence of the others, an aural reversal similar to that which later appears as a stage image reversal when he describes the buckets moving up and down while holding a single crown as the top of the well.

The problems of sound and necessities of hearing are continued in 4.1 as the opening of Richard's line, "Ay, no, no ay," remains ambiguous both in print and on stage and because of this all the more dependent on aural interpretation. The actor must decide how to read the punctuation and playgoers must interpret the homonyms (4.1.201).[31] The First Folio prints the line as, "I, no; no, I: for I must nothing bee" (TLN 2122). Forker describes the line as filled with "ambiguous significances that can only emerge in heard speech."[32] The difficulty of course is that the ambiguities in the line are not erased by the actor's choices; they may be mitigated or clarified, but regardless of the actor's decisions the meaning still relies on playgoers' hearing for the determination of meaning. At the end of the scene, Richard asks Bullingbrook for "one boon":

RICHARD: Then give me leave to go.
BULLINGBROOK: Whither?
RICHARD: Whither you will, so I were from your sights.
(4.1.313–15)

Out of sight in this instance will mean silenced as the scene turns away from both the visual and the auditory. Richard is conveyed to the tower for imprisonment, removed but not banished. After Richard's departure, Bullingbrook announces his own coronation date in two short lines and leaves behind the small faction who plots against him. The brevity of Bullingbrook's pronouncement and his quick departure do not encourage playgoers to identify with him as he departs; the plot against him further bolsters our connection with Richard.

The motifs I have traced in the play, the emphasis on ground and the embodiment of language, in conjunction with the staged spaces of the play reappear and are explored again in Richard's final scene. Much of the strength of the scene for playgoers rests on the fact that we see Richard alone for the first time in the play. He enters alone and his sole occupation of the stage establishes him in control of the space despite his clear proclamation that he is in prison. His initial attempts to "people this little world" imagine corporeal existence for his own thoughts, but only through the frame of voicing those thoughts (5.5.9). When his thought "Persuades me I was better when a king; / Then am I king'd again, and by and by / Think that I am unking'd by Bullingbrook (5.5.35–7). For playgoers, his descriptions remind us of the events we have already seen, presenting verbal descriptions shaded by the images from 4.1. Richard is pleased and surprised to have the visit from the Groom, who visits "To look upon my sometimes royal master's face" (5.5.75). Although the keeper turns him out, the leaving Groom remarks, "What my tongue dares not, that my heart shall say" (5.5.96). Here at the end of this play so invested in the organs of speech and the possibilities of saying and unsaying, Richard believes that the meat the keeper brings is poisoned. If he were right, the death would fittingly happen by mouth. After he is struck down, Richard's death speech is short, but he accuses Exton: "thy fierce hand / Hath with the King's blood stain'd the King's own land" (5.5.109–10). In this moment, Richard describes the corporeal merging with the land, a merging toward which so many of his earlier stage actions gestured. He returns to the earlier imagery of rising and falling powers when, dying, he exclaims, "Mount, mount, my soul! thy seat is up on high, / Whilst my gross flesh sinks downward, here to die" (5.5.111–12). Exton immediately regrets his actions and departs bearing the body of the dead king. Given Richard's attempts to save himself, the presence of the hired murderers, and Exton's awareness of his own deed, playgoers understand this moment as a tragic ending.

A Midsummer Night's Dream does not need a normalizing character because playgoers have in hand all of the strands of the plot. As playgoers, *Richard II* tantalizes us with the notion that we have as much information as any character, but we are not actually offered sufficient details to be able to fully predict events in the play. As mentioned before, playgoers are not presented with enough information to adjudicate between Bagot and Aumerle in 4.1. Likewise, we do not have enough information in 1.1 to adjudicate between Bullingbrook and Mowbray. In part, these gaps have to do with the generic constraints of history plays. Over the course of the play, we might identify the Duke of York as our normalizing character, whose late appearance in the play (in 2.1) surprisingly helps to support that role. His absence from act one might be to facilitate doubling of the role with Mowbray, who departs in 1.3 not to return.[33] Partly because of his delayed appearance, York provides a voice of moderation. He urges Gaunt, "deal mildly with his youth, / For young hot colts being rag'd do rage the more" (2.1.69–70). In response to York's moderating encouragement, Gaunt refers to Richard's inability to properly apprehend the situation when he says, "My death's sad tale may yet undeaf his ear" (2.1.16).

Given the numerous mentions of tongue and voice in the play, it is noticeable that York in 2.1 focuses on ears and hearing when he describes the young king. In response to Gaunt's hope, York disagrees:

> No, it is stopp'd with other flattering sounds,
> As praises of whose taste the wise are fond,
> Lascivious metres, to whose venom sound
> The open ear of youth doth always listen; (2.1.17–20)

York's complicated description here imagines that sounds have a physical presence that can block other sounds. Auditory perception does not depend on physically opening or closing the ears; we have little choice about whether we hear sounds. York's description introduces the much more controlled perception of taste through his punning on "taste." York's complex enunciation of how Richard is misled introduces directional language, which ties together hearing, sight, and the breath required to produce words:

> Where doth the world thrust forth a vanity—
> [...]
> That is not quickly buzz'd into his ears?

> Then all too late comes counsel to be heard,
> Where will doth mutiny with wit's regard.
> Direct not him whose way himself will choose,
> 'Tis breath thou lack'st, and that breath wilt thou lose. (2.1.24–30)

The dispute between will and wit depends on "wit's regard," and "regard" connotes both "to consider" and "to view." Leading or misleading depends on being directed, in a particular direction. The connection between hearing and location or dislocation in York's speech develops through the senses and ends with the suggestion that Gaunt's words will be insufficient. We see York's intimation borne out in the remainder of the play, and even in the remainder of this scene we see York more thoroughly taking on the role of the normalizing character. After Richard says he will seize Gaunt's "plate, coin, revenues, and moveables," it is York who upbraids the king (2.1.161).

In the final act of the play, York finds himself in a position to act in a way that makes clear his loyalty to the newly crowned Henry. In 5.2, 5.3, and 5.4, we see a series of events that depend heavily on elements of stagecraft to make them compelling in the complex ways they resonate with the overriding concerns of the play. At the same time, these three scenes move the play, and Henry's kingship, into the episodic realms of the history play. In 5.2 and 5.3, the Duke and Duchess of York discuss the crowd's responses to Richard and Bullingbrook, uncover the traitorous plot of their son, make arguments before the king, and receive a pardon. In the very short 5.4, Exton convinces himself that Bullingbrook wishes for the death of Richard. These three scenes exemplify the ways stagecraft elements can shift the generic understanding of the play.

The opening of 5.2 shows that playgoers are involved with a domestic scene between the Duke and Duchess of York, as the Duchess asks for further description of "our two cousins coming into London" (5.2.3). The entrance of their son Aumerle interrupts the Duke's sad description of Richard's "face still combating with tears and smiles" (5.2.32). Despite the Duke's attention being gripped by his own retelling of the scene in the street, he is aware enough of his son to descry the letter Aumerle has incompletely concealed about his person. The Duke's immediate cry of "Treason, foul treason! Villain, traitor, slave!" (5.2.72), demonstrates his absolute willingness to act on his own description of himself as "To Bullingbrook are we sworn subjects now" (5.2.39). The Duke's assertion of loyalty correlates to an immediate embodiment in his reactions to his son's perfidy. The scene ends in a mad scramble as the Duke calls for his boots and departs, and the Duchess urges their son:

> After, Aumerle! Mount thee upon his horse,
> Spur post, and get before him to the King.
> And beg thy pardon ere he do accuse thee.
> I'll not be long behind; though I be old,
> I doubt not but to ride as fast as York. (5.2.111–15)

As playgoers we are left with no doubt but that she will try to ride as fast as York; the scene sets the characters in motion. The opening of the next scene places us already at the castle with King Henry. As playgoers we have outpaced their fastest riding and find the King fretting over the behavior and absence of his son. When Aumerle enters, his shortened first line, "Where is the King?"(5.3.23), in the midst of the play's regular verse, verbally demonstrates his agitation. Twenty lines later the Duke pounds on the door, and the King allows him to enter. Another thirty-five lines pass before the Duchess arrives to pound on the door as well. The King voices what the playgoers have already discerned: "Our scene is alt'red from a serious thing, / And now chang'd to 'The Beggar and the King'" (5.3. 79–80). Henry's comment functions in several ways here. Initially, it alters how Aumerle and York understand the situation; Henry's description of Aumerle as "My dangerous cousin" must be taken as doubting his dangerousness (5.3.81). More importantly for playgoers, Henry's comment aligns him with playgoers as we struggle to follow the shifts in tone and genre.

In 5.3, we have moved away from the tragic images of Richard's passage into London and moved on to something else, something generically different. Charles Forker points out that Henry's continued rhyming, "together with the kneeling of each of the suppliants at various points, produces an undeniable shift towards comedy."[34] However, the farcical possibilities of the scene do not jar with the generic possibilities of the history play. Although 5.2 and 5.3 are often cut in production, 5.3 is particularly important for shifting Henry into alignment with playgoers' perspective, that of an outside viewer musing on the generic possibilities of the scene. The very brief 5.4

shows Exton convincing himself that he will be acting on the King's desire in his attack on Richard. As has been frequently pointed out, this short scene helps to make sense of the attack on Richard in 5.5. For playgoers, it also moves us away from the Duchess' concern for her son and back to the machinations and political strife that drive the history play. The immediacy and the brevity of 5.4 ensure that playgoers have Richard's probable fate in mind when he enters in 5.5. This knowledge also helps to build empathy for Richard's situation as he works through his solitary questions. Simultaneously, 5.4 returns playgoers to the plot of a history play while heightening the tragic possibilities of Richard's confinement. The complex stage images of these scenes reiterate and embody the recurring concerns of the play as a whole.

In Jeremy Lopez's deft reading of the imagery of the final scene 5.6, he points out that "Bringing the coffin onstage literalizes Richard's process of self-consumption, and the fantasy of nothingness."[35] The framing of the scene ensures that playgoers understand that Henry has complete control of the space, that the dead will be buried, and that finally the play gestures toward the motion of history itself. When 5.6 opens, Henry asks York for updates on the rebels, and Northumberland's nearly immediate entrance offers news that "I have to London sent / The heads of Salisbury, Spencer, Blunt, and Kent" (5.6.8). Fitzwater enters after Henry's very brief two-line response and describes how he has "from Oxford sent to London/ The heads of Brocas and Sir Bennet Seely" (5.6.13–14). Again, after a short two-line response from the King, another loyal nobleman Harry Percy enters with news of the Abbot of Westminster's death and the living Carlisle for "kingly doom and sentence" (5.6.23). This continual iteration of entrances with news of moved and moveable bodies cements Henry's power and establishes his kingly behavior. Only Exton enters with a dead body. Although he presents his prize in much the same terms as the other noblemen, only in this instance are playgoers faced with the physical property of a coffin. More than the process of Richard's self-consumption (in Lopez's terms), the stage image ensures that playgoers see the events and images as perpetuating the motions of history. As the traitor's voices are silenced through beheading, Richard's bodily difficulties will be buried. Again the stage image provides a disparate visual effect. Although Henry claims "my soul is full of woe / That blood should sprinkle me to make me grow" and plans a "voyage to the Holy Land, / To wash this blood off from my guilty hand," the final stage image is a surprisingly bloodless one (5.6.45–6, 49–50). Finally, playgoers see not the stage space filled with dead bodies but the exits of soldiers after a coffin.

Notes

1. Exton speaks in a soliloquizing mode after the death of Richard in 5.6; others are necessarily present since Exton's final words are orders about the removal of the other bodies while he removes Richard's body. In general, I assume an early modern style stage that requires (among other things), in the absence of curtains, the removal of all bodies from any scene but the final one. The first four lines of his six-line closing could be given as an effective aside, with the final two lines addressed to the other still-living characters on stage.
2. Later in this chapter, I return to Richard's 5.6 soliloquy. I draw a firm distinction around soliloquy here and insist on the character being alone on stage; Janette Dillon's *Shakespeare and the Staging of English History* (Oxford: Oxford University Press, 2012) argues for a wider use of the term soliloquy, particularly in connection with *Richard II*, 89–91.
3. For a useful exploration of the available different objects called "perspectives" in the period, see Allan Shickman, "The 'Perspective Glass' in Shakespeare's *Richard II*," *Studies in English Literature, 1500–1900* 18.2 (1978), 217–228.
4. Scott McMillin has argued that in *Richard II*, we might read the moments focused on eyes and weeping as attempts to manifest a nothingness that cannot be made tangible, the production of absence and vacancy. "Shakespeare's *Richard II*: Eyes of Sorrow, Eyes of Desire," *Shakespeare Quarterly* 35.1 (1984): 40–52. The quotation in the text appears on page 41.
5. Jeremy Lopez, *The Shakespeare Handbooks:* Richard II (Basingstoke: Palgrave Macmillan, 2009), 30.
6. Charles Forker, (ed.), *Richard II*, by William Shakespeare (London: Thomson, 2002), 65.
7. Brian Walsh, "The dramaturgy of discomfort," in *Richard II: New Critical Essays*, ed. Jeremy Lopez (London: Routledge, 2012), 181–201, 190.
8. Jonathan Baldo's *Memory in Shakespeare's Histories: Stages of Forgetting in Early Modern England* (London: Routledge, 2012) reads memory and forgetting in *Richard II* to offer a modified notion of the kingship the play displays, 10–50.
9. E.M.W. Tillyard, *Shakespeare's History Plays* (London: Chatto & Windus, 1951), 251.
10. Charles Forker notes that the early exit is problematic and explores the possibilities that the First Folio stage direction (which does not appear

in the quarto) was added either mistakenly or at least with infelicitous results. Forker, *Richard II*, 198n, 509n.
11. This formulation of the ending of the scene is paralleled in some ways by 1.2 in *Hamlet* when Hamlet remains after Claudius and his court depart.
12. Helena's soliloquy appears at the end of 1.1 in *A Midsummer Night's Dream*.
13. Phyllis Rackin, "The Role of the Audience in *Richard II*," *Shakespeare Quarterly* 36.3 (1985), 262–281, 268.
14. Baldo, *Memory in Shakespeare's Histories*, 29.
15. Janette Dillon has noted that "the descent from the walls to the base court at Flint Castle is the turning point of the play and a microcosmic visual enactment of its central concern. As a reversal of the tableau placing the monarch at the apex of the social order, familiar from the street pageantry of royal entries, it has all the more power to shock" (*Shakespeare and the Staging of English History*, 47).
16. *Henry VI, Part Two* and *Henry VI, Part Three* both have interesting instances of appearances above. See *2H6* 4.9 and *3H6* 4.7, 5.1, and 5.6.
17. The line abbreviates "the" in order to fit it on one line. It seems unlikely that the decision to make it one line rested with the setting of the type, since an empty line above the stage direction *"Enter Richard and Yorke"* remains available (TLN 2083).
18. Forker's note on these lines remarks on the clear foreshadowing of the immediately following mirror incident.
19. The two definitions come from Forker's note; Forker, *Richard II*, 2.1.102 fn.
20. These definitions are from the *Oxford English Dictionary*: "waste, n. II.5.a" and "waste, n. I.1.a" respectively.
21. Henry S. Turner not only provides a useful summary of recent scholarship on the connections between "plot" and "plat" but also (and more importantly) develops the links between early modern mathematical and scientific discourses and the correlative dramatic manifestations. *The English Renaissance Stage: Geometry, Poetics, and the Practical Spatial Arts 1580–1630* (Oxford: Oxford University Press, 2006).
22. In his third series Arden edition, Forker offers "enquired of"; Forker, *Richard II*, 1.1.8fn.
23. "Tongue" occurs twenty-six times in *Richard II* and "tongues" four more times. The play with the next most frequent use of the word is *Henry the Sixth, Part Two*, where it appears sixteen times. There are interesting correlations between these two plays not the least of which is this similarity in the emphasis on the organ of speech.
24. See Forker's longer note on this passage; Forker, *Richard II*, 97.
25. Lopez, *The Shakespeare Handbooks*, 11. Lopez goes on to offer another suggestion: "they might be performed in such a way as to emphasize the guiding hand of the poet, the deliberately artificial way in which similar verbal conventions of chivalric confrontation are being employed by two different characters."
26. Jane Kingsley-Smith, *Shakespeare's Drama of Exile* (Basingstoke: Palgrave, 2003) 56. Kingsley-Smith reads Romeo's banishment as being essentially

about "speechlessness," which links that banishment to Mowbray's exile in interesting ways.
27. Michael Grene, *Shakespeare's Serial History Plays* (Cambridge: Cambridge University Press, 2002), 170.
28. Grene, *Shakespeare's Serial History Plays*, 171.
29. Lopez, *Shakespeare Handbooks*, 55. Lopez also notes staging decisions that could increase the visual parallels between 4.1 and the opening scene of the play.
30. See Forker's note on this line and his longer note on the earlier line 2.1.16n.
31. I quote from Evans' edition here; Forker prints: "Ay, no. No, ay;" (4.1.201).
32. Forker, *Richard II*, 4.1.201n, 61.
33. Mowbray must have been a doubled role; his taxing part would need a competent actor, and it is difficult to imagine that such an actor would not have been used in the later acts.
34. Forker, *Richard II*, 5.3.78-81n.
35. Jeremy Lopez, "Eating *Richard II*," *Shakespeare Studies* 36 (2008): 207–228, 215.

3
Narrative and Spatial Movement in *Hamlet*
"To find his way"

The opening act of *Hamlet* directs our attention to the nature of the Ghost and the disorienting story it has to tell, while more subtly setting the stage with a different kind of disorientation, that of place. The first scene opens with the question "Who's there?" (1.1.1) and much critical discussion has focused on the various personal identifications the "who" might call into question in the play. Maynard Mack noted that "Hamlet's world is pre-eminently in the interrogative mood," calling attention to how the play "reverberates with questions, anguished, meditative, alarmed."[1] Rather than the "who" of the opening line of the play, I shall take up the question of "there" with its spatial indeterminacy, particularly as it exists for playgoers as a locational marker and also as an important part of the interrogative mood of the play. In many instances, characters' spatial interactions establish the position of the playgoers; this spatial specificity develops the narrative momentum of a play, a momentum toward the final stasis of the ending.

The previous chapters have explored how, in different fashions, *A Midsummer Night's Dream* and *Richard II* interact with the visual elements presented to playgoers. *A Midsummer Night's Dream* relies on playgoers' visual perceptions to raise, at the end of the play, a larger question about the validity of those perceptions. While *Richard II* encourages playgoers with verbal descriptions of visual spectacles, these descriptions often undermine or appear at odds with the staged images. Some of these differences rest on generic expectations; comedic endings encourage a renewal, circling around, and beginning again (whether with marriages or promised marriages, or reunions). The episodic nature of the history play aspects of *Richard II* support the disparities between description and action, a difference inherent between historical events and staged representations of historical events. The generic elements of *Hamlet* that make it a tragedy are intrinsically tied to the ways the play and the characters control or attempt to control space in the play. The stage spaces encourage a momentum toward the final events, but these final events spiral in on the stasis of the ending.

The opening question of *Hamlet*, "Who's there?" (1.1.1), puts playgoers spatially with Barnardo and Francisco in a confused location. Horatio and Marcellus arrive into this state of confusion; the dislocation is then compounded by the arrival of the Ghost. These dislocations often depend on characters merging descriptions of space and time. What we see here in the opening of the play are characters intent on knowing and holding their locations, the primary role of a guard or "watch." Although Barnardo opens the play with the question of "Who's there?," Francisco repeats the question, "Who is there?" when Horatio and Marcellus enter (1.1.14). Horatio's response, "Friends to this ground," attempts to connect them to the ground of the country on which they stand, but all of these characters are uncertain about themselves (1.1.15). Before Francisco exits, he says that "Barnardo hath my place" referring to his role as watch as a physical location (1.1.17). They all use language connected to locations despite apparently being unable to perceive the other characters clearly. The meetings and comings and goings of these characters at the very opening of the play develop the uneasiness of the location. When asked if it is Horatio who arrives, Horatio responds, a "piece of him" (1.1.19). Harold Jenkins notes that "the hand he offers is solid enough, but the dark which conceals the rest of him enables him to reserve full participation."[2] The opening of the play destabilizes the playgoers' notions of place, while simultaneously emphasizing the importance of space.

As discussed earlier, the difficulties of transporting playgoers were noted by Sidney in his *Defence of Poesy* (1595), where he claims that, while watching a play,

> you shall have Asia of the one side, and Afric of the other, and so many under-kingdoms, that the player, when he cometh in, must ever begin with telling where he is, or else the tale will not be conceived[....]. By and by we hear news of shipwreck in the same place: and then we are to blame if we accept it not for a rock.[3]

Sidney's approach includes him as a member of the playgoing crowd who attempts to follow the verbal constructions meant to produce a landscape (or a seascape). Yet Sidney's concerns may be overcome by playgoers accustomed to the very conventions that he decries. Most playgoers will not resist these locational devices I am most interested in here. In a discussion of the presence (or absence) of scenery, Harley Granville-Barker makes the point that an "audience is passive, if expectant, imaginatively lazy till roused, never, one may be sure, at pains to make any effort that is generally *un*necessary to enjoyment."[4] In the same way that playgoers may not consciously calculate slight slippages in time frames, the space of the theater can function through subtle frames of action.

In his illuminating book *The Necessity of Theater*, Paul Woodruff examines how theater both constructs and depends upon delineated space and time. As he explains, though we might measure time with a clock or calendar, "The best way to measure time in theater, however, is by plot. Clock time does not guarantee something worth watching from beginning to end. A good plot does. A well-made plot will catch the audience's attention at the start and sustain it through to the end."[5] Woodruff also remarks that theater demands a demarcated space, and he offers two ways that theater commonly measures out that necessary area.[6] He claims, "the most common way is to draw a line before the time begins," thus marking out the space of the stage to separate the actors from the playgoers; the second way, as he puts it, "is to see where the actors go."[7] Sidney has already marked for us the physical parameters of the stage by noting that the player "cometh in;" Sidney's description relies on the existence of an offstage area. Where the actors go helps to mark onstage and offstage as different spaces, but close attention to the actors' movements on the stage itself reveals internal boundaries within the onstage area. We might take Woodruff's suggestion one step farther, to fold in the questions of the time measured by plot, and pay attention to where the *characters* go. Initially, the actors and the playgoers share a temporal reality (whether we are watching a clock or not); the characters however exist in the time frame of the plot. One goal of theatre is to transport playgoers into this plot time frame. Bruce R. Smith uses the term "characterlogical space": "Overt indications of characterological space are coordinated in complicated ways with fictional space. Hamlet the character inhabits all of *Hamlet* the play's fictional locations [...] as well as locations beyond the scenes [...]. In this respect, Hamlet occupies more space than any other character in the play."[8] Whether or not playgoers consciously take note of the locations of characters, these frameworks and parameters function in the theater space to develop the narrative momentum. D.A. Traversi has asserted that the structure of the theater focused attention specifically on "the *action*" and that this structure required of playgoers "not only that they watch and listen, but that they participate."[9] This participation, I suggest, has to do with the engagement with the time and space of the play in terms the play itself establishes. In *Hamlet*, the framing of locations engages the conscious or unconscious awareness of the playgoers and develops our understanding and the meaning of events presented on stage. After examining some of the ways the characters experience space in the play, I return at the end of this chapter to questions of how playgoers reconcile these experiences.

Placing ghosts

When Marcellus says that he has asked Horatio "along/ With us to watch the minutes of this night" (1.1.29–30), he links the passage of time and physical space of the play. Similarly, Barnardo's description of the passage of the previous night depends on astronomical markers for temporal locations. These astronomical markers more commonly measure space:

> When yond same star that's westward from the pole,
> Had made his course t'illume that part of heaven
> Where now it burns, Marcellus and myself,
> The bell then beating one— (1.1.36–9)

Barnardo's speech breaks off here because of the entrance of the Ghost – a Ghost not contained by the space that the characters inhabit and, in this instance, not halted by Barnardo's description of the time marked by the bell. The Ghost's appearance interrupts a rather expansive description, not hastily presented, which emphasizes time and place. Noticeably, Barnardo's speech leads the playgoers toward the not-given movement of the absent verb; we have been given the when, where, and even the who, but the expectation-filled delay of awaiting the verb increases our interest, only to be interrupted by the actual physical movement of the Ghost's entrance.

In this first appearance to playgoers (and to Horatio), the Ghost remains on stage for a short eleven lines. Barnardo observes, "See it stalks away" and Horatio implores, "Stay! Speak, speak, I charge thee speak" (1.1.50, 51). The characters onstage do not consider following the Ghost, and Marcellus' comment, "'Tis gone, and will not answer" seems to offer closure for the ghostly incident (1.1.52). Horatio announces the second appearance of the Ghost, indicating again its location, "lo where it comes again!" (1.1.126). Marcellus and Horatio have decided to strike it, "if it will not stand" (1.1.141). The crowing of the cock and the attempts to halt the Ghost's progress put an end to the appearance. As the onstage characters attempt to understand the Ghost's location, their shortened, repetitive speech re-emphasizes the spatial confusions and dislocation:

BARNARDO: 'Tis here.
HORATIO: 'Tis here.
MARCELLUS: 'Tis gone. [*Exit Ghost.*] (1.1.142–4)

The repetition of "here" and the finality of "gone" leave the playgoers in the same, suddenly emptied, space as these three characters.[10] After deciding they will tell Hamlet of the spirit, Marcellus claims, "and I this morning know/ Where we shall find him most convenient" (1.1.175). Marcellus is the first of many characters in this play to claim to know Hamlet's location; Marcellus happens, of course, to be right.

When Hamlet returns with them to watch, his own interactions with the Ghost establish location as a prime concern and carefully mark that location for the playgoers. Hamlet's calls of "come" and "come" (1.5.116) draw Horatio and Marcellus first toward where the Ghost speaks to Hamlet and then to the space where the Ghost issues orders from under the stage to "swear" (1.5.155). When the Ghost cries out again, Hamlet's response, "*Hic et ubique*? Then we'll shift our ground. / Come hither, gentlemen" (1.5.156–7), directly raises questions of *where* the events occur. At the same moment, the playgoers move with Hamlet and the other characters, even though Hamlet repeatedly insists on changing locations. We experience these changes in location. The characters do not leave the stage but enact all of the changes of place in view of the spectators: "Once more remove, good friends" (1.5.163).[11] In *A Midsummer Night's Dream*, the necessity for Lysander and Demetrius to follow Puck and move to different locations on the stage is clarified through the First Folio's unusually explicit stage directions with the note, for example, of *'shifting places.'*[12] Here the necessity for movement rests in Hamlet's own speech. *A Midsummer Night's Dream* allows the dislocations of sight lines of affection and space to merge into one another, while keeping the playgoers outside the experience; both *Hamlet* the play and especially Hamlet the character insist on playgoers' participation in the confusing attempts to follow the subterranean ghost. In *Hamlet*, the characters' movements sustain our experience by keeping the confused characters in front of the playgoers. Before making him swear to secrecy about any possible "antic disposition" (1.5.172), Hamlet insists to Horatio, "But come—/ *Here*, as before" (1.5.168–9), and moves the playgoers to the space that Hamlet and Horatio revisit.[13]

Many scholars have noted the sense of enclosure endemic in this play. In his illuminating reading of *Hamlet*, David Hillman asserts, rightly I think, that, "More than any other work in the Shakespearean corpus, the play's world is, through and through, one of claustrophobic, enclosed spaces, of nunneries, closets, nutshells and the like."[14] The claustrophobia in the play stems from the characters' constant concerns over space and access to other characters. Traversi notes that, after the revelation of the Ghost, "a claustrophobic sense of Renaissance court intrigue permeates the action."[15] Oddly, these early scenes with the Ghost occur outside buildings, whether on the ramparts or on some waste land, rather than in contained confined spaces bounded by walls. Much of the confining and constricting tenor of these scenes depends on the ways the characters speak about space and attempt to firmly locate themselves and one another. In both early instances of the Ghost, but particularly in the opening scene, the characters' repeated attempts to halt, stop, or bring to a standstill events or other characters produce the enclosed effect. When the Ghost appears in the enclosed space of Gertrude's closet, the effects are even more claustrophobic and confining.

Before the reappearance of the Ghost in 3.4, Hamlet's conversation with Gertrude introduces spatial constructs and quickly merges these questions of direction and location with questions of visual sensibility. The queen tries to change the direction of Hamlet's conversation.

Hamlet's retort negates the queen's entreaty and shows the spatial imperative in her language:

QUEEN: Come, come, you answer with an idle tongue.
HAMLET: Go, go, you question with a wicked tongue. (3.4.11–12)

As he reverses her language and mimics her repetitions, he returns us to the questions of movement and direction with his reversal of "come" to "go."[16] His next repetition includes the possibility of showing her herself: "Come, come, and sit you down, you shall not boudge; / You go not till I set you up a glass / Where you may see the inmost part of you" (3.4.18–20). In some ways this scene matches the call for a mirror in 4.1 of *Richard II*. In that instance, Richard himself asks for "a mirror hither straight, / That it may show me what a face I have / Since it is bankrout of his majesty" (4.1.265–7).[17] When the mirror arrives, he demands, "Give me that glass, and therein will I read" (4.1.276–7). Richard imagines that he will be able to read the representation he will see in the mirror to decipher the changes in himself and his position; he asks for the mirror as a means of self-examination. In *Hamlet*, Gertrude seems to have little interest in a mirror. Marvin Rosenberg notes that in productions of *Hamlet* a mirror is often present and that stage business forcing Gertrude to look in an already present mirror or making a mock thrust with a knife leads to Gertrude's outcry, "Thou wilt not murther me?" (3.4.21).[18] Being forced to look in a mirror at this point in their discussion may not, in production, be sufficient to raise the question of murder. Granville-Barker claims that "it is not that threat" of looking in a mirror "which frights her, but plainer danger."[19] While a mirror may be present in some productions, in the text of *Hamlet* neither the spectator nor Gertrude is offered a chance to see the queen in a mirror. Gertrude's outcry, Polonius' response, and Hamlet's stabbing of him through the arras interrupts the possibility.

After Polonius' death, Hamlet returns to the question of a vision of oneself; he says, "Look here upon this picture, and on this" (3.4.53). Hamlet refers to the portraits of the old king and of Claudius as if they are mirrors in which Gertrude will see herself. There are varied ways of playing this scene. John Russell Brown describes that, "At one time, he pointed to portraits on the wall of the 'closet', and later, to miniatures hanging around his and Gertrude's necks, or to two coins that he draws from his pocket. In modern-dress productions, photographs have been used, either carried in a wallet or pocket book or found in a newspaper or journal."[20] Philip Edwards remarks that, "A favourite practice is for Hamlet to have a locket of his father as a pendant, and to seize a similar locket, of Claudius, which hangs around Gertrude's neck."[21] Importantly, visual representations need to appear. Using the portraits as mirrors, his descriptions of the two men emphasize their physical appearances, and he demands, "Have you eyes?" and "ha, have you eyes?" (3.4.65, 67). While Richard imagines his own appearance must be altered by his experiences, Hamlet uses the differences between the two men to try to show Gertrude the alterations he believes she has wrought on herself. While the sightlines in *Richard II* complicate the mirror scene, any staging of Hamlet showing Gertrude the two portraits raises its own issues for playgoers. Once again, sightlines preclude playgoers seeing the three aspects involved here: Hamlet's face, Gertrude's face, and the images presented as portraits. Thompson and Taylor note that "some commentators have argued that the audience needs to see the pictures to judge for themselves, but this may not be necessary, given that they have seen both the Ghost and the King in person."[22] Given the difficulties with available sightlines, only large portraits would sufficiently allow playgoers to judge for themselves. Surely the point here in the scene is to follow Hamlet's readings of the portraits regardless of his accuracy.

Before the appearance of the ghost in the scene, Hamlet already questions Gertrude's ability to see while taxing her to see as he sees, encouraging her through his careful descriptions to see with his eyes.[23] John Russell Brown claims that during the showing of the portraits, "the change of focus alters how he speaks" and asserts that "Having both portraits in his gaze, perhaps in his hands, brings more measured and ordered speech until he turns away from them to address his mother."[24] Brown's description emphasizes the choices an actor must make about where to direct his own gaze during these descriptions. After cataloguing the differences he thinks she ought to see, Hamlet reminds himself that she must have use of her senses, "sense sure you have, / Else could you not have motion, but sure that sense/ Is apoplex'd" (3.4.71-3).[25] Despite his assertion that her movement demonstrates working senses, he demands:

> What devil was't
> That thus hath cozen'd you at hoodman-blind?

> Eyes without feeling, feeling without sight,
> Ears without hands or eyes, smelling sans all,
> Or but a sickly part of one true sense
> Could not so mope. (3.4.76–80)

The confusion of senses here depends on Hamlet perceiving an inappropriate separation rather than appropriate merging and use of more than one sense; he quickly moves from a disconnection of sight from feeling to hearing without touch or sight. We might be reminded of the confusion of senses catalogued by Bottom when he awakens, convinced he has dreamt his strange experiences, and claims, "The eye of man hath not heard, the ear of man hath not seen, man's hand is not able to taste, his tongue to conceive, nor his heart to report, what my dream was" (*A Midsummer Night's Dream* 4.1.211–14). In the instance of Hamlet's harangue, he describes Gertrude's insensibilities in terms that make it clear that he believes all the senses must perform appropriately together to allow for proper reason. It is in this enclosed, confined space that Hamlet can explore these sensory questions in ways avoided in the rest of the play. Importantly, these descriptions work on Gertrude:

> O Hamlet, speak no more.
> Thou turn'st my very eyes into my soul
> And there I see such black and grained spots
> As will not leave their tinct. (*Hamlet* 3.4.88–91)

The visual introspection Hamlet forces on Gertrude shows her visual markers of her own culpability. Because of her capitulation to looking inward, this point in Gertrude's responses to Hamlet seems to me the most likely place for her to change her mind about where her loyalties ought to lie.[26]

The appearance of the Ghost expands the questions of perceptual veracity. Closeted with the queen, Hamlet, and the corpse of Polonius, playgoers necessarily experience the Ghost as does Hamlet, since we see and hear that which the queen cannot.[27] The actor Michael Pennington usefully points out that Gertrude's inability to see the Ghost "is partly a subtlety of Shakespeare's – Gertrude has simply wiped old Hamlet out, forgetful of his body and spirit, and for that reason is blind to him now – and partly a stage expediency: he does not plan a lengthy discussion of the Ghost after he has left, but he does want Gertrude to be convinced of Hamlet's derangement."[28] The subtlety here depends a great deal on the visual aspect of the characters' literal experiences becoming metaphorical for the playgoers. During Hamlet's descriptions of the portraits, he argues that Gertrude's sense of sight was inaccurate when she married Claudius; for playgoers, the appearance of the Ghost offers a twisting argument against the blindness of love, inability to perceive, and metaphorical blindness. Gertrude's experience becomes a spatial and visual blank when she asks Hamlet about "bend[ing] your eye on vacancy" (3.4.117). "Forth at your eyes your spirits wildly peep," she exclaims, locating the appearance of madness emitting from his eyes. Frightened, she asks, "*Where*on do you look?" (3.4.124). Hamlet insists on the existence of the Ghost and tries to get Gertrude to see the Ghost by pointing out both his appearance and the possibility of the Ghost's visual perception: "look you how pale he glares" (3.4.125). His exhortation to the Ghost "Do not look upon me" (3.4.127), shows Hamlet relying on Andreas du Laurens' "emission" theory of vision.[29] Hamlet fears not what the ghost will see, but the possible effect of the glare. He describes the glare as a movement of its own: "this piteous action" (3.4.128). Gertrude's interruption of Hamlet's discourse to the Ghost offers a return to the clearer, more pointed speech she assumed at the beginning of the scene. The short lines of the exchange attempt to return the scene to what Gertrude sees as reality:

QUEEN: To whom do you speak this?
HAMLET: Do you see nothing there?
QUEEN: Nothing at all, yet all that is I see.
HAMLET: Nor did you nothing hear?
QUEEN: No, nothing but ourselves. (3.4.131–3)

This exchange is remarkable in the scene for its directness and the brevity of the questions. It is at this remark, "Do you see nothing there," that Hamlet must be certain that Gertrude cannot see the Ghost. In the briefly clear moment at the center of this exchange, Gertrude's perfectly even line of verse stands out with its thumping pentameter asserting her conviction of her own perceptions.[30] Since Gertrude clearly cannot see the ghost, Hamlet's insistence on the exact location and repetition of "look" as the Ghost exits becomes noticeable: "Why, look you *there*, look how it steals away" (3.4.134); "Look *where* he goes, even now, out at the portal" (3.4.136). Hamlet points out to playgoers the obvious corporeal movement, engaging playgoers to understand our experience of the Ghost in the same way he does.

Placing and misplacing a prince

Hamlet's speech and interactions with the Ghost accentuate the notions of space functioning in the play, while the later scene with the Ghost and Gertrude emphasizes the visual aspects of the characters' realities. Although Hamlet orients himself within these spatial systems, this engagement does not allow other characters to be able to locate him. Claudius' attempts to control or fix Hamlet's location create much of the narrative tension of the play, and a great deal of Claudius' uneasiness emerges through his ineffective attempts to *find* Hamlet. Claudius' concerns about Hamlet's whereabouts appear early in the play. In 1.2, the king focuses on where other people go and also manages to demonstrate that he can control the movements of those people. Claudius is on stage for 128 lines in this scene, and most of these lines are his. He takes care of various pieces of court business, which are (in the order he addresses them): formal announcement of his wedding; presentation of news of young Fortinbras' demands for lands lost to old Hamlet; dispatch of messengers to old Norway; acquiescence in Laertes' departure for France; and finally a request that Hamlet not return to Wittenberg. Claudius claims that his letters will encourage Old Norway to "suppress / [young Fortinbras'] further gait herein" (1.2.30–1). Claudius grants Laertes' suit for "leave and favor to return to France" (1.2.51). In both of these instances, Claudius shows his control over the comings and goings of others.

When it comes to Hamlet's "intent / In going back to school in Wittenberg," Claudius claims, "It is most retrograde to our desire, / And we beseech you bend you to remain / Here in the cheer and comfort of our eye" (1.2.112–13, 114–16). To be under Claudius' "eye" has an ominous ring to it, but as Jenkins notes it is a "frequent metonymy for the royal presence."[31] Later in the play, these metonymic aspects shade into the literal. Noticeably, Claudius maintains the formal second person pronoun when addressing Hamlet, and while it might be that he speaks for himself and Gertrude, more likely he uses the royal third person to refer to himself alone. "Retrograde" means, literally, travelling backward, which Claudius conjoins with the rather convoluted "we beseech you bend you to remain."[32] We cannot be certain if Claudius uses the first "you" in the subject position before the verb "bend" or in the object position after "beseech." In other words, does Claudius say, "we beseech you and bend you to remain," or "we beseech you to bend yourself to remain"?[33] In either case, Claudius encourages Hamlet to bend in the direction Claudius wishes, the direction that would not be retrograde. Hamlet only agrees after the queen adds her much more personal entreaty, "I pray thee stay with us, go not to Wittenberg" (1.2.119). Hamlet makes clear that he agrees to the queen's and not the king's request when he says "I shall in all my best obey you, madam" (1.2.120). Claudius' response, "Why, 'tis a loving and a fair reply, / Be as ourself in Denmark" (1.2.121-2), increases the uneasy sense that Hamlet's response has been what he wished, but not as he wished it were framed. The "ourself" in his response makes clear the royal third person that refers only to himself. Despite showing himself perfectly in control of his royal affairs when he ably dispatches messengers and grants leave for Laertes' departure, Claudius less successfully attempts to control Hamlet's movement.

We might also look to the very beginning of Claudius' appearance for another way that he controls movement in this scene. His first two sentences of the scene are both somewhat long and organized in a fashion that only allows the movement, the main verb, to occur at the very end of the sentence. In the first sentence, clause follows upon clause until finally we reach "we with wisest sorrow think on him/ Together with remembrance of ourselves" (1.2.6-7). The waiting for the verb is more noticeable in the second sentence, particularly because the verb itself is divided:

> Therefore our sometime sister, now our queen,
> Th'imperial jointress to this warlike state,
> Have we, as 'twere with a defeated joy,
> With an auspicious, and a dropping eye,
> With mirth in funeral, and with dirge in marriage,
> In equal scale weighing delight and dole,
> Taken to wife; (1.2.8-14)[34]

If we can understand Claudius through his syntax here, we know he attempts to control movement; we see this syntactical control manifested through action in the remainder of the scene.

In 2.2 Claudius maintains his tenuous hold on the comings and goings of others. Clearly Rosencrantz and Guildenstern have arrived in response to his "hasty sending" (2.2.4). The return of Voltemand and Cornelius makes clear that some time has passed since 1.2, but more importantly we see Claudius' earlier dispatch followed through. It is in this long scene 2.2 that Polonius reveals, to Claudius and Gertrude, Hamlet's letter to Ophelia and suggests it is love that causes Hamlet's madness. Claudius has no suggestion, but rather asks Polonius, "How may we try it further?" (2.2.159). Clearly Claudius and Gertrude do not expect Hamlet to appear where they are, since they have sent Rosencrantz and Guildenstern out (at line 39) to be taken to him. The king and queen exit in response to Polonius' "Away, I do beseech you, both away" (2.2.169). Claudius has already agreed to Polonius' plan, but this dismissal of the king strikes an odd note in a scene where Claudius ought to be in control of the space. When choreographing the meeting with Ophelia, Claudius requests Gertrude's departure,

> For we have closely sent for Hamlet hither
> That he, as 'twere by accident, may here
> Affront Ophelia. (3.1.29–31)

To "closely" send demarcates the necessity of secrecy and the spatial imperative that Hamlet will be confined "here," where Claudius wants the confrontation to occur. The attempt to contain Hamlet in that space – and its confused outcome – helps to convince Claudius that Hamlet cannot be fixed in place. Claudius has "in quick determination/ Thus set it down: he shall with speed to England / For the demand of our neglected tribute" (3.1.168–70). Polonius understands the king's point and adopts Claudius' locational language when he suggests that if Gertrude, "*find* him not, / To England send him" (3.1.185–6). Despite the political end Claudius offers as an excuse, Polonius extends another possibility for being certain of Hamlet's whereabouts: "or confine him where / Your wisdom best shall think" (3.1.185–7).

After the upheavals of the play-within-the-play, Claudius realizes Hamlet's dangerousness and correlates it with his spatial movement: "nor stands it safe with us / To let his madness range" (3.3.1–2).

Thompson and Taylor note "range" as "roam freely," which helps to clarify the movement Claudius envisions here.[35] Claudius tells Rosencrantz and Guildenstern:

> Arm you, I pray you, to this speedy viage,
> For we will fetters put about this fear,
> Which now goes too free-footed. (3.3.24–6)

In this instance, Claudius conflates the distance of the voyage into a possibility of containment; his own spatial sensibilities become confused. Although he says he will "fetters put about this fear," he will not in fact be confining Hamlet; instead, he will essentially be banishing him. Banishment through a "speedy viage" becomes fettered imprisonment in Claudius' description.[36] Andrew Hiscock has argued, rightly I think, that "With the to-ing and fro-ing of Rosencrantz, Guildenstern, Voltemand, Cornelius, Polonius, Ophelia and indeed Gertrude to her chamber, Claudius seeks to express his power by monitoring all the dark corners of his palace and beyond, rendering them knowable, organized and ruled spaces."[37] Hiscock's readings center on a discourse of space based on "obsessive interest in control" rather than on the narrative movement developed through stage spaces I explore here, but his point about Claudius' fascination with controlling characters' movements and having knowledge of spaces helps to clarify some of Claudius' actions.[38]

Even at the opening of 4.1, when Claudius appears completely in control of the space, his primary concern seems to arise from not being able to locate Hamlet. The arrangement of the characters on the stage insists that the action takes place in the private space of Claudius and Gertrude. Although Rosencrantz and Guildenstern arrive with the king, they are immediately sent away. The king's focus on Hamlet's whereabouts appears both in his question to the queen, "Where is he gone?" (4.1.23), and in his immediate attempt to locate him when he sends (the returned) Rosencrantz and Guildenstern to "go seek him out" (4.1.36). In 4.3 the king's focus remains on locations, "I have sent to seek him, and to find the body" (4.3.1); he demands of Rosencrantz, "But where is he?" (4.3.13); and he demands of Hamlet, "where's Polonius?" (4.3.16) and again, "Where is Polonius?" (4.3.32). As the king attempts to orient himself, he makes clear his awareness of the dangers of

Hamlet's peripatetic movement: "How dangerous is it that this man goes loose!" (4.3.2).

Hamlet's absence in 4.5, both from the scene and from Denmark, is centrally important to this reading of the play.[39] The control of the stage spaces in the scene often do not make sense and increase the feelings of madness brought on by the presence of Ophelia with her mad songs. When the queen first enters, she is protesting that she will not see Ophelia and that she wishes to be kept separated from her. Horatio convinces her that Ophelia's behavior "may strew/ Dangerous conjectures in ill-breeding minds" (4.5.15). In a rare moment alone on stage, the queen (in lines marked by Evans as an aside) possibly addresses the playgoers and explains her worries over the increasing suspiciousness: "To my sick soul, as sin's true nature is, / Each toy seems prologue to some great amiss, / So full of artless jealousy is guilt, / It spills itself in fearing to be spilt" (4.5.16–20).[40] Her concerns over containment and spillage infect the remainder of the scene. Once Gertrude has acquiesced to seeing her, Ophelia enters almost immediately; it has taken only four lines for the Gentleman to fetch her or to allow her entrance (since he does not return with her).[41] Clearly whatever power the queen has to keep Ophelia away, it does not keep Ophelia at a very great distance. The king enters at line 37, completely unannounced and certainly not in control of the space or the events there. He sends Horatio after Ophelia when she departs: "Follow her close, give her good watch, I pray you" (4.5.74–5). When Claudius explains his worries to Gertrude, he lists off the various events (Polonius' death, Hamlet's departure, Polonius' hushed-up burial, Ophelia's madness) and then follows with the news of Laertes' return in terms that reveal more about Claudius' worries than about Laertes' actions:

> Last, and as much containing as all these,
> Her brother is in secret come from France,
> Feeds on this wonder, keeps himself in clouds,
> And wants not buzzers to infect his ear
> With pestilent speeches of his father's death,
> Wherein necessity, of matter beggar'd,
> Will nothing stick our person to arraign
> In ear and ear. O my dear Gertrude, this,
> Like to a murd'ring piece, in many places
> Gives me superfluous death. *A noise within.* (4.5.86–96)[42]

His repetitive use of "ear" and discussion of speeches emphasizes aural effects even before he is interrupted by the noise within. In response, the Queen asks, "Alack, what noise is this?" (4.5.97). After two more lines, a messenger enters with the news of Laertes' arrival, and Laertes himself enters after a short ten lines more. Upon his entrance, Claudius does not have control of the stage space; he has at this point clearly completely lost control of the court space as Laertes comes with guard. Laertes' entrance (even without his guard in attendance) shifts control of the space to him, but only for a brief time. It is yet another stage direction for "*A noise within*" (4.5.154; TLN 2904) that marks the return of Ophelia. This time it is Laertes, in an echo of Gertrude's earlier response, who questions, "How now, what noise is that?" (4.5.155). The First Folio stage directions for the second entrance appear as "*A noise within. Let her come in, / Enter Ophelia*" (TLN 2904–5). Reasonably, many editors have assigned "Let her come in" as dialogue; we might however read these as stage directions that ensure a pause for a stage door opening before the entrance of Ophelia. This instance of extending the stage direction may allow Laertes a pause to match Gertrude's earlier hesitation, repeating and extending the action as Laertes seems to repeat Gertrude's responses from earlier in the scene. Ophelia enters alone despite the king's earlier order that Horatio "Follow her close" (4.5.74). Ophelia is in the scene for 46 lines before she exits leaving Laertes and the king and queen to exit together at the end of the scene. Gertrude does not speak for the final ninety lines of the scene and has nothing at all to say when Ophelia returns.[43] Claudius has lost control of the situation and space of the stage; the queen likewise has little control over events. We know that she physically grasps at Laertes since Claudius twice admonishes her ("Let him go, Gertrude" (4.5.123; 4.5.127). But there is no indication of what Gertrude does for the remainder of the scene. Her last comment in the scene is "But not by him," attempting an intervention against Laertes' accusations and meaning that Polonius' murder was not committed by Claudius (4.5.129). John Russell Brown has traced this increasing separation of Gertrude and Claudius from one another through the change in the ways they end the scenes in which they both appear. Over the course of the play and particularly at their exits, Brown notes Gertrude's increasing "immobility and silence" and Claudius' "self-concern, haste, and insistence."⁴⁴ From the beginning of the play, Claudius has focused his energies on knowing and controlling Hamlet's location. Despite having (he thinks) achieved the removal of Hamlet, Claudius in that absence has lost control of the stage space.

As Claudius puts in motion a plan to engineer Hamlet's death, his movements and control of others' movements become more convoluted. In 4.7, before Laertes knows of his sister's death, Claudius convinces him to augment and adopt Claudius' plan for engaging Hamlet in a match of rapiers. To encourage Laertes in his desire for revenge for his father's death, Claudius raises an image that harkens back to Hamlet and Gertrude's exchange in 3.4. Claudius asks, "Laertes, was your father dear to you?/ Or are you like the painting of a sorrow,/ A face without a heart?" (4.7.107–9). Claudius unknowingly raises the image of a "painting." However, these are the same sorrows that Claudius complained that Hamlet was extending past the normal mourning period. Although Claudius does not reveal an awareness of his own duplicity here, his later question comes closer to parallels with his own experiences.⁴⁵ When Laertes says he is willing "To cut his throat I'th'church," Claudius responds, "No place indeed should murther sanctuarize,/ Revenge should have no bounds. But, good Laertes, / Will you do this, keep close within your chamber" (4.7.126, 127–9). Edwards notes that "Claudius' remark runs in two directions at once," since a murderer such as Hamlet ought not to be offered sanctuary in a church, but revenge ought not to be bounded.⁴⁶ More interesting for the point here, Claudius makes these claims about aptness of place and the lack of boundaries on revenge and then immediately begins to set out the plan that would require firstly that Laertes "keep close within your chamber." Despite Laertes' compliance with the plan, Claudius still cannot be certain enough of his location. After the queen's description of the death of Ophelia, a speechless Laertes departs: "Adieu, my lord, / I have a speech a' fire that fain would blaze, / But that this folly drowns it" (4.7.189–91). Immediately after this, Claudius lies to the queen:

> Let's follow, Gertrude.
> How much I had to do to calm his rage!
> Now fear I this will give it start again,
> Therefore let's follow. (4.7.191–94)

His insistence that he and Gertrude follow Laertes does not arise from the reason he offers her; he has fueled Laertes' desire for revenge and developed the plot that will offer him the chance to reap that revenge. His desire to follow Laertes displays, even if hidden from Gertrude, his intention to track Laertes' movements.

Placing the playgoers

Critical readings of *Hamlet* have often gestured toward the spatial elements in the play even when not tracing the ways characters understand space. Traversi, for example, made this claim: "*Hamlet* is – to put the matter briefly – a masterpiece of exploration, and the initial effect of obscurity which it is apt to make upon us is a necessary part of the price we pay for participating in the process of relentless probing by which this exploration is conducted."[47] Traversi points to the probing and searching that characters experience, but these are equally true of the readers' or playgoers' experiences in following the narrative movement. The "exploration" of the unknown terrain of obscurity in the play develops, for playgoers, through their participation in the temporal experience of the spatial elements of the play as a whole. Other critics have likewise noted these effects without delving into the specific elements of the play which produce them. In discussing reading the play, Inga-Stina Ewbank, for one, remarked that "In the study, [...] the play so readily presents itself spatially and thematically."[48] The effects of the play I am most interested in here develop through a combination of the characters' experiences of space and playgoers' (or readers') experiences of the play in production. While the division is certainly not a perfectly clear one, I shall return to particular moments in the play that develop their effects through the playgoers' perceptions of space.

Playgoers may experience some of the dislocations that Claudius himself fears; however, certain movements between scenes, and the movements of the messengers, offer other markers and experiences of space that may keep us from that dislocation. In the shift between 1.1 and 1.2, the playgoers find themselves in a court where Claudius firmly holds his place as a political leader. Claudius enters and establishes the space as his own by repeatedly using the third-person pronoun and calling himself "the throne of Denmark" (1.2.48).[49] The members of the court form Claudius' immediate audience, but the speeches function for the playgoers in a similar fashion. The opening of 1.2 establishes the restricted space of Denmark before Hamlet has a chance to comment on its narrow confines.[50] When Claudius and the court clear the space that the King has so firmly established as his own, Hamlet is left behind with the playgoers. The arrival of Horatio, Marcellus, and Barnardo halts Hamlet's speech: "But break, my heart, for I must hold my tongue" (1.2.159). We know where they have been and what they have seen. Despite Horatio's comment (at the end of 1.1) that he knows "where we shall find" Hamlet (1.1.180), it takes these men 180 lines to transport themselves the distance that we have already been moved by the shift in scenes.[51] Stephen Booth has pointed out that, "Throughout the play, the audience gets information or sees action it once wanted only after a new interest has superseded the old," and he uses the example of 1.2, showing that, "By the time they arrive 'where we shall find him most conveniently' the audience has a new concern – the relation of Claudius to Gertrude and of Hamlet to both."[52] Booth makes the important distinction that "In *Hamlet* the audience does not so much shift its focus as come to find its focus shifted."[53] The control of space in the structure of the play itself moves playgoers through these shifts. Often the shifts in location are complicated for playgoers through the characters' use of language connected to place and location.

The shift between 1.4 and 1.5 exemplifies the questions of location presented to playgoers. We arrive in 1.4 with Hamlet, Horatio, and Marcellus before the Ghost's arrival. The Ghost's insistent gestures urge a change of place that raises serious concerns for Marcellus and Horatio. "Place" becomes the compelling notion in Horatio's description:

> The very *place* puts toys of desperation,
> Without more motive, into every brain
> That looks so many fadoms to the sea
> And hears it roar beneath. (1.4.75–78)

His use of "fathom" links comprehension or understanding to linear measurements of distance in this desperate description. Hamlet leaves, insisting that he will follow the Ghost; Horatio and Marcellus then leave shortly after, Marcellus saying "Nay, let's follow him" (1.4.91).[54] Surprisingly, the opening of 1.5 establishes that the playgoers have done what Horatio and Marcellus want to do: caught up to Hamlet and the Ghost. Hamlet's speech-provoking question to the Ghost initially emphasizes place: "*Whither* wilt thou lead me?" (1.5.1).[55] The playgoers have already arrived or been transported to Hamlet and the Ghost; it takes Horatio and Marcellus about 110 lines to traverse that space. C. Walter Hodges has offered a possible staging of these entrances and exits that depends on a continuity developed through maintaining a coherent use of the stage doors.[56] Hodges argues for the ghost entering from one door and exiting the other door repeatedly, to establish circularity to the scenes, and then making his final exit through the trap to be under the stage for the voice below. Although Hodges does not consider the lagging Horatio and Marcellus, the point about clarity for playgoers becomes particularly cogent in his illustration.

Although Horatio and Marcellus take a while to locate Hamlet, in 2.2 Rosencrantz and Guildenstern take even longer. Although playgoers may not consciously register that the messengers take as long as they do to arrive, the effect remains integrated into the construction of the stage space. The queen orders, "Go some of you,/ And bring these gentlemen where Hamlet is" (2.2.36–7). At 2.2.39 the stage direction calls for Rosencrantz and Guildenstern's exit. Problematically, Hamlet appears in the "lobby" (2.2.161) when he enters at 2.2.167 reading a book. Nearly fifty lines later, Rosencrantz and Guildenstern encounter Hamlet when they enter at 2.2.219. Rather than following their circuitous 185-line route, the playgoer has access to Hamlet's location and the knowledge that the messengers are on their way.[57] Booth points out, "Except for brief periods near the end of the play, the audience never has insights or knowledge superior to Hamlet's or indeed different from Hamlet's. Instead of having superiority *to* Hamlet, the audience goes into the second act to share the superiority *of* Hamlet."[58] Playgoers' connections with Hamlet continue through most of the third act as well.

In 3.2 the entrances and exits are complicated in interesting ways, which develop the control of stage space increasingly under the sway of Hamlet. This complex scene includes: Hamlet's last minute instructions to the players and their exit, Polonius' short appearance with Rosencrantz and Guildenstern and confirmation that Claudius and Gertrude will see the play, Hamlet's dismissal of Rosencrantz and Guildenstern to hurry the players, Hamlet's discussion of the play with Horatio, the entrance of the court to see the play, the performance of the play-within-the-play, the King's frantic call for light and the exit of all but Hamlet and Horatio, Hamlet's call for music, Rosencrantz and Guildenstern's entrance with the request that Hamlet visit his mother, the entrance of the players with recorders, Polonius' entrance with the repeated message that Hamlet visit his mother, Polonius' exit, the exit of everyone but Hamlet, and finally Hamlet's exit. As this description makes clear, Hamlet holds the stage for the entirety of the scene as all of the other characters in the play arrive to him; only Fortinbras and Laertes are absent from this scene.[59] Despite Claudius' attempts to control stage spaces over the course of the play and even before his interruption of the play-within-the-play, the scene has already spatially asserted that Claudius is out of his element.

Horatio's first appearance in 3.2 reassures us that he acts as a normalizing character for playgoers. At the beginning of the play, he and the other members of the watch confirm the appearance of the Ghost before we see Hamlet interact alone with the Ghost. In this scene, after describing Horatio as the perfect friend, Hamlet remarks on the upcoming performance, saying, "One scene of it comes near the circumstance/ Which I have told thee of my father's death" (3.2.76–7). Despite his refusal to convey to his companions of the first act his experiences with the Ghost, he has clearly in the intervening period revealed these important details to Horatio. After the revelatory reaction prompted by the play, Hamlet and Horatio are again left alone, and Hamlet confirms: "O good Horatio, I'll take the ghost's word for a thousand pound. Didst perceive?" (3.2.286–7). Horatio's unequivocal, "Very well, my lord" and "I did very well note him" (3.2.288, 290), agree with Hamlet's understanding of events and reiterate for playgoers the understanding we are meant to have both of the events and of their relationship.

The events of the closet scene 3.4 change the tempo of the scenes that follow it. In Evans' edition act four is divided into seven scenes; the first four of these leading up to Hamlet's departure are each less than 70 lines. While the locations of the scenes do not depart from Denmark, the increasing speed of scene changes marks an increase in the narrative movement. A similar increase in narrative momentum appears in act four of *Antony and Cleopatra*, where the accelerated motion of numerous short scenes in widely disparate locations creates an accelerated narrative.[60] These frequent shifts dislocate the playgoers from seeing a lengthy narrative space and, instead, foreshorten the events into an experience of rapid motion. In *Hamlet*, the series of short scenes depends less on vast changes in location and more on the shifts in appearances of characters.[61] The longest scene in the act is 4.5, a scene that demonstrates the spatial confusions of the stage and the court in the absence of Hamlet. As the play draws nearer to its conclusion, the increasing quickness with which the messengers move speeds the pace of the play's action for playgoers. In 4.6, when the sailors arrive, Horatio moves the messengers on their way quickly: "Come, I will give you way for these your letters" (4.6.32). These letter carriers move more quickly than any other messengers in the play; 4.6 includes only two more lines before their exit and then a brief 36 lines into 4.7 where the messenger delivers to Claudius the letter that informs him of Hamlet's return. The playgoer does not see Osric being given his orders, and since Osric has no starting point, he arrives in 5.2 without any perceptible passage of time or space.

The narrative events of the play move more and more quickly forward, as the events themselves collapse to a confined space in a way that has not happened before in the play. In the final act, the increasing pace of the narrative and quickness of the messengers combine with spatial fixity to produce a disorienting effect on the playgoer. Earlier, in 3.1, Hamlet links the afterlife to a spatial location when he describes the "something after death" (3.1.77) as "the undiscover'd country, from whose bourn/ No traveller returns" (3.1.78–9). In 5.1 we become immersed in conversations around mortality and space. The locations of the bones found in the graves, the placement and lasting powers of the dead bodies, the physical labor of preparing a place for the dead body, and the concerns about the burial location of suicides fix the playgoers to this physical location rather than allowing us to form a part of Ophelia's funeral train. Hamlet's description of the skull attempts to fix the location of human individuality: "Here hung those lips that I have kiss'd I know not how oft. Where be your gibes now, your gambols, your songs, your flashes of merriment, that were wont to set the table on a roar?" (5.1.188–91). Even in the moment of considering the corpse of Alexander, Hamlet focuses on the physical locations of existence:

HAMLET: To what base uses we may return, Horatio! Why may not imagination trace a noble dust of Alexander, till' a find it stopping a bunghole?
HORATIO: 'Twere to consider too curiously, to consider so.

HAMLET: No, faith, not a jot, but to follow him thither with modesty enough and liklihood to lead it: Alexander died, Alexander was buried, Alexander returneth to dust, the dust is earth, of earth we make loam, and why of that loam whereto he was converted might they not stop a beer-barrel? (5.1.202–12)

This discussion returns us to questions of the ground and location itself through the travel of Alexander's dead body being reintegrated into the world. As playgoers we remember the similar discussion of Polonius' body feeding worms. In this moment though the descriptions are tied to the place and properties of this place through the skull and the corporeal realities of the gravediggers. We are even more closely tied to this space that we have occupied with the gravediggers, receiving news about Ophelia's burial, before Hamlet and Horatio enter (at 5.1.56). Hamlet and Horatio engage with the space, and the men they find there, and their subsequent concealment serves to remind us of our role as spectators for the arriving funeral procession. Unlike many other characters who hide themselves in this play, there is no indication in the text that Hamlet and Horatio are concealed from the playgoers; they do not exit the stage. Instead, Hamlet and Horatio maintain the continuity of the space the playgoers are so firmly grounded on.

In the instance of *Hamlet*, the narrative events hurry forward as we remain with a non-moving Hamlet. His location seems known to the other characters, and the members of the court locate him with ease. Hamlet's location is fixed in the space, and he is in view of the playgoers for the entire remainder of the final act. We are located in a viewing position that Claudius, Polonius, and even Rosencrantz and Guildenstern seem to desire for much of the play, a position where we can see him at all times for all of his actions. E.T. Schell made the point, in connection with questions of rhetorical and mimetic intention in the play, that "if we cannot trust Hamlet's perspective, there is no perspective in the play that we can trust. And while the modern theater has opted for structural ambiguity, Shakespeare's theater did not."[62] This structural fixity of early modern theater, depended on by early modern playwrights, helps to develop the experience of space for playgoers. We cannot overestimate the effect of Hamlet's location in the final act. He occupies the center of the space at the end of the play; he remains on stage for the entire final scene as the events are brought to him in that place. This staging of events supports the narrative momentum and acceleration of the end of the play. Moreover, it is worth noticing that increased speed arises simultaneously with stasis. This staged space at the end of the play forms the center of an enclosed, but dislocated, narrative space. The circling into a hurtling stasis produces much of the inward movement of the whole play. Possibly this final stasis gives rise to the debate around Hamlet's inaction. In terms of plot, he's not an inactive character: he seeks out a ghost, writes a section of a play, engages the players to play it, harangues Gertrude, stabs Polonius, travels, writes and switches letters, convinces pirates to return him home, and engages in a duel. In terms of plot, he is active. His halting movement toward the necessary vengeance only achieves its goal at the static closure of the end of the play. The spatial structures that function through our perceived locations appear more clearly in an early modern staging where elaborate scenery and properties do not contribute to the spatial divides. The emptiness of an early modern stage facilitates these frames; however, even in a stage with full scenery, the links remain between the spatial elements that close in at the end and the circling elements of Hamlet's internal struggles.

Notes

1. Maynard Mack, "The World of Hamlet," *Yale Review* 41.4 (1951–1952): 502–523, 504.
2. In Harold Jenkins' second series Arden edition (London: Arden/ Methuen, 1982), the line to which this note is appended appears at 1.1.22.
3. Sir Philip Sidney, *The Defence of Poesy*, in *The Oxford Authors: Sir Philip Sidney*, ed. Katherine Duncan-Jones (Oxford: Oxford University Press, 1989), 243.
4. Harley Granville-Barker, *Preface to Hamlet*, (New York: Hill and Wang, 1957), 9.
5. Paul Woodruff, *The Necessity of Theater: The Art of Watching and Being Watched* (Oxford: Oxford University Press, 2008), 109.
6. Ibid., 110.
7. Ibid., 112.
8. Bruce R. Smith, "Taking the Measure of Global Space," *Journal of Medieval and Early Modern Studies* 43.1 (2013), 26–48, 36.
9. D.A. Traversi, *An Approach to Shakespeare* (New York: Anchor, Doubleday, 1969), xxi. I quote from the revised and expanded third edition of the book, which was originally published in one volume (New York: Sands and Company, 1938).

10. Albert Cook has noted (in relation to this passage) that the boundary "between life and death" is "freely crossed by the ghost who confronts those on stage by evading an ordinary stabilization in space"; Albert Cook, "Space and Culture," *New Literary History* 29.3 (1998), 551–572, 565.
11. In a longer note on the Ghost's entrances, Harold Jenkins points out that the "shifting locality of the voice adds to the impression of a subterranean demon" (Jenkins, *Hamlet*, 458).
12. This stage direction appears in the First Folio *A Midsummer Night's Dream* at TLN 1460. I discuss this scene in Chapter 1.
13. Emphasis mine.
14. David Hillman, *Shakespeare's Entrails: Belief, Scepticism and the Interior of the Body* (Basingstoke: Palgrave, 2007), 82. Hillman argues that the "paradigmatic sceptic's question of what lies behind or within [...] occupies a number of the play's characters" and suggests that these "within and without" boundaries of bodies in *Hamlet* connects with what he terms "visceral knowledge" (82).
15. Traversi, *An Approach to Shakespeare*, 29.
16. Emrys Jones, in *Scenic Form in Shakespeare* (Oxford: Oxford University Press, 1971), traces connections between this mother-son scene and Shakespeare's earlier mother-son scene between the Bastard and Lady Faulconbridge in *King John* (100).
17. See Chapter 2 for a discussion of this scene.
18. Marvin Rosenberg, *The Masks of Hamlet* (Newark: University of Delaware Press, 1992), 657.
19. Granville-Barker, *Preface to Hamlet*, 111. John Russell Brown remarks that "he may catch hold of his mother roughly and this makes her cry out for help [...]. But his very look and tone of voice may be sufficiently frightening to motivate this reaction." John Russell Brown, *The Shakespeare Handbooks:* Hamlet (Basingstoke: Palgrave, 2006), 90–91. In their third series Arden edition (London: Arden/Thomson, 2006), Ann Thompson and Neil Taylor note that while the lines indicate that Hamlet forces her to sit, "theatrical tradition has not needed the authority of this text to inject violence, often erotically charged, into this scene." This note appears at 3.4.17 in their edition.
20. Brown, *Handbooks:* Hamlet, 92.
21. In Philip Edwards' updated New Cambridge Shakespeare edition of *Hamlet* (Cambridge: Cambridge University Press, 2003), this note appears at 3.4.53.
22. This note appears in Thompson and Taylor's third series Arden edition at 3.4.51.
23. This issue of seeing with another's eyes arises in a different register in *A Midsummer Night's Dream*; see Chapter 1.
24. Brown, *Handbook:* Hamlet, 92.
25. Scholars have debated the reasons for the exclusion of these lines from the First Folio; see Thompson and Taylor's note for a brief description of these controversies (3.4.69-74 fn).

26. Brown notes on 3.4.89-103 that "By some point – varying with each change of cast and probably, with each performance – Gertrude has listened and her mind has changed" (Brown, *Handbook: Hamlet*, 92). In Simon Russell Beale's discussion of playing Hamlet in John Caird's production (2000–2001), he describes how "We found that, by the end of a scene in which an important relationship could have been destroyed, precisely the opposite has happened." Simon Russell Beale, "*Hamlet*" in *Players of Shakespeare 5*, ed. Robert Smallwood (Cambridge: Cambridge University Press, 2003), 145–177, 173.
27. My description assumes a physical presence on stage in the role of the Ghost.
28. Michael Pennington, *Hamlet: A User's Guide* (New York/London: Limelight Editions/ Nick Hern Books, 1996), 102.
29. See Chapter 1 where I discuss Laurens' descriptions of "emission" and "reception."
30. It is in response to this line of Gertrude's that Harley Granville-Barker remarks, "so speak the spiritually blind." Granville-Barker, *Preface to Hamlet*, 114. While Evans prints these as shared lines (as represented here), other editors have frequently printed them as shortened lines; see Thompson and Taylor, Edwards, and Jenkins.
31. Jenkins, *Hamlet*, 1.2.116fn.
32. The *Oxford English Dictionary* offers, "Directed or moving backwards; in a direction contrary to the previous or usual motion; retreating" under its definition of "retrograde, adj. 2.a."
33. This ambiguity would disappear if Claudius had used second person familiar pronouns here. Jenkins asserts "not '(we) bend you' as a reinforcement of 'we beseech you,' but 'bend yourself,' i.e. submit yourself" (Jenkins, *Hamlet*, 1.2.115fn).
34. Evans and Edwards end this sentence unit with a semi-colon; Jenkins, Thompson and Taylor, and others use a full-stop.
35. Thompson and Taylor, *Hamlet*, 3.3.2fn.
36. This connection between banishment and imprisonment demonstrates a different conflation than the one made by Mowbray in *Richard II*. Importantly, it is in Mowbray's response to his own banishment that he calls it an imprisonment; see Chapter 2. Patricia Parker's illuminating work on "delation" and "dilation" shows another way that spatial confusions (between enclosures and revelations) function in the play. Parker's larger argument ties these resonances and confusions to concerns in the period with views of bodies, espionage, and expansion of geographical knowledge. Patricia Parker, *Shakespeare from the Margins: Language, Culture, Context* (Chicago: University of Chicago Press, 1996).
37. Andrew Hiscock, *The Uses of this World: Thinking Space in Shakespeare, Marlowe, Cary and Jonson* (Cardiff: University of Wales Press, 2004), 24.
38. Ibid., 25.
39. Hamlet does not appear on stage until 5.1, but letters make his presence felt. In 4.6, Horatio receives Hamlet's letter from the sailors; in 4.7, Claudius receives Hamlet's letter from a messenger.

40. Marvin Rosenberg calls this speech Gertrude's "one pure soliloquy." Rosenberg, *The Masks of Hamlet*, 760.
41. Productions have often added a lengthier pause here allowing Gertrude time alone on stage; the text's imperative requires only the space of the four lines.
42. This stage direction appears in the First Folio at TLN 2834.
43. Rosenberg has pointed out that, "since many of their lines must touch on the raw of Gertrude's conscience and on her feelings – caring or hostile – toward the three, and also must relate to her absent son, her mute contributions to the scene can be eloquent" (Rosenberg, *The Masks of Hamlet*, 761).
44. John Russell Brown, "The Setting for Hamlet," in *Stratford Upon Avon Studies 5:* Hamlet, eds. John Russell Brown and Bernard Harris (London: Edward Arnold, 1963), 163–184, 171.
45. The parallel for Claudius is the aptness of inciting a son to revenge the death of his father; playgoers may see parallels with 3.3 here.
46. Edwards, *Hamlet*, 4.7.126fn.
47. Traversi, *Approaches*, 22.
48. Ewbank's larger argument focuses on questions of "translation" and how much in the play is determined through language and the attempts to translate, which often can be read as a failure of language itself. Inga-Stina Ewbank, "*Hamlet* and the Power of Words," *Shakespeare Survey* 30 (1977): 56–78, 60.
49. Jenkins notes that "Claudius effects an identification of his audience with himself" (1.2.2 fn). In regard to this same scene, Thompson and Taylor note the elision between Claudius and the court.
50. Robert E. Wood has noted that Hamlet's assertion that "I could be bounded in a nutshell, and count myself a king of infinite space – were it not that I have bad dreams" (2.2. 254–6) uses "metaphoric language drawn from the lively Renaissance debate concerning the boundedness of space." Robert E. Wood, "Space and Scrutiny in *Hamlet*," *South Atlantic Review* 52.1 (1987), 25–42, 36.
51. Mariko Ichikawa's *Shakespearean Entrances* carefully explores the configuration of stage movement and the passage of time on stage particularly as it relates to entrances and exits. The movement I am interested in here also considers the passage of time as offstage characters perform certain actions. Mariko Ichikawa, *Shakespearean Entrances*, (Basingstoke: Palgrave Macmillan, 2002).
52. Stephen Booth, "On the Value of *Hamlet*," in *Reinterpretations of Elizabethan Drama*, ed. Norman Rabkin (New York: Colombia University Press, 1969), 74–93. The essay is reprinted in *Critical Essays on Shakespeare's* Hamlet, ed. David Scott Kastan (London: Prentice Hall, 1995), 19–42. I quote from Kastan's reprint where these quotations appear on page 22.
53. Booth, "On the Value of *Hamlet*," 23.
54. Ichikawa points out that in the First Folio "There is no break in the action between the two scenes now numbered 1.4 and 1.5, though Hamlet's

first speech after his re-entrance suggests some change in location" (71). Ichikawa supposes that if "while Horatio and Marcellus are still moving towards the door from which the Ghost and Hamlet have made their exit, the Ghost and Hamlet enter through the opposite door" then the "audience would never be aware of any scene change" (71). I would suggest that even in the case of overlapping entrances and exits, the spatial frame here would require that the Ghost and Hamlet have traveled some distance.
55. Emphasis mine.
56. C. Walter Hodges, *Enter the Whole Army: A Pictorial Study of Shakespearean Staging: 1576–1616* (Cambridge: Cambridge University Press, 2004), 119–121.
57. Tom Stoppard's *Rosencrantz and Guildenstern are Dead* (1967) takes advantage of this absence of location and opens with "two Elizabethans passing the time in a place with no visible character." Tom Stoppard, *Rosencrantz and Guildenstern are Dead* (New York: Grove Weidenfeld, 1967), 11.
58. Booth, "On the Value of *Hamlet*," 31.
59. I refer to main characters here and discount the absence of characters such as Osric, Voltemand, and Cornelius who may well round out the court presence during the performance of the play.
60. The quick succession of short scenes after Antony's preparation for battle in 4.4 includes multiple locations and very short bursts of activity. John Wilders' Arden edition marks a total of fifteen scenes in the fourth act; the Oxford text edited by Wells and Taylor includes sixteen through a different act break. John Wilders, ed., *Antony and Cleopatra* by William Shakespeare (London: Arden/ Routledge, 1995). Stanley Wells and Gary Taylor, eds. *William Shakespeare: The Complete Works* by William Shakespeare (Oxford: Oxford University Press, 1986).
61. This dependence on locations separated by vast distances in *Antony and Cleopatra* relate to that play's relationship to blurred distinctions and difficult boundaries.
62. E.T. Schell, "Who Said That—Hamlet or *Hamlet*?," *Shakespeare Quarterly* 24.2 (1973), 135–146, 145.

4
Place, Perception, and Disorientation in *Macbeth*
"A walking shadow"

The static tragedy at the end of *Hamlet* depends on playgoers' experience of the staged space defined by Hamlet's movements. In *Macbeth*, the relentless forward movement of the narrative sweeps playgoers along with Macbeth himself as he realizes, "I am in blood/ Stepp'd in so far" (3.4.135–6). As playgoers, our sense of location depends a great deal on how Macbeth experiences his own reality, and this reality develops from Macbeth's confused perceptions of his location. When Lady Macbeth publicly hears of Duncan's murder, her response is "Woe, alas! / What! in our house?" (2.3.87–8). Critics have found this response baffling; she has had time to think of something better to say. Eighteenth-century editors generally see this as a blunder on the part of Lady Macbeth, a mistaken lack of preparation for an inevitable discovery.[1] George Lyman Kittredge claims it is "A natural expression for an innocent hostess, horrified at the thought that such a thing has happened to one of her own guests."[2] More likely, and more sensibly, her comment relates to the facts of location. It may be a hostess' concern that cloaks the commentary, but the playgoers already have knowledge of Lady Macbeth's involvement with the murder; playgoers can only see this comment as some attempt to appear innocent to the other characters. Macbeth, offstage for Lady Macbeth's reception of the news, does not respond directly to her commentary. On the difference between their public responses, William Warburton remarks that, "on the contrary," Macbeth "now labouring under the horrors of a recent murder, in his exclamation, gives all the marks of sorrow for the fact itself."[3] However, Banquo's immediate response to Lady

Macbeth's outcry emphasizes the oddity of her concern about place: "Too cruel any where" (2.3.86).

In the midst of the confused revelation of Duncan's murder, Lady Macbeth's comment rings an odd note both for the characters on stage and for the playgoers. This and other moments that similarly emphasize location point to a larger concern of the play – a constant fixation on location, both in mentions of place and the attempts to perceive one's own whereabouts. The characters, particularly Macbeth, consistently comment upon and wonder about location and movement. The play as a whole depends, for the development of its narrative movement, on these concurrent emphases on location and related sensory confusions. Macbeth's moral and psychological deteriorations manifest through his inability to accurately perceive his location and direction. Other characters' experiences and reiterated comments about location exacerbate Macbeth's deterioration.

Macbeth's locations

The first appearance of Macbeth on stage shows him entering with Banquo as they travel into a location already occupied by the witches. Macbeth's first line echoes the witches' words, saying "so foul and fair a day I have not seen" (1.3.38), and shows his immersion in circumstances beyond his control.[4] In response, Banquo asks a traveler's common question for information about the distance to their destination: "How far is't call'd to Forres?" (1.3.39). Similar questions in other plays, *Richard II* for example, offer instances of characters establishing a mode of movement that the playgoers need to understand for the scene to make sense. This unanswered are-we-there-yet question gets lost in the surprise of seeing the witches; worry about exact location disintegrates into questions about and exclamations on the witches' appearance. Location threatens to turn into dislocation; the supernatural interferes with the normal movements of characters. Macbeth, after hearing the first of the witches' proclamations, attempts to stop their movement; his imperative "stay" halts them both in their chanting and presumably from moving on to some other place (1.3.70). His emphasis on a directional orientation of their information ("say from whence/ You owe this strange intelligence") matches his concern that the witches "stop our way" (1.3.75–6, 77). "Way" in this instance refers directly to their course or pathway of travel rather than their means of travel. When the witches disappear, Banquo appropriately asks not how or why, but "Whither are they vanish'd?" (1.3.80). Macbeth's immediate response links "whither" to a failure of perception: "what seem'd corporal melted" (1.3.81). To "seem," in Shakespeare's plays, nearly always implies false appearance leading to misperceptions. Hamlet's cavil at Gertrude's use of "seems" offers an important negating example: "seems, madam? nay it is, I know not 'seems'" (1.2.76). Claudius counters Hamlet's description of "that within which passes show" (1.2.85) by arguing that Hamlet's mourning is "To reason most absurd" (1.2.103). This comparison between that which "seems" and the overriding "reason" that urges clarity of thought, asserts that misperceptions might be corrected by the reasoning faculties. Indeed Macbeth's comment that "what seem'd corporal melted" elicits Banquo's suggestion that the failure of perception might be a failure of reason (1.3.81). Banquo voices the possibility that they have "eaten on the insane root/ That takes the reason prisoner" (1.3.84–5). Reason and awareness of location ought to provide understanding. In this instance, as in so many that follow, inchoate location combines with sensory confusion to undermine reason.

Macbeth's first soliloquy, in 1.7, begins the conflations of time and location that increase over the course of the play. Macbeth is separated in this scene from the main action taking place offstage. The First Folio stage direction reads: *"Ho-boyes. Torches. Enter a sewer, and divers Servants with Dishes and Service over the Stage. Then enter Macbeth"* (TLN 472-4). Interrupting his soliloquy, Lady Macbeth enters twenty-eight lines later and remarks: "He has almost supp'd. Why have you left the chamber?" (1.7.29). Most likely then Macbeth enters from the same door the servants have recently exited. Macbeth must have been in the chamber with Duncan and the other guests and left. In other words, Macbeth leaves the place where most of the other characters are gathered and seeks this emptied place for his soliloquy, in contrast to many characters who are often left alone on stage as other characters exit. Rather than the emptying of a filled stage to leave a character in control of a space as we saw in Helena's soliloquy in the opening scene of *A Midsummer Night's Dream* or the departure of the members of the court in the instance of Hamlet's first soliloquy, in 1.7 of *Macbeth* the space actively filled by other characters is offstage. Noise and spectacle establish the existence of the other characters elsewhere without those characters occupying the stage.

Macbeth's first soliloquy noticeably emphasizes the location of the events he contemplates – despite his own dislocation from events happening offstage. In this soliloquy he uses "here" in a variety of ways important for both this particular speech and for larger questions in the play:

> If it were done, when 'tis done, then 'twere well
> It were done quickly: if th'assassination
> Could trammel up the consequence, and catch
> With his surcease success; that but this blow
> Might be the be-all and end-all – *here*,
> But *here*, upon this bank and shoal of time,
> We'd jump the life to come. – But in these cases,
> We still have judgment *here*; that we but teach
> Bloody instructions, which, being taught, return
> To plague th'inventor: this even-handed Justice
> Commends th'ingredience of our poison'd chalice
> To our own lips. He's *here* in double trust[.] (1.7.1–12 emphasis added)

Initially, "here" is "upon this bank and shoal of time," a marker of chronology; this temporal notation has oddly geographical realities. After the rhetorical reversal of "But," Macbeth's assertion that "We still have judgment here" complicates matters considerably. Is it "here" in this emptied location Macbeth occupies in that moment? Or is it "here" in Macbeth's own mind? Kittridge explains that this "here" refers to "in this world," presumably as the contrary location to "the life to come" from the previous line.[5] Kenneth Muir notes without clarification that "judgment here" refers back to both earlier uses of "here."[6] In line 12, Macbeth uses "here" to denote location in his description of Duncan's stay. In this speech, "here" initially refers to the chronological moments, shifts through a more complex notion of the location of choice, and rests in the questions raised by Duncan's immediate physical location in the Macbeth's household.

Angus Fletcher's description of the function of soliloquy offers some useful ways of thinking about how this particular soliloquy of Macbeth's works. Fletcher says,

> In a soliloquy, the speaker enhances the role of separation from the self, to increase incorporation into the self, through a liminal loosening of all conventional stereotypes. The soliloquy is defenseless. [...] In the great dramatic soliloquies of Renaissance drama, there is thus a special poignancy in that the audience is made fully aware of the vulnerability of such a speaker, who is in a single speech enacting a much larger social drama.[7]

Macbeth's soliloquy separates him from himself insofar as it allows him to voice, and playgoers to experience, the wanderings of his mind. The defenselessness of the speech increases with Macbeth's awareness that he ought to be elsewhere. This moment separates him from the duties he ought to be performing as a host; even as he simultaneously ponders the ultimate inhospitable act.[8] Macbeth's vulnerabilities – perceptual incapacities, the possibilities for inhumane actions, uncontrollable locations, and erratic movements – all appear in this soliloquy.

When Macbeth is next alone on stage, he asks, "Is this a dagger, which I see before me[?]" (2.1.33). Again, the soliloquy is framed by other characters' earlier participation with the scene's space. Banquo and Fleance's occupation of the place before Macbeth's entrance emphasizes the liminal nature of the place; it is one that must be guarded, and Banquo throws out the demanding question of a guard to a stranger, "Who's there?" (2.1.10). This is of course the same as the opening line of *Hamlet* where the liminal space is soon occupied by a ghost. Macbeth takes control of the place by ordering the others to leave, and he remains in a location both inexact and unguarded. When he sees the dagger before him ("I have thee not, and yet I see thee still"), he grasps and clutches at empty air as most productions stage it (2.1.35). As an object of comparison or protection, he draws his own dagger and says, "Thou marshal'st me the way that I was going" (2.1.41). His confusions over locating the non-existent dagger encourage him to accept direction from either the phantom dagger or the dagger he draws. He links his attempt to disregard that direction to the confusion of his perception: "Mine eyes are made the fools o' th' other sense/ Or else worth all the rest" (2.1.44–5). Despite these problems of perception, Macbeth continues the description of his choices and actions as a pathway when he describes his own and "murther's" possible movement through the night:

> [...] wither'd Murther,
> Alarum'd by his sentinel, the wolf,
> Whose howl's his watch, thus with his stealthy pace,
> With Tarquin's ravishing strides,[9] towards his design
> Moves like a ghost. (2.1.52–6)

Murder personified here strides and "Moves like a ghost," and yet even his sentinel participates in the oddities of perceptual confusion. It is the audible howl of the wolf that acts as "watch" with that position's implied reliance on the visual.

Macbeth's vision leads him to movement and the movement has a direction determined by the dagger. He immediately begins to describe his movement, although he can remain in one area of the stage to deliver this speech. Macbeth's reiterated vision of the dagger does not note that the dagger might be appearing in different positions. "Thou marshal'st me the way I was going" has been read as the phantom dagger directing toward Duncan's chamber; if this reading informs production decisions, the imagined dagger would be fairly static. Macbeth gives the remainder of his speech in relation to that still point. Marvin Rosenberg's illuminating descriptions of choices made in a variety of productions make clear that, while the actor might choose to hide his eyes, step back from the location of the dagger, or otherwise introduce movement in the scene, the imaginary dagger usually remains in a static position and movement locates itself in relation to that point.[10] Indeed, Macbeth worries about his own location and others' awareness of it. He hopes that the "firm-set earth" will "Hear not my steps, which way they walk, for fear/ The very stones prate of my where-about" (2.1.56, 57–8). "Hear" and "here" are confounded in this instance; his "where-about" becomes an indefinable location.

Macbeth's deteriorating spatial orientation appears even more clearly after Duncan's murder. After Lady Macbeth leaves to return the daggers to their "proper" place, Macbeth hears knocking: "Whence is that knocking?" (2.2.56). He claims that "every noise appals" him, (2.2.57), but the real problem here seems to be that he cannot tell from where it comes. When Lady Macbeth returns, she does not have this same problem; she remarks quite specifically the location of the knocking: "I hear a knocking/ At the south entry" (2.2.64–5). Lady Macbeth has no difficulties locating the source of the sound that Macbeth finds so frightening.[11] Evelyn Tribble, in the context of a comparison with Kurosawa's film adaptation, discusses the effects of the "soundscape" (to use Bruce R. Smith's term) of *Macbeth*.[12] Tribble's descriptions of the instinctual "startle" response are particularly useful for thinking about how the play depends on immediate sensory responses from the characters. Tribble explains that the association between "sound and fear" includes "the capacity of sound to startle, to stir a physical response and to prompt an orienting response, a search for the source of the sound."[13] Lady Macbeth's awareness of the origin of the sound shows that Macbeth's startle responses inaccurately respond to the noise.

Macduff's horrified descriptions of Duncan's death continually assert that the event – and, more importantly, the perception of the event – disrupts normal perceptual function. Initially, it is unspeakable, neither "tongue nor heart/ Cannot conceive nor name thee" (2.3.63–4). He warns other characters that to see it, will "destroy your sight" (2.3.71). At Lady Macbeth's entrance, he urges deafness, since "'Tis not for you to hear" (2.3.85). If accurate perception leads to comprehension, he imagines that the reverse must hold; incomprehensible horror must make the organs of perception inaccurate. David Lucking links Macduff's descriptions of the "unnameable" in 2.3 to Macduff's actions in his later confrontation with Macbeth, where Macduff "discover[s] in effect that words are not after all entirely impotent even when they are obliged to grapple with the unspeakable."[14] However, Macduff's incoherence in 2.3 depends more on the way the body functions. In other words, the problem in that moment rests in the organ of speech rather than in language. In *Richard II*, performative accusations are the central location for the conflation of tongue, breath, and words; in *Macbeth* these conflations occur in instances when characters find events incomprehensible to the senses.

Compared to Macduff's insistence on the incomprehensibility of the events, Macbeth and Lady Macbeth separately attempt the appearance of innocence. As we have already seen, Lady Macbeth's insistence on the location of these events "in our house" sits oddly in the scene. And, despite Macduff's predicted alteration in the organs of perception, Macbeth's active response returns to the possibilities of movement he emphasized so heavily in his earlier evocation of "Murther." Macbeth describes killing Duncan's chamber guards as a movement: "Th' expedition of my violent love/ Outrun the pauser, reason" (2.3.108–9). Although generally glossed as "haste," the word "expedition" also calls to mind a journey, movement toward a destination.[15] After the departure of the banquet guests in 3.4, Macbeth describes his plan as a forward movement:

> I am in blood
> Stepp'd in so far that, should I wade no more,
> Returning were as tedious as go o'er.
> Strange things I have in head, that will to hand,
> Which must be acted ere they may be scann'd. (3.4.135–139)

The distance he has traveled makes it useless to turn back; only the corporeal experience will allow him to understand his own actions. Since he describes the actions and decisions as one long endeavor of wading, the continuation on his journey implies not only the inevitability but also the bodily aspects of the experience. These "strange things I have in head" can only be comprehended after experienced.

Means of perceiving space

Although early modern medical treatises and more general texts of the period usually describe five senses (sight, touch, taste, smell, and hearing), the additional sense of locomotion was described by Julius Caesar Scaligar in 1557.[16] A nearly contemporaneous dramatic representation, Thomas Tomkis' *Lingua* personifies the five senses battling against speech (the character Lingua) as she attempts and fails to gain standing as one of the senses.[17] This representation of the various senses combating one another may not have influenced the construction of Macbeth's dilemmas. However, the discussions of the senses in the period had not settled completely the questions of modes of perception functioning within the human body. The inclusion of Macbeth's heightened and disordered sense of his own movement coincides with similar disorder of his other senses. Additionally, early modern descriptions of movement, even of objects other than one's own body, depended in tangible ways upon human perception. In the absence of readily available accurate devices, measurement of distance, for example, still relied on the understanding that a fathom was the length of a man's outstretched arms, a unit of length and a measuring tactic that depended on the sense of touch and the corporeal realities of anatomy.

For Macbeth, Banquo's clarity of direction, and the physical and moral certitude it implies, becomes worrisome: "He hath a wisdom that doth guide his valour" (3.1.52). Further dilemmas arise for Macbeth because of that guidance and certitude of direction. When planning Banquo's murder, Macbeth recognizes that he might "With bare-fac'd power sweep him from my sight" (3.1.118), a removal that might mean banishment or death. As a reigning monarch, Macbeth has control of the location of his subjects since banishment offers the option of removal. Exile, a power mechanism not used in this play, has public elements that Macbeth cannot afford to use. The more stealthy elements he employs, the murderers, describe themselves in terms usually applied to directionless or wearied travelers. One claims he will be reckless because "I am one, my liege, / Whom the vile blows and buffets of the world/ Hath so incens'd" (3.1.107–9). The other describes himself as, "so weary with disasters, tugg'd with fortune" (3.1.111). Caroline Spurgeon used this last description as one piece of evidence to support her assertion that,

> [Shakespeare's] use of verbs of movement is a study in itself, and one of his outstanding characteristics is the way in which by introducing verbs of movement about things which are motionless, or rather which are abstractions and cannot have physical movement, he gives life to a whole phrase.[18]

In this instance, "tugg'd with fortune," the verb of movement encourages us to read "fortune" as a personification, enlivening the imagistic qualities and also reminding us of the resistance to fortune. Although Spurgeon's point refers to many plays, in *Macbeth* particularly, verbs of movement are introduced in unexpected constructions. Despite, or perhaps because of, this rhetorical and physical movement, Macbeth introduces stasis as desirable certitude:

> [...] Better be with the dead,
> Whom we, to gain our peace, have sent to peace,

Than on the torture of the mind to lie
In restless ecstasy. Duncan is in his grave;
After life's fitful fever he sleeps well. (3.2.19–23)

Almost immediately, that previously desirable stasis turns into imposed restraint. After hearing that Fleance has escaped, Macbeth describes himself trapped: "But now I am cabin'd, cribb'd, confin'd, bound in/ To saucy doubts and fears. – But Banquo's safe?" (3.4.23–4). The indeterminate location of Fleance traps Macbeth in a motionless state of doubt and fear. The murderers understand Macbeth's real concern when he asks about Banquo. In fact, they remark his location – he is "safe in a ditch" (3.4.25) – before describing the injuries inflicted upon him.

Macbeth's eventual response to the appearance of Banquo's ghost recalls his assurance to himself about Duncan's whereabouts. "The time has been, / That when the brains were out, the man would die,/ And there an end; but now they rise again" (3.4.77–9). Initially, the spatial anomaly alerts Macbeth to the existence of the ghost; what ought to be an empty space appears filled: "The table's full" (3.4.45). This appearance of Banquo's ghost shakes Macbeth's remaining faculties for locating himself: "if I stand *here*, I saw him" (3.4.73 emphasis added). The doubt rests in whether he can accurately locate himself, and then this doubt extends to his senses. He questions how others "can behold such sights" and "remain unmoved" (3.5.113). Macbeth's vision of the ghost muddles further his confidence in his senses to correctly apprehend the realities around him.

Without confidence in his ability to accurately perceive his own surroundings, Macbeth offers up all faculties for organized movement in exchange for an answer from the witches:

> answer me:
> Though you untie the winds, and let them fight
> Against the Churches; though the yesty waves
> Confound and swallow navigation up;
> Though bladed corn be lodg'd, and trees blown down;
> [...]
> Even till destruction sicken; answer me
> To what I ask you. (4.1.50–61)

The witches call forth the apparitions who deliver the messages to Macbeth, but they insist repeatedly that Macbeth must not speak. When the second apparition repeats his name three times, Macbeth responds, "Had I three ears, I'd hear thee" (4.1.78). This line has not excited much commentary, but it succinctly draws attention to both the sense organ and the sense itself, in this moment which must be as visually stimulating as it is aurally. Despite his earlier claim that he is willing to see the natural order disordered, Macbeth refuses to believe the possibility that Birnam Wood can "Unfix his earth-bound root" (4.1.95). The disorder and doubleness of nature in the play has been widely remarked.[19] The movement of "Great Birnan wood to high Dunsinane hill" (as the apparition phrases it) seems to be a final disordering of the possible natural markers of location (4.1.93–4).[20] One expects, either when moving through a landscape or when remaining still, that geographical features of the landscape will remain relatively fixed. Rather than an assertion of natural order, this disorder presents the ultimate un-navigable terrain.

Other characters in the play similarly describe difficulties negotiating their surroundings. Rosse, delivering his warning to Lady Macduff, describes the quandary of Macbeth's subjects who find they cannot know their own positions and have no way to control their own directions.

> I dare not speak much further,
> But cruel are the times when we are traitors,
> And do not know ourselves; when we hold rumor
> From what we fear, yet know not what we fear,
> But float upon a wild and violent sea
> Each way, and move. (4.2.17–22)

These moves depend on metaphorically unchartable waters.[21] When Rosse delivers the news of the death of Macduff's family, he attempts to halt the senses themselves from working. "I have words/ That would be howl'd out in the desert air, /Where hearing should not latch them" (4.3.193–5). These nameable events must be articulated, but they would be better done in an open and empty landscape where hearing cannot locate them. Rosse describes himself as someone who hopes his own words will be unable to navigate the only appropriate terrain for unleashing them. In turn, a recipient sense of hearing in a listener will be unable to accurately perceive them. The sleepwalking scene shows the most extreme case of a character losing control of the senses.

DOCTOR: You see, her eyes are open.
GENTLEMAN: Ay, but their sense are shut. (5.1.24–5)

The watchers can only conclude that Lady Macbeth's senses are useless and, after this point, Macbeth's disintegration soon follows.

Many commentators have remarked on the confusion of Macbeth's senses in the play. From the opening scenes, the stagecraft elements of the play as a whole confuse and consistently undermine Macbeth's own sense of space and location. Macbeth's entrances in act five noticeably depart from the previous sections of the play; only in the final act does he enter to an empty stage. However, these solitary and controlling entrances only happen after he is unable to separate time and space in any meaningful fashion. Macbeth describes the perceptual confusions and near dissolution of his senses:

> I have almost forgot the taste of fears.
> The time has been, my senses would have cool'd
> To hear a night-shriek; and my fell of hair
> Would at a dismal treatise rouse, and stir
> As life were in't. (5.5.9–13)

The disintegration of his ability to separate time and space through the use of his senses culminates in his response to the news of Lady Macbeth's death. His comment that "she should have died hereafter" provides fodder for critics trying to make sense of his ambiguous speech. In this instance, when Macbeth uses "hereafter," the English language aids him in the confusion of space and time; we might say "nowadays" but we do not (nor have we ever) used "now-after." The "here" of "hereafter" both connects and confuses spatial and temporal locations.

> She should have died hereafter;
> There would have been a time for such a word.—

> To-morrow, and to-morrow, and to-morrow,
> Creeps in this petty pace from day to day,
> To the last syllable of recorded time;
> And all of our yesterdays have lighted fools,
> The way to dusty death. Out, out, brief candle!
> Life's but a walking shadow; a poor player,
> That struts and frets his hour upon the stage,
> And then is heard no more: it is a tale
> Told by an idiot, full of sound and fury,
> Signifying nothing. (5.5.17–28)

His line following "hereafter" again emphasizes the location of time: "*There* would have been a time for such a word" (5.5.18). The multiplied "to-morrows" imply a movement forward into a future of multiple next days, yet the reiteration also presents a static day-after-this-one. The "to-morrows" "*creep* [...] in this petty *pace*" – the movement of time appears as motion across areas that can be paced out. Time past offers direction to fools who are offered a lighted "way" or pathway "to dusty death." Time and its movement are translated here into spatial relationships. The "walking shadow" offers an image of impossible motion without the body to cast the shadow. Separations between body and reflection have disintegrated.

After this disintegration of spatial certainties and temporal existence, Macbeth has useless control of an empty stage space in act five. This meaningless control throws into relief his trapped circumstances, and his description reveals his loss of control of time and space. When Macbeth enters in 5.7 he claims that, "They have tied me to a stake: I cannot fly, / But, bear-like, I must fight the course" (5.7.1–2). "Course" (as Muir and others gloss) is the "bout or round between the bear and the dogs;" but "course" is also "path" or "way."[22] Macbeth claims he is "tied to a stake" or fixed to a location, and that he knows his location. Yet a short battle – and only twelve lines – later he leaves the stage. In the final act of the play, Macbeth operates in what Henri Lefebvre describes as a "monumental space." In Lefebvre's descriptions of the production of social space, he emphasizes ways particular activities – in conjunction with spatial realities – produce functions of space. "Monumental space," one classification he offers of a social space, produces complexities that "involve levels, layers and sedimentations of perception, representation, and spatial practice which presuppose one another, which proffer themselves to one another, and which are superimposed upon one another."[23] Only in the final moments of the play can we reasonably describe Macbeth's actions taking place in a "monumental space," which has been developed through the control of space over the course of the previous action of the play. He is not a monarch who establishes his power through the convening of audiences and courtly functions; we see those practices by Richard and Bolingbrook in *Richard II* and by Claudius in *Hamlet*. Instead, Macbeth's power to command a "monumental space" appears only after his other means of controlling or perceiving space disintegrate. The layers of "perception, representation, and spatial practice" built into the play coalesce into Macbeth's experiences and decisions of the final act.

Macbeth's short victorious battle against Young Siward shows Macbeth functioning as he will in his final scene where he rejects the possibility of dying "On mine own sword" (5.8.2). Immediately after the battle with Young Siward, Macbeth exits and, in quick succession, two short vignettes increase the speed of the events of the play and finalize the difficulties of location that have plagued Macbeth throughout. In brief appearances, first Macduff and then Malcolm and Old Siward appear as they search for Macbeth in the melee of the battles. These characters emphasize their own awareness of their locations, and they depend on sounds to direct their movements.

Macduff has a clear direction, and he comments on his own knowledge of Macbeth's whereabouts. Fittingly, this speech is the only time Macduff appears on stage alone in the play – a minor soliloquy in the midst of the battles. He claims his "wife and children's ghost will haunt" him if he fails to find Macbeth; he is drawn away by the awareness that "There thou shouldst be;/ By this great clatter, one of greatest note/ Seems bruited" (5.7.16, 20–22). Macduff clearly knows which way he needs to go, and he knows this from correctly hearing and interpreting the noise around him. His senses function as they ought, and he interprets what "seems bruited" in what turns out to be a correct fashion. In this instance, "seems" bends to reason. Malcolm and Old Siward are similarly directive in their descriptions of their own movements. Siward directs Malcolm, "This way, my Lord" (5.7.24). The brevity of their appearance (fifteen lines) bolsters the impression that these movements are purposeful and direct.

It is in the next scene, of course, that Macbeth is slain. Macbeth's disintegration, his dislocation from his own sense of time and place, prepares playgoers for his death.

Playgoers' understanding of space

In Thomas de Quincey's 1823 "On the Knocking at the Gate in Macbeth," he centers the essay on a particular effect most easily perceived through production of the play:

> From my boyish days I had always felt a great perplexity on one point in Macbeth: it was this: the knocking at the gate, which succeeds to the murder of Duncan, produced to my feelings an effect for which I never could account: the effect was – that it reflected back upon the murder a peculiar awfulness and a depth of solemnity: yet, however obstinately I endeavoured with my understanding to comprehend this, for many years I never could see *why* it should produce such an effect.[24]

What makes de Quincey's starting point interesting, for this discussion, is that he attempts to understand an otherwise incomprehensible effect on playgoers and explores how the play achieves that effect. In his description, understanding arises from reasoning, while feelings might not be understood in these same kinds of questions. Thus he begins his exploration by claiming that, "The mere understanding, however useful and indispensable is the meanest faculty in the human mind and the most to be distrusted."[25] As an example to demonstrate his point about understanding, he offers linear perspective: "Ask of any person whatsoever, who is not previously prepared for the demand by a knowledge of perspective, to draw in the rudest way the commonest appearance which depends upon the laws of that science [...] he will be utterly unable to make the smallest approximation to it."[26] De Quincey claims that the person involved in the experiment would be allowing his or her understanding to overrule the evidence of the person's eyes, which have clearly seen this quotidian effect. The distinction between "understanding" and "feeling" relies on "feeling" as that which depends on the senses themselves; in this instance, vision. His own difficulty understanding the effect in the play remained a question: "my understanding could furnish no reason why the knocking at the gate in Macbeth should produce any effect direct or reflected: in fact, my understanding said positively that it could *not* produce any effect [...] But I knew better: I felt that it did."[27] De Quincey essentially drops the question of visual perspective from the rest of his essay, but the inclusion of it at the beginning of the essay points to the ways that confusion of perspective can produce an effect on stage – or at least provides an opening to discussion of these effects.

De Quincey offers two important conclusions in his essay that go some way to describing the root of the effect he feels at this moment in the play. Firstly, he emphasizes the way the scene (and the play) insists on the playgoer experiencing the feelings Macbeth experiences. As he puts it, the poet "must throw the interest on the murderer: our sympathy must be with *him*; (of course I mean a sympathy of comprehension, a sympathy by which we enter into his feelings, and are made to understand them; – not a sympathy of pity or approbation."[28] The playgoers' sympathy with Macbeth depends on entering into the feelings and the realities of the character in particular moments. Secondly, de Quincey argues that the knocking offers a resumption of action that jolts the playgoer. He uses the word "reaction" to describe what he understands as a revivification of events on and off stage:

> Hence it is that when the deed is done – when the work of darkness is perfect, then the world of darkness passes away like a pageantry in the clouds: the knocking at the gate is heard; and it makes known audibly that the reaction has commenced: the human has made its reflux upon the fiendish: the pulses of life are beginning to beat again: and the re-establishment of the goings-on of the world in which we live, first makes us profoundly sensible of the awful parenthesis that had suspended them.[29]

What de Quincey points to are the ways the scene manages to establish the playgoers within the staged space of the action, allowing us to forget the certainty of offstage actions to such an extent that the resumption of those offstage activities startles us with a reality and clarity. The offstage events become part of the "goings-on of the world in which we live," which at that moment are the reality of the play itself.

Actors are often in an unusual position for understanding how playgoers perceive the events of a play. Antony Sher played, in quick succession, Leontes in *The Winter's Tale* and then Macbeth in *Macbeth*. His perceptive comments, as he compares the two characters, point to some of the other ways the play achieves a strange kind of clarity through Macbeth's character. Despite the confusion of senses and sensory perceptions in *Macbeth*, the confusions of the play are often produced through what Sher describes as a terrible awareness. Sher remarks, "But the profound difference between [Macbeth and Leontes] is that Macbeth remains horribly sane throughout; he watches himself throughout, increasingly appalled by what he sees. He never enjoys the wild, almost liberating oblivion that Leontes knows."[30] Sher specifically refers here to the confused oblivion of Leontes' disordered meter and sense in the early scene in *The Winter's Tale* when Leontes' becomes utterly (and wrongly) certain of his wife's infidelity. As Sher puts it, "in *The Winter's Tale*, Shakespeare shows how certainty can be a kind of madness. In *Macbeth* he shows how uncertainty is very human."[31] In *Macbeth*, playgoers experience the uncertainty of Macbeth because we, as playgoers, experience those uncertainties with him. Sher provocatively suggests that, "Macbeth is tortured by sanity, by clarity, by both consciousness and conscience. Even when he sees visions like Banquo's ghost, or the apparitions, or the air-drawn dagger [...], even on these occasions he remains a sane man peering at assorted nightmares."[32] Sher's determination that Macbeth remains a sane man depends on a definition of sane that involves playgoers in the otherwise insane experiences of Macbeth. Sher's discussion is, I think, useful here because he considers how playgoers understand Macbeth's experience. Obviously, Macbeth as a character is rather more (and less) than sane or insane. His interactions and decisions and experiences are presented in a series of staged events to convey the narrative and presumably to elicit responses from playgoers. The appearances of the supernatural in a play do not noticeably figure into whether we understand a character as sane or insane. Although in *Hamlet* Ophelia's behavior strewing flowers and singing songs denotes madness, in *A Midsummer Night's Dream* Oberon and Puck's use of the magic flower does not. Partly, we understand these events in particular ways because of how the other characters in a play describe those events. Claudius, Gertrude, and Laertes make clear that we must understand Ophelia's behavior as signs and demonstrations of insanity. Puck does not question the effectiveness of the magic flower in *A Midsummer Night's Dream* and playgoers have proof nearly immediately of its efficacy.

Playgoers' responses must be informed by the ways characters in the play respond, even if only to reject mistaken apprehension. During the banquet scene, Lady Macbeth's response to Macbeth's perception of the ghost produces several effects. After she demands, "Are you a man?" (3.4.57), this exchange follows:

MACBETH: Ay, and a bold one, that dare look on that
                  Which might appall the devil.
LADY MACBETH: O proper stuff!
                  This is the very painting of your fear;
                  This is the air-drawn dagger which you said
                  Led you to Duncan. (3.4.64–8)

Playgoers receive several pieces of important information through this exchange. Clearly, Lady Macbeth cannot see Banquo's ghost, but her exclamation "O proper stuff" dismisses the experience of it. Most of the contemporaneous definitions of "stuff" connect the word to "material" or "matter," which is exactly what Lady Macbeth dismisses here, the material reality of Banquo's ghost.[33] Playgoers are also upbraided by her description here. Not only is the materiality dismissed, but we also quickly understand that some not-staged scene has occurred wherein Macbeth describes his experiences of seeing the dagger. This knowledge on the part of Lady Macbeth makes playgoers aware of her rather complete knowledge of events we experience alone (as it were) with Macbeth. In this instance, the supernatural elements are dismissed by Lady Macbeth and dismissed in a fashion that demonstrates her awareness of Macbeth's previous experiences.

Effects on playgoers are difficult to generalize because productions, in their performance choices, and groups of playgoers, in their perceptions of those performance choices, differ vastly. However, the attempt to consider some of these effects often leads to a better understanding of how the drama functions. In *Macbeth*, playgoers experience some of the same dislocations the characters experience. The careful control of places and locations in the play heightens the already controlled areas of the stage on which the actions take place. However, the playgoer, continually aware (particularly in this play) of off-stage events, usually has more information and at different times than most of the characters. This discussion of the play and characters has so far focused on places and locations as the characters experience them within the frame of the play. What remains is to explore some of the ways the playgoer experiences the stage space as the play's events unfold through the narrative movement. Susanne Langer says that although "It has been said repeatedly that the theater creates a perpetual present moment [...], it is only a present filled with its own future that is really dramatic."[34] The "virtual future" (to use Langer's term) created by drama functions through the defined spaces of the action. In the case of drama, that space includes the stage, the playgoers, the characters, off-stage action, entrances and exits. The inexorable constant temporal movement of performance ensures a feeling of the perpetual present, which depends on its own future. The playgoers' experiences of that perpetual present and, I suggest, the staged spaces determine the possibilities for that dramatic future. Although individual production choices vary widely, careful attention to some spatial aspects of the play and the effects on the playgoer illuminate some of the ways the play produces narrative movement.

Although the first two scenes of the play neither include Macbeth on stage nor establish his location, they offer some directional markers about how we (as playgoers) are meant to understand locations. D.J. Palmer has explored the visual impact of the play and stresses the importance and frequency in *Macbeth* of visual expressions prescribed through commentary by other characters. Palmer points out, for example, that Banquo's commentary on Macbeth's initially physical reaction to the witches and their prophecies "draws the attention of the audience to Macbeth, who is silent himself."[35] The directional markers for playgoers at the opening of the play extend beyond the visual impact and prepare us in important ways for the appearance of Macbeth. The Captain in 1.2 describes how "with his brandish'd steel" Macbeth "carv'd out his passage" in the battle (1.2.17, 19). The Captain describes Macbeth knowing how to make a path, a passage, with direction. This description seems to establish Macbeth as a character who knows where he is going. This scene with the captain appears between two scenes with the witches. The opening scene with the witches' first appearance emphasizes location "Where the place?" (1.1.6) and the impending meeting at that location: "There to meet with Macbeth" (1.1.7). Early in the play, we hear constant iterations of means of location. The witches reappear (in 1.3) and with "ports," "quarters," and "shipman's card" describe a soon-to-be "tempest-tossed" sailor (15, 16, 17, 25). These are directional markers and descriptions that offer another version of some of the dislocations that Macbeth himself suffers later in the play. The witches describe themselves as being exceptionally mobile, they are "Posters of the sea and land" (1.3.33). "Posters" are not simply travelers; they deliver items or news in particularly expedient fashion. These portents of misunderstood direction prepare us for these concerns before Macbeth appears.

Most of the act one scenes establish the locations aurally, in what Bruce R. Smith calls "the establishment of the auditory field of the play."[36] In the first six of the seven scenes in act one, the First Folio stage directions establish locations with sounds: in 1.1 and 1.3 thunder precedes the witches' appearances; in 1.2, 1.4, and 1.6 sounds associated with royal pageantry precede the entrance of the king and others.[37] In 1.5, however, no sound accompanies Lady Macbeth as she enters "alone with a letter" (1.5.0 SD). She herself provides the aural location by reading the letter to the audience. Alan Stewart has shown how Macbeth's letter in 1.5 brings Macbeth on stage with Lady Macbeth while emphasizing his absence. As Stewart has pointed out, the use of the letter "spatially figur[es]" "the Macbeths as singular" and that the letter's "textual content, uttered in Lady Macbeth's voice" helps to collapse the characters into one.[38] He asserts that "Beyond its spatial figuring of the Macbeths as singular (a representation not possible by any other means), the letter plays with time, collapsing present and future."[39] The experience of collapse works for playgoers, but it also has the effect of disembodying Macbeth. Appropriately, Lady Macbeth produces this disembodiment of a character who has not yet appeared with her. For the playgoers, it presents a contrasting version of someone who has already been described as overtly physical in his military activities. His voice presents itself on stage through his wife's ventriloquism in an early instance of his corporeal indeterminacy.

For playgoers, the effect of Macbeth's entrance in 1.7 depends on pageantry and aural cues, and then the scene immediately removes those elements. We have been located, but we are aware that the pageantry has moved on past this space of the stage, leaving it emptied when Macbeth enters. If Macbeth, through this device, appears at one remove from the other action, the playgoer appears at two removes. The pageantry and (presumably) off-stage noise ensure that we must be aware of the events happening elsewhere, even if the noise does not continue through the scene. This double remove matches the incessant doubling of language in the play and confuses our sense of which events might be central to the narrative.

D.J. Palmer argues that, in the case of Duncan's murder off-stage and Lady Macbeth's awareness of events, "instead of distancing the deed from us [...] the effect is to intensify its sacrilegious horror."[40] The horror increases through the imagined rather than the represented. While we are protected from witnessing the image, that very protection maintains the possibility that the vision of it might "destroy [...] sight," as Macduff fears (2.3.71). In some instances, however, the play offers the playgoers double visions of events by reporting events already witnessed by the spectators. Lady Macbeth's remark about the "air-drawn dagger" offers another description of an event staged for the playgoers (3.4.61). Frequently noted cases of double reporting include Macbeth's letter to Lady Macbeth detailing the witches' prophecies, Banquo's murderers' reports of their activities, and the reporting of the killing of Macduff's family. These events are peculiar in other ways too; the playgoer has seen these events staged and thus has knowledge prior to these recapitulating descriptions. The details of the witches' prophecies may come as a surprise, but we know the witches await Macbeth with specific intent; we hear the planning of Banquo's murder; and we know Macbeth plans to surprise Macduff's household and "give to th' edge o' th'' sword/ His wife, his babes" (4.1.151–2). The prior knowledge, view of the event, and presence at the delivery of the news of these last two events involve the playgoer in ways denied to, for example, Lady Macbeth. The playgoer's awareness is greater than that of any of the characters. In some fashion, this awareness makes the playgoer complicit in the actions.

In the case of the murders of Macduff's household, not only is the playgoer aware of each segment of the series, but the events are experienced with such rapidity that Macbeth complains that "Time, thou anticipat'st my dread exploits:/ The flighty purpose never is o'ertook / Unless the deed go with it" (4.1.144–6). His own quick actions are framed as necessary for his own resolve; he claims, "This deed I'll do before this purpose cool" (4.1.154) and then exits after two more lines. In 4.2 at Macduff's castle, the murderers enter after a quick 80 lines of dialogue split between Lady Macduff and Rosse and Lady Macduff and her son. In 4.3 Macduff, safely in England, receives Rosse and the news of his family's death. The rapidity and quick succession of these events show Macbeth's plan exactly carried out. It also presents a useful example of the discontinuities in the playgoers' experience of the passage of narrative time. Kittredge points out that "we reckon the interval, not by clock and calendar, but in terms of our emotional exhaustion."[41] Although he offers this description as a dismissal of various attempts to work out a coherent time scheme for the narrative events of the play, it does point to how playgoers' responses to the play depend heavily on an emotional experience. A. R. Braunmuller elucidates some ways the characters in the play experience time, saying, "struggling with time and its consequences – birth and death, usurpation and punishment – Lord and Lady Macbeth sense time 'at odds' with itself, time *now* conflicting with time *then* and time to *come*."[42] For playgoers though, the "virtual future" of the play depends on the speed of staged events. Emma Smith points out how, for playgoers, the increase of the speed of events depends on the gap between the playgoers' knowledge of future events and the staged realization of those events. As Smith says, "By the time we get to the plan to exterminate Macduff's line, the gap between thinking and doing has entirely collapsed."[43] While playgoers might experience the emotional exhaustion Kittredge describes, Paul Woodruff's notion of measuring time in the theater "by plot" might be more useful for exploring how the play achieves the effect on playgoers.[44]

With this play, part of the temporal confusion for playgoers arises from the ordering of the narrative events within the structure of the play, an ordering Braunmuller calls "rather strange."[45] Whether we perceive the temporal center of the play at the banquet scene or at the regicide, these are, Braunmuller convincingly argues, either untypical or subordinate positions for events of central importance.[46] Emrys Jones sees the play divided into three sections where Duncan dominates the first two acts, Banquo the third act, and Macduff the fourth and fifth. Jones points out the parallels in the openings of the first and fourth acts that help to set off the third act as its own section. Most importantly for the point here, this description shows how the events around Banquo's death are set into their own section of the play.

Banquo's death plays an important role in the ways the playgoers can orient themselves to the actions and dilemmas in the play. Frequently, Shakespeare's plays present a "normalizing" character who is able to either transcend the circumstances or at least outlast them and present the playgoers with information or material that might be considered more reliable than other information available. As I discussed in an earlier chapter, Horatio in *Hamlet* offers an example of such a character. Horatio sees the ghost of Old Hamlet, which helps convince playgoers that the ghost exists; likewise, Banquo confirms the existence of the witches in *Macbeth*. Thus, the normalizing character seems at the beginning to be Banquo, Macbeth's original confidante. The murder of Banquo turns the action of the play beyond the irrevocable events, and the playgoer remains with no single character to maintain that function. Jones' divisions of the play emphasize Duncan's and Macduff's absence from the part of the play that allows that removal of Banquo. The playgoers become unmoored from the normalizing elements of the narrative.

The playgoer also experiences the later hallucinatory misperceptions that Macbeth experiences. When the witches appear at the beginning of the play, Banquo serves to verify for the playgoer that the witches are real. The playgoer must accept the world of the play as one with supernatural beings who have a corporeal existence. When the dagger appears to Macbeth, the playgoer does not see the dagger and no other characters verify its existence. The playgoer must conclude, as Macbeth quickly does, that the dagger is a hallucination. This instance serves to separate us from Macbeth's experience while still involving us in the experience – one only revealed through Macbeth's soliloquized thoughts and perceptions. When Banquo's ghost appears at the banquet, we (the playgoers) and Macbeth see the ghost. Lady Macbeth and the guests, who might act as witnesses to establish reality, do not see the ghost. As Macbeth's perceptions have disintegrated into hallucination, our own have followed suit. The First Folio stage directions read, "*Enter the Ghost of Banquo and sits in Macbeths place*" (TLN 1298). The text specifically calls for the entrance of an actor here, a corporeal embodiment invisible to the other characters. The playgoers can no longer trust characters to act as witnesses, a dislocation made all the more disconcerting by the murdered Banquo's earlier role as the normalizing character. We are trapped in Macbeth's interiority in the banquet scene because we do know what his disordered senses perceive; we deny the reality of the other characters despite needing to accept these other versions to make sense of the events of the play. As playgoers, we simultaneously experience both the corporeal embodiment of the ghost and yet understand Lady Macbeth's dismissal of that experience as "O proper stuff!" (3.4.59).

The swiftness of *Macbeth*, which has been frequently remarked, depends on multiple aspects of the play. It is exceptionally short. And, as Emrys Jones comments, its "scenic forms are marked by extreme economy."[47] In *Hamlet*, playgoers are moved forward to an essential stasis through the long final scene of the play. As events coalesce to the ending, characters and playgoers converge in the final location fixed by Hamlet's control of the space of the stage. In *Macbeth*, playgoers are denied that centralized stasis. In the last act, this effect partly depends on both the brevity and the large number of scenes. The combination ensures that scene changes are fast; we are quickly shifted from one location to another. None of the scenes of the final act is longer than eighty lines. As playgoers we may not be perfectly aware that the sleepwalking scene begins the final act and is the longest scene in the act. However, it begins the final series of scenes that end the play, a recognizable series as it occurs.

Our own sense of time as an audience – a sense that never functions perfectly with any play – experiences some of the same deterioration that Macbeth and other characters in the play experience. Macbeth offers to "let the frame of things disjoint" in favor of having the stasis of death; the playgoer experiences the disjointed frame (3.2.16). Despite understanding events through what Paul Woodruff calls "plot time," we are rushed forward through different locations, through an indeterminable passage of time, through the off-stage death of Lady Macbeth and finally to Macbeth's death. The playgoers' awareness becomes attached in important ways to Macbeth's awareness; in this play replete with tellings and retellings of events, we only learn of the death of Lady Macbeth at the same time Macbeth does. We have known of most other events in the play at the moment of their happening. In this instance, we are aligned with Macbeth's experience when his senses become most confused. The ultimate disjointing of Macbeth's perceptions comes with his death and decapitation. The First Folio stage directions note "Enter Macduffe, with Macbeths head" (TLN 2504). This complete dissolution of Macbeth's perceptions appears as a compelling visual spectacle on the stage.

The concentrations of spatial constructions in the narrative, the playgoers' awareness of certain events, the changing and dislocating descriptions of location, and the consistent return to questions of place, all contribute to the narrative movement in the play. The construction of space through these intersections includes Lady Macbeth's outcry at the news of Duncan's death and alters how we might see place and location functioning. When Macduff offers Macbeth's head to Malcolm he says, "I see thee compassed with thy kingdom's pearl" (5.9.23). Macduff confirms Malcolm's kingship and metaphorically refers to a kingdom in order. "Compassed" or encircled offers the closure the narrative demands even as it opens out to the wider locating questions of the play. That closure, circling back, forms an essential narrative element in different ways in *The Tempest*, questions I shall take up in the next chapter.

Notes

1. For example, Warburton offers this explanation. William Warburton, ed. *Macbeth* in *The works of Shakespear in eight volumes* Vol. 6 (London: J&P Napton, 1747).
2. George Lyman Kittredge, ed. *Macbeth* (Boston, MA: Ginn and Co, 1939), 144.
3. I include Warburton's note here since many eighteenth-century editors followed suit; Warburton, 367. Samuel Johnson, for example, quotes Warburton's note in full and without commentary. Samuel Johnson, ed. *Macbeth* in *The plays of William Shakespeare in eight volumes, with the corrections and illustrations of various commentators; to which are added notes by Sam Johnson* (London: J. and R. Tonson, 1755), 367–484.
4. David Kranz, in his discussion of the verbal patterning of the play, points out rhetorical and rhythmic elements that make this line particularly memorable in its repetition: "Fricative alliteration reinforces the repetition, and the completely monosyllabic nature of the line crisply highlights its iambic meter" (346). David Kranz, "The Sounds of Supernatural Soliciting in *Macbeth*," *Studies in Philology* 100, no.3 (2003), 346–383.
5. Kittredge, 171. William Carroll similarly notes "in this world" for the use; A.R. Braunmuller does not comment on the use of "here" in this passage. William Carroll, ed., *Macbeth* by William Shakespeare (Boston, MA: Bedford, 1999); A.R. Braunmuller, ed., *Macbeth* by William Shakespeare (Cambridge: Cambridge University Press, 1997).
6. Kenneth Muir, ed. *Macbeth* by William Shakespeare (London: Thomson, 1962).
7. Angus Fletcher, *Time, Space, and Motion in the Age of Shakespeare* (Cambridge, MA: Harvard University Press, 2007), 92.

8. Geraldo de Sousa, in his exploration of boundaries, architecture and the Macbeths' perceived safety gained from walls, notes that the Macbeth's house "becomes a deadly trap for unsuspecting guests." Geraldo de Sousa, *At Home in Shakespeare's Tragedies* (Farnham: Ashgate, 2010), 154.
9. The First Folio text reads "sides" here and the textual debate offers "slides" and the now more-popular "strides" as optional readings for what appears to have been a misprinting. Either way, "slides" and "strides" both convey the movement important to the speech. Hinman, *Macbeth*, TLN 635.
10. Marvin Rosenberg, *The Masks of Macbeth* (Newark: University of Delaware Press, 1978), 305–309.
11. Marvin Rosenberg notes in his discussion of productions the clarity at this particular moment of the differences in perception between Macbeth and Lady Macbeth. Rosenberg, *The Masks of Macbeth*, 147.
12. Bruce R. Smith, *The Acoustic World of Early Modern England: Attending to the O Factor* (Chicago: University of Chicago Press, 1999).
13. Evelyn Tribble, "'When Every Noise Appalls Me": Sound and Fear in *Macbeth* and Akira Kurosawa's *Throne of Blood*," *Shakespeare* 1.1–2 (2005), 75–90, 79.
14. David Lucking, "Imperfect Speakers: Macbeth and the Name of King" *English Studies* 87. 4 (2006), 415–425, 423.
15. The *Oxford English Dictionary* defines "expedition" as "speedy performance or prompt execution" (1.a) and "A journey, voyage, or excursion made for some definite purpose" (2.b).
16. An example of a medical text that depends heavily on the division of five senses, Helkiah Crooke's *Mikrokosmographia* (London: William Jaggard, 1615) compiles and translates much of the anatomical material available in the period. Julius Caesar Scaliger, *Exotericarum Exercitationum Liber Qvintvs Decimvs, de Svbtilitate, ad Hieronymvm Cardanvm* (Lvtetiae [Paris]: Michaelis Vascosani, 1557).
17. Thomas Tompkis, *Lingua, or The Combat of the Tongue and the Five Senses for Superiority* (London: N. Okes, c1607). *Macbeth* is usually dated to 1606, although Alfred Harbage lists 1606–1611 as limits; for Tomkis' *Lingua*, Harbage offers limits of 1602–1607. Alfred Harbage, *Annals of English Drama 975–1700*, revised S. Schoenbaum (Philadelphia: University of Pennsylvania Press, 1964). In his introduction, Kenneth Muir suggests that *Lingua* echoes *Macbeth* rather than the reverse (xvii).
18. Caroline Spurgeon, *Shakespeare's Imagery and What It Tells Us* (Cambridge: Cambridge University Press, 1965), 51.
19. See, for example, Mary McCarthy, "General Macbeth" *Harper's Magazine* (June 1962), 35–39; reprinted in *Macbeth* ed. Sylvan Barnet, 2nd rev. edn. (New York: Signet, 1998), 157–167.
20. G. Blakemore Evans (ed.) maintains "Birnan," rather than the common revision to "Birnam," based on the singular First Folio use of "Great Byrnam Wood" (TLN 1636); *The Riverside Shakespeare*, 2nd edn (Boston, MA: Houghton Mifflin, 1997).
21. The desire to hold "rumor" or loose speech away from articulation of feared events fits into a pattern explored by Arthur Kinney of a culture

of surveillance, both in this play and in the wider culture of Jacobean politics. Arthur Kinney, "Macbeth's Knowledge," *Shakespeare Survey 57* no.1 (2004), 11–26.
22. Muir, *Macbeth*, 5.7.2. See *Oxford English Dictionary*, "course" (n.) 2.a and 11a. The nautical term in this period means "the direction in which, or point of the compass towards which, a ship sails" (*OED* "course" (n.) 12.a).
23. Henri Lefebvre, *The Production of Space*, trans. Donald Nicholson-Smith (Oxford: Blackwell, 1991), 226.
24. Thomas de Quincey, "On the Knocking at the Gate in Macbeth," originally published in the October 1823 issue of *The London Magazine* and collected in *The London Magazine July to December 1823 Vol VIII* (London: Taylor and Hessey, 1823), 353-6. The quotation appears on pages 353–354.
25. de Quincey, "On the Knocking," 354.
26. Ibid., 354.
27. Ibid., 354. An apparent typographical error in the printing omits the end stop added to the quotation.
28. In his rather contentious footnote, de Quincey makes a point about the proper and improper use of the word "sympathy" and argues that its proper meaning is "as the act of reproducing in our minds the feelings of another." de Quincey, "On the Knocking," 355.
29. Ibid., 356.
30. Antony Sher, "Leontes and Macbeth," in *Players of Shakespeare 5*, ed. Robert Smallwood (Cambridge: Cambridge University Press, 2003), 91–112, 99.
31. Sher, "Leontes and Macbeth," 107.
32. Ibid., 111.
33. See the *Oxford English Dictionary*'s definitions for "stuff, n.1."
34. Susanne Langer, *Feeling and Form* (Upper Saddle River, NJ: Prentice-Hall, 1977), 307. Emrys Jones quotes from this section of Langer to assert that the "virtual future" is the "*subject*" of *Macbeth* in the early scenes. Emrys Jones, *Scenic Form in Shakespeare*, 1971 (Oxford: Oxford University Press, 1985), 206.
35. D.J. Palmer, "'A new Gorgon': Visual Effects in *Macbeth*," in *Focus on Macbeth*, ed. John Russell Brown (London: Routlege & Kegan Paul, 1982), 54–69, 58.
36. Smith, *Acoustic World*, 276.
37. The stage directions in the First Folio are: "Alarum within [...]"; "Flourish"; and "Hoboyes and torches" (1.2, 1.4 and 1.6 respectively) (TLN 15, 278, 431).
38. Alan Stewart, *Shakespeare's Letters* (Oxford: Oxford University Press, 2009), 33.
39. Stewart, *Shakespeare's Letters*, 33.
40. Palmer, "'A New Gorgon,'" 67.
41. Kittredge, *Macbeth*, xvi.
42. Braunmuller, *Macbeth*, 51.
43. Emma Smith, *Macbeth: Language and Writing* (London: Bloomsbury, 2013), 101.

44. Paul Woodruff, *The Necessity of Theater: The Art of Watching and Being Watched* (Oxford: Oxford University Press, 2008), 109.
45. Braunmuller, *Macbeth*, 24.
46. Braunmuller connects his discussion of the central moment of the play to George Walton Williams' assertions about the temporal center. Braunmuller, *Macbeth*, 25.
47. Jones, *Scenic Forms*, 195.

5
Direction and Space in *The Tempest*
"Through forth-rights and meanders"

The Tempest is a play rooted in the metaphoric and descriptive language of early modern travel writing. Although most critical approaches that link the play and travel literature limit themselves to colonialist discourses, the play in fact draws on a wide spectrum of travel writing of Shakespeare's period: instructions for travelers on the continent, narratives of shipboard travel, diplomatic imperatives, descriptions of trading possibilities, treatises of navigational methods, comportment advice for young men, and encouragement for colonizing missions. Reading *The Tempest* with attention to the modes and experiences of travel portrayed onstage reveals a structural pattern based on spatial confusion that continues throughout the play and does much of the work of producing meaning. While *The Tempest* relies on some of the language, events, and descriptions of the contemporaneous shipwreck on the Bermudas of the Virginia-bound *Sea Venture*, the meaning of the characters' movements on the island can be found in the larger spectrum of contemporary discourses of travel.[1]

Most of the travel in *The Tempest* occurs as characters move about the island on foot; characters also rely on standard metaphors of travel and use directional language in their conversations. Rather than mapping them on colonialist projects of the period, *The Tempest*'s characters more clearly emerge from within the contemporary discourses of travel. If we explore the "characterlogical space," to use Bruce R. Smith's term, as a space to be traversed using contemporary modes of movement, we can better understand how the structures of location and movement in the play develop a particular experience for the playgoers.[2] While we, as playgoers attending productions, may not recognize the development of the different modes of travel, the structures built into the play alter how we understand it in production. In this chapter, I am returning to the discourses and contemporaneous materials that develop an understanding of perception that I already discussed in connection with *A Midsummer Night's Dream*. This discussion of *The Tempest*, rather than focusing on vision, uses materials describing utilitarian realities and modes of travel.

When Gonzalo, in 3.3, remarks that he can "go no further" because his "old bones ache," he gives voice to the experiences of the weary foot travelers who move through Prospero's spatial confusions (3.3.1, 2). His lament opens the scene:

> By'r lakin. I can go no further, sir,
> My old bones aches. Here's a maze trod indeed
> Through forth-rights and meanders! By your patience,
> I needs must rest me. (3.3.1–4)

The "maze" they try to traverse takes them "through forth-rights and meanders." As the *Oxford English Dictionary* notes, "forth-rights" refers to a "straight course or path."[3] In this instance, "forth-rights" contrasts with "meanders" to illustrate the tracks of their movement with connotations of the intent behind that movement. "Forth-rights" refers to the straight course but also to directness; "meanders" refers to the circuitous course but also to convoluted thought. Gonzalo and most of the characters describe their own travels in ways that mirror extended experiences of movement. This chapter focuses on the different forthright and meandering movements in *The Tempest*. The play's staged incidents of travel and the fractures in time and space the characters experience on the island undergird the structures of the play. Distinguishing between the modes of travel presented in the play also illuminates at least two topics that figure in current critical discussions: the power relationships between characters and generic questions raised by the play's relation to Shakespeare's other late works.

The colonialist readings of the play, common in post-eighteenth-century staged productions and in twentieth-century critical discussions, rely heavily on interest in Caliban's compelling character, often obscuring other considerations of travel in the play. David Lindley (in his Cambridge edition of the play) traces post-eighteenth-century productions (after Dryden and Davenant's adaptations had been replaced by Shakespeare's text) and shows that "audiences have found it difficult to resist some degree of sympathy for Caliban, and reviewers have complained at representations which failed to bring out the suffering and pathos the part can sustain." The desire to stage *The Tempest* as a play mostly concerned with Caliban's enslavement appeared, as Lindley points out, in early staged versions. Responses to those productions show that, on stage, "colonial readings of the play were already in place at the beginning of the twentieth century."[4] Playgoers have always been interested in Caliban, even in Shakespeare's time. The Scrivener, in the Induction to Ben Jonson's *Bartholomew Fair* (1614), offers the articles from the author and explains, "If there be never a servant-monster i'the Fair, who can help it? he says; nor a nest of antics? He is loath to make nature afraid in his plays, like those that beget *Tales*, *Tempests*, and such drolleries."[5] Aside from Jonson's seeming dismissal of the "antics" of tragicomedies, this mention reveals a contemporary excitement caused by Caliban's stage presence.

Recent academic interest in colonialist discourses has led to some nuanced and compelling critical readings of the power relations between Prospero and Caliban. For example, Peter Hulme reads Caliban and Prospero in the context of other pairs of colonized and colonizing individuals – some literary and some historical figures. However, Hulme explains that, in this instance, while using some texts "usually considered as significant works of literature," his reading requires that "their status as 'literary' texts is put into suspension."[6] Less nuanced readings of the play in the service of providing examples of colonialist endeavors may be misleading about the fuller effects of the play. For instance, in an otherwise carefully framed discussion, Ania Loomba's *Colonialism/ Postcolonialism* claims that, "In *The Tempest*, for example, Shakespeare's single major addition to the story he found in certain pamphlets about a shipwreck in the Bermudas was to make the island inhabited before Prospero's arrival."[7] Loomba's assertion that "That single addition turned the adventure story into an allegory of the colonial encounter" illustrates ways that narrowly colonialist readings raise problems, particularly in productions.[8] The insistence that the play functions as an allegory confines the meaning of the play to emergence only through an understanding of the allegorized people or ideas outside the play.

Direction and Space in The Tempest   129

In addition to narrowing the play to a *roman a clef*, the insistence on allegory also empties meaning from characters who do not fit into the allegory. For example, Ferdinand, who never interacts with Caliban, disappears entirely from allegorical colonialist readings. Although this chapter centers on questions connected to travel and movement in *The Tempest*, ground heavily trodden by critics interested in post-colonialist readings, my focus here connects more closely to the characters' experiences of space and the underlying structures of the play.

Framing spaces

Explorations and contemporary travelers' narratives had profound effects on the ways space and location could be portrayed in early modern plays. John Gillies shows that,

> [w]hat has been called 'the Shakespearean moment,' then, was also the moment of the new geography's most monumental statements. By the same token, it also represented the last flowering of the old 'cosmography,' because both Ortelius and Mercator conceived of geography in cosmographic terms.[9]

In other words, the cosmographical and geographical concerns were coexistent and informed one another. These modes of describing explorations, the narratives generated by the travelers, the maps upon which they relied, and the means for describing their own bodies' movements all contribute to representations of space and location in early modern plays. *The Tempest*, as has been widely noted, maintains the unities of time, place, and action; it presents events occurring in the time consumed by the playing of the play, takes place (after the opening shipwreck) in a confined space easily framed by the stage, and maintains the order of events as they occur in the narrative. *The Tempest*'s structural formalities and maintenance of the unities of time and place forge bonds that connect temporal and spatial realities in production. Prospero's insistence on the speed with which events must take place reminds playgoers of the passage of time on the island and in the theater. Despite the maintenance of the unities, characters' descriptions of their own locations and movements disrupt time and space and reveal the play's fracturing of the construct.

In addition to the structural order imposed by maintaining the unities, *The Tempest*'s nine scenes (see Figure 5.1) mirror one another and tighten the plot's structure. *The Tempest*'s relatively few scene breaks establish a repeating pattern of character activity divided into nine distinct scenes, as indicated below. Although act and scene divisions are not always marked in early modern plays, for this description, I assume clearing the stage of actors marks a scene break and often establishes a new location for the ensuing action.[10]

While playgoers may not process the specifics of this mirroring in the scenes, this organizing structure, in combination with the insistent physical enclosure of the movements on the island, and the emphasis on the passing of time create expectation for closure at the end of the play. Emrys Jones has pointed out some effects that underlying structures have on playgoers. He claims,

> while the spectators are being absorbed into the visible and audible world of the play, they are also being exposed to the influence of patterns which, though themselves neither visible nor audible, are none the less powerfully coercive. These patterns are in fact the means whereby the action of the play is carried deep into the audience's mind.[11]

Scene 1	1.1	Wrecking of the ship	
Scene 2	1.2	Prospero, Miranda, and Ferdinand	
Scene 3	2.1	Gonzalo consoles Alonso for loss of his son	Antonio and Sebastian plot to kill Alonso
Scene 4	2.2	Drunken antics of Caliban, Stefano and Trinculo	Caliban takes a new master
Scene 5	3.1	Miranda proposes marriage to Ferdinand	
Scene 6	3.2	Drunken antics of Caliban, Stefano and Trinculo	Caliban plots to kill his old master
Scene 7	3.3	Gonzalo consoles Alonso for loss of his son	Antonio and Sebastian plot to kill Alonso
Scene 8	4.1	Prospero, Miranda, and Ferdinand	
Scene 9	5.1	Restoration of the ship	

Figure 5.1 The scenes of *The Tempest*

Direction and Space in The Tempest 131

The complex structural patterning of the scenes in *The Tempest* produces for the playgoers an experience not unlike Gonzalo's maze. The shape may not be apparent when within the pattern, but the order and structure become clear when viewed as a whole.

Structurally, of the nine scenes of *The Tempest*, Miranda's betrothal to Ferdinand in the fifth scene forms the center of the play. The framework of the play makes this scene central and emphasizes the moment in the narrative. Four evenly matched scenes appear on either side of the moment when Miranda proposes marriage to Ferdinand and he tells her that, "I, / Beyond all limit of what else i' th' world, / Do love, prize, honor you" (3.1.71–3). The scenes on either side of that central moment match one another. The first scene presents the shipwreck and arrival on the island; the final scene mirrors these events when it describes a return to the ship and the plans for departure. In the second scene, Prospero and Miranda appear and Ferdinand believes he has lost his father; in the penultimate scene, Prospero and Miranda appear and Ferdinand believes he takes Prospero as a new father.

On either side of the central betrothal scene, the same characters appear. Initially, Trinculo and Stephano drunkenly carouse and Caliban takes a new master; immediately after the betrothal scene Trinculo and Stephano drunkenly carouse and Caliban goads the others in a plot to kill Prospero, his old master. In the third and seventh scenes Antonio and Sebastian likewise plot to kill Alonso and Gonzalo and are interrupted both times by Ariel. Some of the scenic mirroring presents reversals. In the second scene, Ariel demands freedom; in the penultimate scene Prospero promises freedom. The playgoer travels a narrative plot line, passing through scenes that after the betrothal are reversed as the play comes to a close; the characters appear and reappear in a mirroring fashion that reverses at the central betrothal scene. This matching of scenes and appearance of characters structurally establishes the betrothal as the center of the play's actions.

Locating characters

The betrothal scene forms the narrative center; more importantly, the characters describe their own movements and direction differently in the two halves of the play. This change, I suggest, internally fractures the time and space in *The Tempest*, changes the reading of

Ferdinand's role in the plot, and links the play's narrative movement to Shakespeare's other romances in important ways. Prospero and Miranda's use of temporal and spatial language in their conversations offers a clue to how direction functions on Prospero's island. And the shipwrecked characters, in the first half of the play, use abstract terms to address their locations and movements: terms unrelated to the specifics and necessities of their plights. In the second half of the play, these dislocated characters show an awareness of the necessity of directions, even if many of the characters do not achieve clear direction. Through the characters' movements – some effective, some ineffective – the play finally presents an enclosed, internally fractured time and space. The most problematic and misdirected characters are those who are lost without realizing it, who are unable to find their way, and who choose improper guidance when they do recognize the need for direction. This underlying emphasis on direction may encourage the allegorical readings related to moral direction that the play has engendered.[12]

Prospero's role in the play has been compared to that of a "director," a word with obvious links to "direction." As Waldo McNeir puts it, "it is as if [Prospero] controls both space and time."[13] Particularly in Prospero's early narrative to Miranda, the scene relies heavily on directional language for the phatic parts of the narration. The scene consistently repeats spatial imperatives to move the conversation and the narrative. The difficulty of this long scene of exposition is widely discussed; it presents problems for any actor. David Lindley points out that the scene "is rendered more difficult by the fact that throughout its length [Prospero] is never engaged in conversation, speaking either to himself, or else aggressively to dominate."[14] Some scholars read Prospero's insistent demands for Miranda's continued attention as unnecessary for the onstage characters. McNeir assumes that Miranda is completely attentive "throughout and needs no urging" and "these warnings are in reality meant for the audience, for we must miss no word of Prospero's revelations."[15] This stance could easily be undermined in production where Miranda could be nodding off to sleep, aimlessly wandering about, or otherwise physically showing her lack of attention. The text itself, however, does not prescribe any particular movements for the actors in the portion of the scene where Prospero explains the past to Miranda. Jeremy Lopez suggests that "expository scenes, especially at the beginnings of plays, are, I think, inefficient and indirect in important ways – ways that perhaps ultimately give a *sense* of directness or efficiency that is more important than the thing itself."[16] This "*sense* of directness" is what I want to pay attention to in this particular scene.

In 1.2, an otherwise static scene, both Prospero and Miranda depend heavily on language that describes movement as conversational markers or as ways of progressing through the narrative. Prospero introduces the narrative saying "thou must now know farther" (1.2.33), pointing to the increased distance of knowledge. On earlier occasions he has halted Miranda's movement by saying, "stay: not yet" (1.2.36). Miranda introduces the distant remembrance of the past ("'Tis far off" 1.2.44) before Prospero asks, "What seest thou else/ In the dark backward and abysm of time?" (1.2.49–50). This phrase, "dark backward and abysm of time," makes time spatial through both of the nouns that take the place of "time." Prospero describes his own role in his brother's rise to power in terms of the possibilities of movement through his books: "And to my state grew stranger, being transported/ And rapt in secret studies" (1.2.76–7). Prospero answers Miranda's encouragement, "Please you, farther" (1.2.65), by describing his own guidance through the time of the narrative he has presented: "Hear a little further, /And then I'll bring thee to the present business" (1.2.135–6). Her hearing becomes a vehicle within which he can guide her to a temporal location, the present.[17]

These spatial descriptions of narrative movement are not all that unusual even in our contemporary speech where "by the way" offers a spatial location for a side comment in a conversation figured as a movement. However, this narrative depends upon these spatial markers in unusual ways related to the fact that banishment and forced travel away from a specific place establish the underlying problems of the play, since the removal from Milan drives the revenge plot of the play. Prospero describes his errors as a ruler as a spatial misunderstanding, "me (poor man) my library/ Was dukedom large enough" (1.2.109–10). The use of spatial markers in the banishment narrative adds movement to stage stasis and provides necessary information of its own. Prospero makes clear to Miranda that she is "ignorant of what thou art, nought knowing/ Of whence I am" (1.2.18–19). Without spatial location – in this instance, Prospero's spatial origins – her own identity cannot be clear. In a particularly effective bit of stage business, the American Shakespeare Center's

2011 production had Prospero (James Keegan) clearing the stage of the properties associated with the ship and storm of the first scene.[18] In this fashion, Prospero's physical actions on stage connected to the seaborne movement, while his rhetorical movement carried the motion of the narrative.

In addition to the narrative for Miranda, Prospero's relationships with both Ariel and Caliban depend on spatial control and temporal awareness. Prospero describes Ariel's imprisonment by Sycorax "Into a cloven pine, within which rift/ Imprison'd, thou didst painfully remain/ A dozen years; within which space she died" (1.1.277–9). Although "space" frequently appears in the early modern period as marking a length of time, the other uses of "space" in this play refer to a three-dimensional expanse.[19] The space of time within which Sycorax died combined with Ariel's physically bounded imprisonment complicates the separations of time and space in this description. Time marks the only boundaries of Ariel's current servitude to Prospero. Although he threatens to imprison Ariel again, Prospero promises "after two days / I will discharge thee" (1.1.298–9). Obviously, Ariel's confinement does not depend on spatial boundaries; he quickly moves between locations on the island and apparently has unlimited range of travel. Caliban's imprisonment seems infinite in duration while his confinement appears to be spatial: "here you sty me/ In this hard rock, whiles you do keep from me/ The rest o' th' island" (1.2.342–4). Control over Ariel depends on temporal duration; control over Caliban depends on allowances of space. These two characters' relationships with Prospero illustrate different versions of Prospero's control of time and space.

In the early modern era, time and space are related through physical and bodily experiences. For example, "telling time" involved counting aloud and calculation of speed onboard a ship , which required counting the "knots" slipping past in the rope. As late as 1637, Richard Norwood's nautical guide *The Sea-Man's Practice* included the explanation that,

> [f]or keeping this account of time, it may be done either by a Sand-glasse for that purpose, or by pronouncing certaine words or numbers: As the time where a man tells twice 60, pronouncing every number as fast as he can conveniently and distinctly, is about a minute[.][20]

Likewise, the playing out of a log-line assumes a physical relationship between measurement and units of distance and speed. Thus, Prospero's dual control of time and space should not surprise us since the two are almost inseparable in the period. Drama constantly integrates different, co-existing, and visible representations of space. Two co-existent dramatic versions of these spaces are the area of the stage within which the actors act, and the space produced by the narrative of the drama. So, while it might be tempting to read Prospero as controlling all time and space of the island, it is useful to see that the play's structural arrangement of the scenes also controls the narrative.

In *The Tempest*, the shipwrecked characters relate to their own locations in tangled ways. Oddly, none of the shipwrecked characters mention being lost. In the first half of the play, most of the shipwrecked characters address their locations and movement in abstract terms – terms removed from the realities of distances and computation of location. Gonzalo's attempt at comforting Alonso depends on all of them imagining themselves *not* lost:

> [...] Our hint of woe
> Is common: every day some sailor's wife,
> The masters of some merchant, and the merchant
> Have just our theme of woe; but for the miracle
> (I mean our preservation), few in millions
> Can speak like us. (2.1.3–8)

The woe arises from the fears for Alonso's son, but Gonzalo conflates the roles of these shipwrecked men. In this description, they become those waiting at home for news of those who travel, and in the same moment they are figured as the survivors. The men have escaped the immediate threat of drowning, but have little way to survive in their new environment. When Gonzalo asserts that "Here is every thing advantageous to life," Antonio immediately undermines the description: "True, save means to live" (2.1.50, 51). Despite Gonzalo's general commentary, none of the shipwrecked men seems particularly concerned about his own sustenance. The men argue over the location of Tunis and Carthage, the possibility of Ferdinand's survival, and the advisability of Alonso marrying Claribel in Africa. But, they do not argue over where they have landed. Fittingly, Gonzalo's musings on his own commonwealth describe a non-existent, utopian no-place.

Antonio uses language based in routes and movement to urge Sebastian toward the usurpation plot. Interestingly, this conversation takes place only while the possible victims are made motionless by sleep. As in Prospero's opening conversation with Miranda, rhetorical motion attempts to counteract the physical stasis. In some ways, this disparity between the rhetorical movement and the physical stasis mirrors the disparity between metaphorical imagery and staged movement in *Richard II*. Sebastian's conviction that Ferdinand is drowned, "I have no hope/ That he's undrowned" (2.1.238–9), offers an opening for Antonio to map out the plot:

> O, out of that no hope
> What great hope have you! No hope, that way, is
> Another way so high a hope that even
> Ambition cannot pierce a wink beyond,
> But doubt discovery there. (2.1.239–43)

Antonio figures the options here as pathways, and ambition itself as an explorer. He echoes Sebastian's phrase "no hope" and changes that despair into a "way" that allows for the introduction of "another way." The lack of direction one way opens the possibility of another pathway. Gonzalo is described as someone who should be killed so that he "should not upbraid our course" (2.1.287). In the early modern era, it is not unusual for "course" to mean "plan" or "direction" in an abstracted sense unrelated to spatial issues.[21] However, this discussion of the usurpation plan uses the language of movement and discovery only to describe events and actions unrelated to any hope of moving off the island.

Even when these characters describe distances, those distances are impossible to traverse. Antonio, blind to their own geographical predicament, imagines that the distance between the King's daughter (in Africa) and the court is more insurmountable than their own distance from Naples. The distance between Tunis and Naples is "A space whose ev'ry cubit/ Seems to cry out, "How shall that Claribel/ Measure us back to Naples?"" (2.1.257–9). Thus, a distance is divided into individual cubits that each can "cry out" against the possibilities of measurement or movement – which are, in this description, the same activities. Antonio enlists distance itself to speak for the impossibility of movement. After Alonso's awakening thwarts the usurpation plot, he orders Gonzalo to "Lead away" (2.1.325). This order encourages movement without specific direction or destination. However, it opens the possibility of movement and the beginning of a realization that some direction may be necessary. Ariel also intimates that Alonso will find some direction after the successful thwarting of the murder plot: "so, King, go safely on to seek thy son" (2.1.327). At the end of this scene, these characters show signs of interacting differently with the space in which they find themselves.

Changed locations

When we see these characters again, they relate differently to their location and the space around them. In 3.3, after the betrothal scene, the shipwrecked characters are still unable to appropriately navigate their search for Ferdinand, but they are aware of the course of their attempts. Gonzalo, as the aged councilor who attempted to mitigate Prospero's situation when he was banished, speaks first in the scene and makes immediately clear that the conditions of travel affect the men. As I have already discussed, Gonzalo complains not only of the physical effects of travel but also of his concerns about the path they are on. His description of a "maze" gives the first indication that these characters realize they are lost and without adequate awareness of their own location. Alonso agrees and, aware of the physical strain of travel, calls himself "attach'd with weariness" (3.3.5). He also recognizes their lack of direction and says, in despair of finding his son, "He is drown'd/ Whom thus we stray to find, and the sea mocks/ Our frustrate search on land" (3.3.5, 8–10). Antonio sees that "they are oppress'd with travail" and renews his plans with Sebastian (3.3.15). The links in "travail" between work and movement emphasize Antonio's realizations that the shipwrecked men are engaged in a struggle that requires effort and knowledge.

This awareness of their plight soon shifts to descriptions of themselves in terms that, at this point in the early seventeenth century, are outmoded. The appearance of the banquet suddenly raises travelers' moldy stories of wonders. Sebastian "will believe/ That there are unicorns; that in Arabia/ There is one tree, the phoenix' throne, one phoenix/ At this hour reigning there" (3.3.21–4), and Antonio says he will now believe that "Travellers ne'er did lie, / Though fools at home condemn 'em" (3.3.26–7). Gonzalo himself considers the effect his story would have if he were to tell it in Naples, and he asks, "would they believe me?" (3.3.28). They all imagine their stories of wonders will confirm outrageous stories and refute long-standing doubts about the truthfulness of travelers' tales. While narratives of travel were constantly being scrutinized for veracity, the increased circulation of verifiable descriptions of travel made it easier to assess the believability of stories brought back. In a letter, probably composed in 1578, Sir Philip Sidney offers travel advice to his younger brother. He steps firmly into the camp of beleaguered travelers who might not be believed when he warns that, "wee Travellers shall bee made sport of in Comedies." Yet he closes his letter by saying, "I will not tell you some absurdities I have heard some Travellers tell," carefully placing himself outside of the camp that might spread such tales.[22] Sidney's advice straddles the difficult positions of both the derided traveler telling tales and the skeptical listener hearing tales. Gonzalo, Antonio, and Sebastian do not express these concerns and are missing the healthy skepticism of the contemporary traveler; instead they imagine themselves functioning as travelers in the outmoded versions of travelers' tales.

Gonzalo continues in this vein when he urges them to believe in the feast since speculating travelers "bring us good warrant of" the reality of such tales as the existence of "such men / Whose heads stood in their breasts" (3.3.49, 47–8). These are the same "men whose heads / Do grow beneath their shoulders" that are described in Othello's travels (*Othello* 1.3.144–5). In the early modern era, tales of these creatures mostly come originally from medieval descriptions included in *Mandeville's Travels*.[23] And, although Sir Walter Ralegh offhandedly gives a second-hand account of being told of their existence in his *Discoverie of Guiana* (1596), Mandeville's narrative had been removed from the second edition of the most important and comprehensive collection of travel narratives of the period, Hakluyt's *Principall Navigations*.[24] These tales lost currency and became suspect as more information became available. Gonzalo, like the other men in this scene, imagines himself as a traveler. These men are no longer as they were in Gonzalo's earlier description, the sailors' wives or merchants waiting at home for news of travelers; however, they use an outmoded way of thinking of themselves as travelers. When Ariel, as the harpy, lectures them on their past sins, they are unable to lift their swords and presumably are stricken motionless. At this moment, the possibility of beginning to move as right travelers – in a purposeful direction – is undermined by their own past actions, as their own notions of travelers are based in earlier ways of thinking.

Stephano and Trinculo illustrate their own confused versions of traveling on the island in drunken antics with Caliban in the two scenes that appear on either side of the central betrothal scene. The opening of 2.2 presents Caliban alone, carrying wood, a staging repeated in Ferdinand's appearance with his burden in the next scene. Frequently in early modern drama, entering alone and delivering soliloquies allows characters to control the space of the stage. In this play, where so much of Prospero's power depends on other characters' belief in his spatial supremacy, these ways of controlling location seem not to work as well. Although Caliban enters alone in 2.2, his speech makes clear that he does not imagine himself to be speaking privately, and his descriptions of places on the island only add to the impression that Prospero controls all since "His spirits hear me" (2.2.3). The appearances of Stephano and Trinculo, and their reunion, amaze Caliban who tries to figure out where they have come from: "Hast thou not dropped from Heaven?" (2.2.137). Neither of them bothers to ask Caliban where they have landed, or even what the island is called. Traveling characters in other plays do ask these types of questions. When Viola in *Twelfth Night* appears, having suffered a shipwreck, she immediately asks the sailors, "What country, friends, is this?" (*Twelfth Night* 2.1.1). In a play more closely related to *The Tempest*, Antigonus in *The Winter's Tale* clearly confirms his location when he lands with the exiled infant: "Thou are perfect then, our ship hath touch'd upon / The deserts of Bohemia?" (*The Winter's Tale* 3.3.1–2).

In *The Tempest*, Trinculo and Stephano do not ask about their location. Nor do they recognize the importance of Caliban's descriptions of the island's resources and his offers to guide them to those. Caliban's offer to "show thee every fertile inch o'th'island" does not register with Trinculo or Stephano (2.2.148). Only after Caliban reiterates "let me bring thee," "I'll bring thee," and finally demands, "Wilt thou go with me?" Stephano agrees to be guided (2.2.167, 170, 172). Importantly, the scene ends with Stephano saying "O brave monster! lead the way" (2.2.188). The three of them reappear immediately after the betrothal scene. The location changes little and, while it is possible they may be drunker than earlier, splitting these actions into two scenes serves mostly to frame the betrothal scene. This framing makes more distinct the differences between the confusions of these characters and the clear direction presented in the betrothal scene.

When they reappear after the betrothal scene, Stephano more quickly understands Caliban's proposal to murder Prospero. Once he begins to understand the possibilities, he uses language that emphasizes direction and guidance to question Caliban's abilities as a guide: "How now shall this be compass'd? Canst thou bring me to the party?" (3.2.58–9). In this question, "compass" means "encompassed," but it raises other meanings since it carries also the implications of the directional device. Trinculo, willing to be led and misled by Ariel's tune, suggests, "Let's follow it, and after it do our work" (3.2.148–9).

The confusion about the order in which they depart at the end of the scene shows the ways that leading and following are confounded by these misdirected characters. The First Folio punctuation of the end of 3.2 has given rise to several editorial decisions:

>   *Ste.* Leade Monster,
> Wee'l follow: I would I could see this Taborer,
> He layes it on.
>   *Trin.*Wilt come?
> Ile follow *Stephano.*   *Exeunt.*   (TLN 1508–12)[25]

Stephen Orgel asserts that "Wilt come?" is addressed to Caliban, who at Trinculo's invitation exits first, followed in turn by Stephano and Trinculo.[26] If this order is used, Caliban needs the extra encouragement from Trinculo to lead them away. Frank Kermode points out the difficulties that arise with the decision to include a comma in Trinculo's line: "I'll follow, Stephano." In his note on the exiting characters, Kermode remarks,

> Trinculo's "Wilt come?" may be addressed to Caliban, and in that case the comma after "follow" should be omitted, as in F. Otherwise "Wilt come?" may be given to Stephano, and then a comma would be required after "follow," as in [Kermode's edition]. Or again, Trinculo's "Wilt come?" may still be addressed to the lingering Caliban, and the reading of "I'll follow, Stephano, remain as in [Kermode's] text.[27]

Virginia Mason Vaughan and Alden T. Vaughan note the controversy and insert a stage direction: "TRINCULO: [to Caliban] Wilt come? I'll follow Stephano."[28] Peter Hulme and William H. Sherman likewise insert the stage direction "to Caliban."[29] A stage production will find ways to sort out the characters' exits and the difficulties that arise. I do not argue for a particular reading of the exits, except to point out the confusion of leaders and followers endemic to the situation. These issues echo, in a different register, the disorderly events onboard the ship at the beginning of the play. The Boatswain asserts that the noblemen have no authority over the "elements" and must remove themselves from the space: "Out of our way, I say" (1.1.21, 26). In the melee of the storm, the proper places – either in status or location – hold no sway. These assertions of place and authority appear and reappear in the play as spatial and directional questions.

Stephano, especially, and Trinculo, by association, show themselves as the unaware, unthinking travelers who wish only to establish their own power in a space they neither explore nor understand. The shift in their ways of speaking about their own movements shows them to be accepting guidance not because of the possibilities that the island offers for their survival but for the more immediate possibilities of power. They assume, erroneously, that "there's but five upon this isle [and] we are three of them" (3.2.5–6). They question neither direction nor distance while agreeing to be led by their inadequate guide.

The central fifth scene contains Ferdinand and Miranda's betrothal, the event that allows the reconciliation at the end of the play. Ferdinand's interactions with space are shown in 1.2 when we first see him. His role as the appropriate traveler is quickly established and continually extended throughout the play. Ferdinand, lured by Ariel's song, moves away from his "odd angle of the isle," and this compulsion depends on the imperative to "Foot it featly here and there" (1.2.222, 379). Ferdinand describes the music that gives him direction and says, "thence I have follow'd it, / Or it hath drawn me rather" (1.2.394–5). He is aware that his own movements seem to be controlled by other forces. Although Prospero describes to Miranda how Ferdinand "strays about to find" those he has lost, we do not see Ferdinand wandering; instead, we see him led by Ariel as Prospero directed (1.2.418). Ferdinand's first request on sight of Miranda attempts to gain information about how to be a traveler in this land where he finds himself:

> Vouchsafe my pray'r
> May know if you remain upon this island,
> And that you will some good instruction give
> How I may bear me here. (1.2.423–6)

His request for "instruction" asks her to provide guidance for his own behavior, his bearing. To "get one's bearings" generally means to locate oneself within a particular space; to "bear oneself" carries implications of behavior, manners, and comportment. The phrases "Instructions for travel" and "Directions for travel" are both commonly used in the early modern era as titles for books describing appropriate comportment while outside one's own country. From his initial encounter with Miranda, he establishes himself as someone concerned with the proper behaviors of a traveler.

In *A Direction for Trauailers* (1592), Sir John Stradling makes clear that "instructions" and "directions" aimed at travelers have little to do with our notion of "directions." Rather than describing where to go, Stradling describes *how* to behave as a proper traveler. Stradling asserts that the most important "vertue of travel, [...] consists in learning to refine our manners, and to attaine to faire conditions; and behaviour towardes all kinde and conditions of men."[30] Ferdinand is not the only Shakespearean traveler who attempts to follow the generally understood precepts of travel. When Antipholus of Syracuse arrives in Ephesus, he plans to spend his afternoon in the normal pursuits of a traveler: "I"ll view the manners of the town, / Peruse the traders, gaze upon the buildings" (*Comedy of Errors* 1.2.12–13). Of course, the confusions of Ephesus distract him from these pursuits, but these plans help establish his normalcy immediately before the misidentifications of that play begin. In 1606, Thomas Palmer directs travelers to "be careful to make observance for the rights, customes, statutes, ordinances, proclamations, decrees, particular lawes and priviledges, liberties & prerogatives of places and persons where happily they shal come."[31] Ferdinand, in his first encounters with islanders of *The Tempest*, attempts to comport himself as a traveler ought by asking a resident how he ought to bear himself.

Ferdinand's initial realization of the oddities of the island shows that he understands the space of travel differently than the other characters. When Prospero charms him, Ferdinand experiences his sudden loss of movement as something like a dream: "My spirits, as in a dream, are all bound up" (1.2.487). Yet, he immediately allows himself an escape not available to any other character in the play:

> Might I but through my prison once a day
> Behold this maid. All corners else o' th' earth
> Let liberty make use of; space enough
> Have I in such a prison. (1.2.491–4)

Ferdinand's descriptions of space are outside the realms of the other characters. His concepts of space are rhetorical and poetic as fits his role outside the usurpation plots, and inside the reconciliation narrative, the narrative that provides the ending of the play. But Ferdinand's love for Miranda, which changes his subjective experience of prison, is not accessible to the other characters. Prospero, controlling time and many of the spaces within which events occur, calls the infatuation between Miranda and Ferdinand a "swift business" that he "must uneasy make" (1.2.451, 2). The quickness of traversing the distance toward betrothal must be slowed for Prospero to be certain it has been properly traveled. That Ferdinand wishes to be a proper traveler is shown by his acceptance of his labors in 3.1 when he bears logs. He describes his feelings to Miranda in terms that emphasize the poetic possibilities of traversing distances, "The very instant that I saw you, did / My heart fly to your service, there resides / To make me slave to it" (3.1.63–5). And he frames his description of his love for her in terms of the size – not of the island – of the world: his love is "beyond all limit of what else i' th' world" (3.1.72). Ferdinand's frames of reference are those of a traveler well-instructed in proper modes of travel.

Ferdinand's character has been dismissed as somewhat uninteresting. He has been described as "pallid in the extreme" and "a very ordinary nice young man," and as a "shorthand sketch" of "the handsome prince who deserves the heroine not just by birth, but by merit."[32] While Ferdinand may not be the most fully drawn of Shakespeare's characters, he does merit the heroine in ways that other Shakespearean young men do not. In *Cymbeline*, for example,

Posthumous' deeply unpleasant accusations and actions toward Imogen tinge their final reunion with serious doubts. Ferdinand seems more closely related to Florizell in *The Winter's Tale*, another son whose betrothal and marriage bind together men whose long-standing disputes propel the narrative. In *The Tempest*, the desire for revenge for the usurpation can only be sated through the betrothal. Prospero, through Miranda, re-establishes his supremacy over his usurping brother, not by regaining his own position (although he seems to gain that as well) but through his daughter's ascent to a higher position than either Prospero or his brother.[33] The change in social location moves both Miranda and Prospero through the socially acceptable modes of ascent: marriage rather than usurpation. Ferdinand, as the correct type of traveler, facilitates that movement.

Ferdinand's descriptions of his "beyond all limit" love are fairly common ones in the period. But, in this circumstance in this play, the descriptions take on an increased resonance, because they differ so markedly from the ways the other characters in the play talk about space and distance. Not only does Ferdinand have different ways of understanding his location, but he shows a flexibility in understanding his own role that leads to the reconciliation of the play. In the wedding masque of 4.1 (the penultimate scene of the play) the goddesses emphasize topographical descriptions both of Ceres' mountains, meadows, banks, vineyard, and sea coast, and of the location for the masque, "Here on this grass-plot, in this very place" (4.1.73). The sudden specificity of location is repeated when the nymphs are called to appear "on this green land" (4.1.130). The masque presents the images of fecundity and harvest that accompany sedentary agricultural production: "Earth's increase, foison plenty, / Barns and garners never empty" (4.1.110–11). These are not the fruits of travel and movement but the outcomes of sustained location. Ferdinand, swayed by this depiction, declares, "Let me live here ever; / So rare a wond'red father and a wise / Makes this place Paradise" (4.1.122–4). In the same way that Ferdinand shows himself to be an apt traveler seeking instruction, he complies with the presented argument for settled location and production of marriage. Prospero appears less certain than Ferdinand of the possibility of constrained movement and, after his often quoted description of the revels ending, he paradoxically attempts to find stillness through motion: "A turn or two I'll walk / To still my beating mind" (4.1.162–3).

Stephano and Trinculo continue to exemplify inexpert travelers as Ariel expertly leads them and Caliban to their uncomfortable rest in "th' filthy mantled pool" until Prospero prepares for their arrival at his cell (4.1.182). Caliban realizes the ineptitude of his followers when they find enticing the "trumpery" placed "For stale to catch these thieves" (4.1.186, 187). Caliban questions their ability to move on their decided course when he asks, "what do you mean / To dote thus on such luggage?" (4.1.229–30). G. Blakemore Evans' note on "luggage" as "encumbering trash" might accurately represent most travelers' feelings at some point in a journey, but the early modern use also includes "inconveniently heavy baggage" for travel.[34] Stephano's joking response to Caliban's complaint about the luggage, "Now is the jerkin under the line. Now, jerkin, you are like to lose your hair, and prove a bald jerkin," refers to "under the line" as south of the equator.[35] Stephano picks up the notion of travel that Caliban introduces, but he immediately turns the reference to a joke based on apocryphal reports of travel rather than considering himself as a traveler.

The final scene brings together the elements of time, space, and travel to provide the reunion and reconciliation that finally mark the play. The emphasis on movement throughout the play and the inability of the shipwrecked men to successfully negotiate their travel combines in the moments of motionlessness in the final scene. Alonso, Antonio, and Sebastian "cannot boudge till [Prospero's] release" and the others are bound near them by their concern (5.1.11). When Prospero capitulates, he frames his forgiveness as action and movement rather than as thought: "The rarer action is / In virtue than in vengeance" (5.1.27–8). Prospero's comment on "virtue" has been noted as the moment of generic shift away from the revenge tragedy to reconciliation; it seems to me more likely that this shift takes place at the center of the play with Prospero's daughter proposing to the king's son.[36]

Prospero's tracing of a magic circle calls up images of Faustus, but more immediately it marks a confined space in terms that resonate with the spatial concerns of the play. Prospero's promise to relinquish his magic depends on navigational terms to describe his own distancing from it:

I'll break my staff,
Bury it certain fadoms in the earth,

And deeper than did ever plummet sound
I'll drown my book. (5.1.54–7)

The length of measure "fathom" comes originally from the distance of outstretched arms and links it to the mental grasp of something fathomable or understandable. Taking soundings is necessary only when wanting to know the depth of the sea floor or wanting to test the depth of understanding. Prospero has circumscribed a confined space and promises to exceed all spaces in his relinquishment of the knowledge he has gained through his staff and book.[37]

This description of depth in "fadoms" verbally recalls Ariel's song to Ferdinand at the beginning of the play.

Full fadom five thy father lies,
  Of his bones are coral made:
Those are pearls that were his eyes:
  Nothing of him that doth fade,
But doth suffer a sea-change. (1.2.397–401)

Part of the strength of this song comes from the repetitions and links in the language (bones, eyes, coral, pearls) between human parts and sea growths.[38] The sea-change then links together human bodies, the sea, and the otherwise incomprehensible enormity of action necessary to move the sea. When Prospero refers back to this song in his description of burying his staff and drowning his book, he links himself to possibilities of change; but more importantly he points to the routes along which that change can take place. When Prospero speaks to the charmed men, he describes their reason as shores filled by the rising sea of understanding:

Their understanding
Begins to swell, and the approaching tide
Will shortly fill the reasonable shores
That now lie foul and muddy. (5.1.79–82)

Despite confining them senseless to the space of the circle, Prospero clearly views them as sovereign when he describes them as being their own earths with tides and shores.

As one of the least culpable of the men, Gonzalo's first words, when he is able to speak, show that he finally realizes the precariousness of his role as a traveler: "All torment, trouble, wonder, and amazement / Inhabits here. Some heavenly power guide us / Out of this fearful country!" (5.1.104–6). Prospero's forgiveness emphasizes the immeasurable virtues of Gonzalo, "whose honor cannot / Be measur'd or confin'd" (5.1.121–2). Prospero's revelation of Ferdinand and Miranda offers Alonso the sight he wishes for; his exclamation of delight, "Now all the blessings / Of a glad father compass thee about!" (5.1.179–80), returns to the measures and perceptions of "encompass." In the same way that Ferdinand and Miranda's betrothal scene appears at the center of the play, the couple now holds the center of the stage in the recessed place beyond the central opening of the *frons*.[39] Gonzalo credits the gods with the blessings he perceives, "For it is you that have chalk'd forth the way / Which brought us hither" (5.1.203–4). The credit here for the pathway and the movement acts as a nod to Prospero who "chalk'd forth" both the circle in which they stand and the paths for journeys they took on the island. Alonso's misdirected usurpation before the action of the play initiates a generic direction, the revenge plot. He shows, at the end of the play, his change in understanding of direction when he finally realizes the importance of finding his way. As he says, "This is as strange a maze as e'er men trod" (5.1.242).

Miranda's own surprise at the people who surround her, "O brave new world / That has such people in it," reminds us of the worlds that the shipwrecked men are shown and fail to navigate appropriately (5.1.183–4). Only Ferdinand masters his role as a traveler in the play, asking for direction and guidance about his bearing and accepting his new place with Miranda. This perspective on the play points out the centrality of Ferdinand, centered physically in his appearances on stage, and also central to the reconciliation that the play achieves at the end. The narrative essentially begins with a revenge plot against a usurping brother, but the final reunions and reconciliation are achieved through the betrothal of Ferdinand and Miranda at the center of the play. Ferdinand's facility as a traveler confirms his role in the resolution of the narrative. Despite the obstacles Prospero presents, playgoers never doubt, because of his asides, that Prospero's objections to the match are meant only to test Ferdinand even if Miranda and Ferdinand believe in the obstacles. The play's scenic arrangements and versions of travelers encourage playgoers to experience the betrothal as the moment of shifting of genre from a possible revenge tragedy to a romance that promises reconciliations.

The implications of the play's reliance on contemporaneous travel writing and the reading of Ferdinand as a centralized character can be highlighted in production. The central placement of Ferdinand in the American Shakespeare Center 2011 production emphasized his centrality to the structure of the play and fitted well with that production's characterization of Ferdinand and Miranda's love as not farcical. Beyond questions of production, this way of reading the play has implications for *The Tempest*'s connections to other Shakespeare plays. Russ McDonald has pointed out that "the spatial limitation for which *The Tempest* is famous reveals immediately that the most significant movement, the travel of which the various journeys are physical manifestations, is internal."[40] In addition to the internal movements, the characters use specific language and spatial navigation to achieve other significant journeys while on Prospero's island – journeys connected to the modes of travel, the ways of mapping, and the notions characters use to understand the world around them. *The Tempest* frequently has been grouped with *Cymbeline*, *The Winter's Tale*, and *Pericles* in the generic category of romances.[41] Although it does not include the geographical and temporal leaps of *Cymbeline*, *The Winter's Tale*, and *Pericles*, *The Tempest* uses similar devices – arising from the wide spectrum of early modern travel literature – to provide temporal and spatial dislocations as vast as those in the other romances. *The Winter's Tale* shifts between Sicily and Bohemia and leaps over sixteen years. *Cymbeline* ranges over wide geographical spaces, and *Pericles* covers long distances and leaps over a substantial gap in time. *The Tempest*, however, confines the characters to an insular space and then requires them to show the same navigational skill and acumen as characters in the other romances with larger geographical expanses.

The simultaneous cosmographical and geographical views of the universe in Shakespeare's time give rise to the mixing of fantastical and quotidian in the romances. It is a geographical universe in which travelers use modern means of measurement, wonder at old tales from past travelers, suffer the physical pains of locomotion, lose their way, attempt to understand their surroundings, and finally depend on a larger cosmographical understanding of how the world functions. Simultaneously, these characters must encounter foreign beings, attempt to find food, be spectators at a masque of goddesses or hear the music of the island. Only through the concurrent understandings of the world as both fantastical and quotidian can the characters succeed. Ferdinand knows he must ask for instruction when he first encounters another being on the island, yet he is also willing to be led by Ariel's music.

Nineteenth- and twentieth-century critics often read the romances in comparison to the tragedies or the histories as being improbably non-realistic, overly magical, too dependent on fairy tale aspects of narratives, and thus as having less to tell us about the human condition. In her review of Sanford Robbins' 1991 production of *The Tempest*, Lois Potter details how a particular acting approach produced for her a new experience of the play. Potter explains that, in part, this experience illuminated for her a possible early modern attraction of tragicomedy as a genre: "not the sentimental drama of wish-fulfillment that it sometimes seems to us but an attempt to bring a classical kind of drama within the range of contemporary audience experience and beliefs."[42] In many ways, the characters in the romances depend on the interrelationships between the theater and a cosmographical view of the world to explore the issues that confront them.[43] The worlds being explored, traversed, and revealed in the early modern era give rise to new ways that individuals, and particularly characters in the romances, can move within their worlds. The romances as a generic group depend on similar narrative moves: journeys and exiles related to domestic and civil authority; explorations of the strengths of marital bonds or separations; quests and epic searches; divine or magical interventions; tests of loyalties; intergenerational conflicts; and recognition, reunion, and regeneration for resolution. Given these aspects of romances, it is hardly surprising that contemporaneous descriptions and modes of travel inflect the construction of the plays. The playgoers' experience of the play arises from these underlying structures: the means and methods of time, space, and perception available through the corporeal representations possible in dramatic performance.

Notes

1. Malone first suggested in 1808 the links between the descriptions of the 1609 wreck and *The Tempest*. Charles Frey's "*The Tempest* and the New World" provides an extensive and compelling discussion of these relationships. "*The Tempest* and the New World," *Shakespeare Quarterly* 30.1 (1979), 29–41. Alden T. Vaughan has more recently and convincingly

insisted on the mistaken nature of assertions that Strachey's letters were not a source for Shakespeare. "William Strachey's 'True Reportory' and Shakespeare: A Closer Look at the Evidence," *Shakespeare Quarterly* 50.3 (2008), 245–273.
2. Bruce R. Smith, "Taking the Measure of Global Space," *Journal of Medieval and Early Modern Studies* 43.1 (2013), 26–48, 36.
3. This usage appears in the *Oxford English Dictionary* as "forth-rights C. n.." The *OED* provides this example from *The Tempest* and a similar usage from *Troilus and Cressida*.
4. David Lindley (ed.), *The Tempest*, by William Shakespeare (Cambridge: Cambridge University Press, 2002), 33, 37.
5. Ben Jonson, *Bartholomew Fair* in *Three Comedies*, ed. Michael Jamieson (New York: Penguin, 1966), 325–460. These lines appear at 114–117 of the Induction.
6. Peter Hulme, *Colonial Encounters: Europe and the Native Caribbean 1492–1797* (London: Routledge, 1992), xiii. See also John Gillies' *Shakespeare and the Geography of Difference* where he insightfully reads Prospero's descriptions of the island against the relevant Virginia pamphlets to illuminate the correspondences between the situations of Miranda and Caliban as "brother and sister, children of ignorance." John Gillies, *Shakespeare and the Geography of Difference* (Cambridge: Cambridge University Press, 1994), 155.
7. Ania Loomba, *Colonialism/Postcolonialism: The New Critical Idiom* (London: Routledge, 1998), 2.
8. Loomba, *Colonialism/Postcolonialism*, 2. In Issue Three of *Early Modern Culture: An Electronic Seminar*, Peter Hulme uses his own work on *The Tempest* to offer an illuminating discussion of some of the dangers of paraphrasing to justify dismissal of particular critical apparatus. Ania Loomba contributes a response to his essay in the same issue of the journal (accessed June 11, 2014 at http://emc.eserver.org/1-3/issue3.html). These discussions center on questions raised by colonialist readings of *The Tempest*.
9. John Gillies, *Geography of Difference*, 35.
10. These are the act and scene breaks that appear in the First Folio. Andrew Gurr has argued that the act breaks in *The Tempest* are a result of the play being specifically written for Blackfriars and that, particularly in the separation between act four and act five, the breaks are required for the time necessary for costume changes. Andrew Gurr, "*The Tempest*'s Tempest at Blackfriars," *Shakespeare Survey* 41 (1989), 91–102.
11. Emrys Jones, *Scenic Form in Shakespeare*, 1971 (Oxford: Oxford University Press, 1985), 8.
12. See, for example, G. Wilson Knight's allegorical readings of the tempest and song themes in *The Shakespearian Tempest*, 1932 (London: Methuen, 1953), 247–266.
13. McNeir primarily situates this comment in a discussion of Prospero's control of the action. Waldo McNeir, "*The Tempest*; Space-Time and Spectacle-Theme," *The Arlington Quarterly* 2.4 (1970), 29–58, 37. Sidney

Homan likewise comments that Prospero /stands at the end of a long line of directors or controlling figures – Petruchio, Oberon, Portia, Helena, Duke Vincentio, Cerimon, Paulina, and Camillo." Sidney Homan, "*The Tempest* and Shakespeare's Last Plays: The Aesthetic Dimensions," *Shakespeare Quarterly* 24.1 (1973), 69–76, 74.
14. David Lindley (ed.), *The Tempest*, 11.
15. McNeir, "*The Tempest*; Space-Time and Spectacle-Theme," 37.
16. The emphasis is in the original, which appears on page 87. Earlier in the same chapter, Lopez points out the disparity in activity between the shipwreck at the beginning and this scene of exposition. His description compares the theatrical possibilities for representing actions (such as the shipwreck) and Prospero's description of another journey and asserts: "The contrast between these two scenes makes quite clear that exposition is more often a choice than a necessity." Jeremy Lopez, *Theatrical Convention and Audience Response in Early Modern Drama* (Cambridge: Cambridge University Press, 2003), 79.
17. Russ McDonald examines the "reduplicative flavor of Prospero's narrative to Miranda" and points out that "Besides furnishing the basic pleasure of echoing sounds, the various kinds of verbal play impart energy and motion to what is dramatically a notoriously static scene." Russ McDonald, *Shakespeare's Late Style* (Cambridge: Cambridge University Press, 2006), 192,193.
18. *The Tempest*, by William Shakespeare, directed by Jim Warren, Blackfriars Playhouse, Staunton VA, June–December 2011.
19. See *OED*: 'space" (n.) I. "denoting time or duration" and II. "an area or extension."
20. Richard Norwood, *The Sea-Mans Practice, Contayning a Fvndamentall Probleme in Navigation, experimentally verified: namely, Touching the Compasse of the Earth and Sea, and the quantity of a Degree in our English measures. Also an exact method or forme of keeping a Reckoning at Sea, in any kinde or manner of sayling. With certayne Tables and other rules usefull in Navigation, As also in the Plotting and Surveying of places. The Latitude of the principall places in England. The finding of Currents at Sea; and what allowance is to bee given in respect of them* (London: George Hurlock, 1637); Wing N1360, H4^v.
21. See *Oxford English Dictionary*: "course" (n.) 22a. "A line of (personal) action, way of acting, method of proceeding."
22. Sidney, Philip, Sir, *Profitable instructions; describing what speciall obseruations are to be taken by trauellers in all nations, states and countries; pleasant and profitable. By the three much admired, Robert, late Earle of Essex. Sir Philip Sidney. And, Secretary Davison 1613* (London: Benjamin Fisher, 1633), STC 6789; these passages appear on G1^r and H3^r-H3^v. The letter is reprinted in *Sir Philip Sidney* edited by Katharine Duncan-Jones (284–287). Duncan-Jones notes: "Copies survive in at least nine MSS, all apparently fairly remote from the original, and in one printed text [*Profitable Instructions*]; Duncan-Jones, *Sir Philip Sidney*, 397.

23. For information on extant manuscripts of Mandeville and the subsequent printings, see Iain Macleod Higgins' *Writing East: The "Travels" of Sir John Mandeville* (Philadelphia: University of Pennsylvania Press, 1997).
24. In *The Discoverie of the Large, Rich and Bewtiful Empyre of Guiana*, Sir Walter Ralegh describes the men who "are reported to have their eyes in their shoulders, and their mouths in the middle of their breasts, & that a long train of haire groweth backward betwen their shoulders." He reiterates the second-hand nature of the report by saying, "for mine owne part I saw them not." Sir Walter Ralegh, *The Discoverie of the Large, Rich and Bewtiful Empyre of Guiana*, ed. Neil L. Whitehead (Norman, OK: University of Oklahoma Press, 1997), 178. The first edition of Hakluyt's *Principall Navigations* appeared in 1589; the second edition in three volumes appeared one volume per year 1598–1600. The bulk of the changes from the first to the second editions were additions and expansions making the excision of *Mandeville's Travels* all the more noticeable as an aberration. Richard Hakluyt, *The Principall Navigations, Voiages and Discoveries of the English nation, made by Sea or ouer Land, to the most remote and farthest distant Quarters of the earth at any time within the compasse of these 1500 yeares: Deuided into three severall parts, according to the positions of the Regions whereunto they were directed* (London: George Bishop and Ralph Newberie, 1589), STC 12625; Richard Hakluyt, *The principal navigations, voiages, traffiques and discoueries of the English nation, made by sea or ouer-land, to the remote and farthest distant quarters of the earth, at any time within the compasse of these 1500. yeeres: deuided into three seuerall volumes, according to the positions of the regions, whereunto they were directed. This first volume containing the woorthy discoueries, &c. of the English ... and the famous victorie atchieued at the citie of Cadiz, 1596. ... By Richard Hakluyt Master of Artes, and sometime student of Christ-Church in Oxford* (London: George Bishop, Ralph Newberie, and Robert Barker, 1598-1600), STC 12626.
25. G. Blakemore Evans punctuates the dialogue in this way:

    STEPHANO: Lead, monster, we'll follow. I would I could see this taborer; he lays it on.
    TRINCULO: Wilt come? I'll follow Stephano. (3.2.150–3)

26. Stephen Orgel (ed), *The Tempest* by William Shakespeare (Oxford: Oxford University Press, 1987).
27. The note in Kermode's text appears at 3.2.150. Frank Kermode (ed.), *The Tempest*, by William Shakespeare (London: Methuen, 1954).
28. Virginia Mason Vaughan and Alden T. Vaughan, (ed.), *The Tempest*, by William Shakespeare (London: Thomson Learning, 2001); the stage direction appears at 3.2.153.
29. Peter Hulme and William H. Sherman, (eds), *The Tempest*, by William Shakespeare (New York: Norton, 2004); the stage direction appears at 3.2.150.
30. Sir John Stradling, *A Direction for Trauaillers. Taken out of Ivstvs Lipsius, and enlarged for the behoofe of the right honorable Lord, the yong Earle of Bedford, being now ready to trauell* (London: Cutbert Burbie, 1592); STC 15696, C1^r.

31. Sir Thomas Palmer, *An Essay of the Meanes how to make our Travailes, into forraine Countries, the more profitable and honourable* (London: Mathew Lownes, 1606); STC 19156, E1ᵛ.
32. The first two quotations are from Bonomy Dobrée, "The Tempest," in *Twentieth Century Interpretations of* The Tempest, ed. Hallett Smith (Englewood Cliffs: Prentice-Hall, 1969), 47–59, 53. The second two descriptions are from Vaughan and Vaughan (eds.), *The Tempest*, 35.
33. Exploring the basis of Prospero's power, Stephen Orgel asserts that "giving away Miranda is a means of preserving his authority, not of relinquishing it." Orgel (ed.), *The Tempest*, 214.
34. See *Oxford English Dictionary*: "luggage" n. 1.a.
35. Evans notes that "The joke involves the popular idea that travellers to tropical countries lost their hair through fevers, or from scurvy resulting from lack of fresh food on the journey" (4.1.236 fn). Lindley notes that "Losing one's hair was [...] associated with sexual disease and its treatment" (4.1.234–5 fn).
36. Marjorie Garber (among other critics) notes this generic shift, after the "revenge plot" beginning, and links "Prospero's conversion from vengeance to 'virtue' [...] through the agency" of Ariel in 5.1. Marjorie Garber, *Shakespeare After All* (New York: Anchor, 2004), 871–872. L.C. Knights remarks that Prospero's comment on virtue "is of course the key. Prospero has come to terms with his experience, and – so far as their individual natures permit – with his enemies." Knights, L.C., "*The Tempest*" in *Shakespeare's Late Plays*, ed. Richard C. Tobias and Paul G. Zolbrod (Athens: Ohio University Press, 1974), 15–31, 28. Virginia Mason Vaughan and Alden T. Vaughan point out that Prospero's "plan for Miranda's marriage to Ferdinand makes it less likely that he intends real harm to her future father-in-law." Virginia Mason Vaughan and Alden T. Vaughan, (eds.), *The Tempest*, 25.
37. Editors do not agree on the point at which Prospero draws the circle to confine the characters. The First Folio stage direction reads: "*They all enter the circle which* Prospero *had made*" (TLN 2011–12).
38. Russ McDonald points out the much of the pleasure from the songs in *The Tempest* comes from "various kinds of echo." McDonald, *Shakespeare's Late Style*, 195.
39. Mariko Ichikawa asserts, I think rightly, that "Clearly, in this scene [5.1], the central opening serves as Prospero's cell." Ichikawa, Mariko, *Shakespearean Entrances* (London: Palgrave Macmillan, 2002), 104.
40. McDonald, *Shakespeare's Late Style*, 143.
41. Gordon McMullen has recently shown some of the difficulties with considering this group of plays as a coherent group of "late plays" with its implication of finality. The greatest difficulty with the grouping remains that three plays, *Henry VIII*, *The Two Noble Kinsmen*, and the lost *Cardenio*, all at least partially written by Shakespeare, followed the plays noted as romances. An earlier grouping maintained *The Tempest*, *Cymbeline*, and *The Winter's Tale* as the "romances" – leaving out *Pericles*, mostly because

George Wilkins wrote parts of it. McMullen notes that scholars argued that the generic similarities of *Pericles* encourage its addition to the (previously) three Romances. He recapitulates the stance as depending on a description of *Pericles* that essentially says, "it is a play about a father and his daughter, involving chivalric motifs, storms and shipwrecks, wide geographical wanderings and powerful emotional wrenches, and it concludes with recognition and reconciliation." Gordon McMullen, "What is a 'late play'?" in *The Cambridge Companion to Shakespeare's Late Plays*, ed. Catherine M.S. Alexander (Cambridge: Cambridge University Press, 2009), 5–27, 8. Frank Kermode uses the term "pastoral tragicomedy" to link the generic structures of *The Tempest* to other non-Shakespearean works of the period. Frank Kermode (ed.), *The Tempest*, by William Shakespeare (London: Methuen, 1954), 59.
42. Lois Potter, "A Brave New *Tempest*," *Shakespeare Quarterly* 43.4 (1992), 450–455, 454.
43. As John Gillies describes, "Renaissance theatre and 'cosmography' are conceptually interrelated. The theater was cosmographic and, to an extent, geographic, in its conceptual character (Shakespeare's Globe Theatre is a striking case in point). Cosmography, for its part, was "theatrical," in the sense that "theater" is an important enabling metaphor. (Thanks in part to the popularity of Ortelius' *Theatrum*, atlases were generically "theaters" before they were "atlases")." Gillies, *Shakespeare and the Geography of Difference*, 35.

Conclusion
Movements of Genre and Other Directions: "As strange a maze"

When we, as actively engaged readers or playgoers, attend to Shakespeare's plays, the stagecraft of the plays develops and controls our experience of the narrative. In order to focus attention on how the plays function for playgoers, these previous chapters have each considered a play as an individual dramatic unit, the way we most frequently encounter them in the theater. However, we can never fully separate individual plays from the implications of the larger Shakespearean canon. If we are attuned to Shakespeare's language and stagecraft, we hear echoes from one character's speeches to another character's, recognize repeated stage images, notice differing outcomes from similar situations, or understand afresh the ways the play moves us through the events of the narrative, involving us in the project of theatrical meaning-making. Since the divisions presented in the First Folio of 1623, we have recognized the usefulness of generic divisions, although we might quibble with those offered by the First Folio that placed, for example, *The Tempest* at the beginning of the comedies and *Cymbeline* as the last of the tragedies. The engagements with playgoers examined in this book offer some ways to elucidate the generic frames upon which we now more frequently depend.

The stagecraft elements of comedic resolution in *A Midsummer Night's Dream* depend heavily on the appropriate pairing of the couples, the probable marriages, and a resumption (based on the reconciliation of Oberon and Titania) of the world's order. Many of Shakespeare's other comedies likewise depend on similar elements for closure. In conjunction with our visual experiences in *A Midsummer Night's*

Dream, the emphasis on vision throughout the play calls attention to how the spectacular can connect to the individual attempts to understand, through sight, a world that does not function as it ought. In *The Comedy of Errors*, the visual errors arise from the circumstance of indistinguishable bodies rather than redirected affection for particular individuals. Despite the lack of magical intervention in *The Comedy of Errors*, the visiting Syracusans fear the possibility of trickery. Antipholus of Syracuse says:

> They say this town is full of cozenage:
> As nimble jugglers that deceive the eye,
> Dark-working sorcerers that change the mind,
> Soul-killing witches that deform the body,
> Disguised cheaters, prating mountebanks,
> And many such-like liberties of sin. (1.2.97–102)

Noticeably, Antipholus of Syracuse has the concerns that ought to worry some of the characters in *A Midsummer Night's Dream*. While the characters in *A Midsummer Night's Dream* do not consider that they might be under a magical spell, they would be right to think it.

No magic intervenes to produce the visual mistakes of *The Comedy of Errors*, but many characters, and especially Antipholus of Syracuse, cannot trust their senses. Despite wooing Luciana and describing her as "mine own self's better part: / Mine eye's clear eye, my dear heart's dearer heart" (3.2.61–2), he undermines the possibility for accurate perception when, in soliloquy, he describes Luciana,

> Possess'd with such a gentle and a sovereign grace,
> Of such enchanting presence and discourse,
> Hath almost made me traitor to myself;
> But let myself be guilty to self-wrong,
> I'll stop mine ears against the mermaid's song. (3.2.160–4)

He figures himself as enchanted and imagines that he requires an Odysseus-like guard against her charms, aural charms in this instance. The misunderstandings of *The Comedy of Errors* depend on visual trickeries of a very different sort than those in *A Midsummer Night's Dream*, and the characters question themselves differently. In both plays, playgoers are offered the distancing awareness of more information than any of the characters in the play. However, the resolution of *The Comedy of Errors* depends on the revelation, to characters and playgoers alike, of the missing family member that completes the final reunion. In this way, *The Comedy of Errors* points forward to the resolutions offered in the romances, while still being firmly grounded in the generic frameworks of comedy.

Given the ways that comedic frames emerge in *A Midsummer Night's Dream*, we might reconsider some of the ways other Shakespearean comedies connect spaces to visual trickery and interchangeability. The changes of location in *The Merchant of Venice* allow Portia and Nerissa to take on different, disguised roles. *The Taming of the Shrew* develops Petruccio's control of space in ways that allow for both his "taming" of Katherine and eventually her own assumption of control of the stage space in her lengthy final monologue, which has troubled many critics' readings of the play. The final wager by the husbands in this play depends on the possibility of controlling entrances and exits as a demonstration of conjugal love. In *Love's Labors Lost*, the agreement to limit the men's interactions with women forms the initial conflict of the play, but this matter becomes a conflict because the men cannot effectively control the space within which they have decided to live. The King and his men's interactions with the Princess and her ladies develop some of the possibilities of interchangeability and the untrustworthiness of visual markers when, for example, the men misread the visually apparent objects they believe might identify the masked women. In many ways, Shakespearean comedy depends on being tricked by vision, but this trickery emerges as something that can be rectified and reconciled for a comedic ending.

Shakespearean history plays depend on building a narrative that can allow us to see what history has in store. In *Richard II*, the play depends on grounding the action in England while constantly questioning the efficacy of necessary speech acts and of visual presentations. In ways discussed earlier, *Richard II* encourages playgoers to reconcile disparate stage images with verbal accounts. In *Henry V*, many of these same kinds of reconciliations are necessary between, for example, description in the Chorus' speeches and the immediately subsequent staged scenes. At the beginning of act two, the chorus assures us that

> Now all the youth of England are on fire,
> And silken dalliance in the wardrobe lies;

Now thrive the armorers, and honor's thought
Reigns solely in the breast of every man. (2.0.1–4).

Despite these descriptions of men rallying to the cause, the actions of Nym and Bardolph in 2.1 do not match the Chorus' report. As Nym puts it, "I dare not fight, but I will wink and hold out mine iron" (2.1.7–8); hardly overwhelmed by patriotic fire, Nym's description shows him unwilling to look directly at the battles he will face. Scenic juxtaposition in *Henry V* is responsible for much of what Norman Rabkin memorably set out in terms of rabbits and ducks.[1] Rabkin explains,

> I am going to argue that in *Henry V* Shakespeare creates a work whose ultimate power is precisely the fact that it points in two opposite directions, virtually daring us to choose one of the two opposed interpretations it requires of us. In this deceptively simple play Shakespeare experiments, perhaps more shockingly than elsewhere, with a structure like the gestaltist's familiar drawing of a rare beast.[2]

This drawing is the one which can either be seen as a rabbit or a duck, but not both at once. I have quoted from Rabkin's well-known essay as a reminder of the way he describes the situation, claiming the play "points in two opposite directions" and emphasizing the referential image as a "structure." In Rabkin's description he implicitly recognizes the ways the play controls our perspectives and vantage points.[3] We might consider these elements in conjunction with similar techniques functioning in other genres of Shakespeare's plays.

Shakespearean tragedy develops an inexorable movement toward that which might well be seen but cannot be avoided. Perhaps most extensively of all the genres, tragedy moves us, controls our perspective, traps us with the trapped experiences of the characters. In the earlier discussions of *Hamlet* and *Macbeth*, the focus on the stage spaces and the characters' discussions of space illuminate the structures that produce effects on us as playgoers. Henry S. Turner's readings of what he calls "spatial cruxes" in *King Lear* reveal the intertwined nature of playgoers' understandings of space and the contemporaneous modes of thought and structure that were available to develop and construct both physical stages and the more abstract stage spaces.[4] The stagecraft of Shakepseare's plays depends on these interconnected understandings and develops our own experience whether as readers or playgoers. Many of Shakespeare's tragedies rely on character misperceptions while simultaneously encouraging playgoers to perceive events or activities in a very different light. Othello asserts that Desdemona "had eyes, and chose me," but he cannot resist Iago's imperative reminders to "look to't" (3.3.189, 200). Othello's misperceptions of Desdemona become articulated, demonstrated misperceptions when Iago orchestrates his conversation so Othello "must conster / Poor Cassio's smiles, gestures, and light behaviors / Quite in the wrong" (4.1.101–3). Iago chooses where Othello will be hidden to observe the exchange, as earlier (in Venice) Iago controls the entrances and noise for the rousing of Brabantio. Iago's control of the staging of Cassio's fight demonstrates Iago's increasing control once the action moves to Cyprus. In many ways, the stagecraft elements of this play develop the spatial and perceptual imperatives that bring about the tragic ending.

The move to tragicomedy or romance in the later period of Shakespeare's career integrates elements of tragedy and comedy into a new kind of entertainment dependent on many of these spatial and locational imperatives, which become their own vocabulary of generic convention. In some cases, such as *The Winter's Tale*, portions of the play seem weighted toward one generic frame or the other as the play moves from the tragic opening acts to the later resolution driven comedy-framed ending. Leontes' visual confusions and spatial control in the early scenes drive much of the tragic beginning of the play. In 1.2 of *The Winter's Tale*, when Leontes becomes (wrongly) convinced of his wife Hermione's betrayal of him with Polixenes, several elements of stagecraft make the scene particularly effective. Leontes' fears of cuckolding arise during what ought to be a stately leave-taking, uncomfortably mixing public and private concerns. Polixenes, planning to depart, opens the scene with formal speeches of gratitude for hospitality during his visit. During these speeches he establishes the basis of the two kings' friendship, institutes his own royalty through the third-person formal pronouns, and demonstrates his own honorable comportment. Leontes' aside initially describes Hermione's behaviors as those that "well become the agent," but these musings soon reveal his burgeoning jealousy as he rereads for playgoers the actions of Polixenes and Hermione: "to be paddling palms and pinching fingers, / As now they are, and making practic'd smiles, / As in a looking-glass" (1.2.114, 115–17). The stage space of the scene requires that we watch Hermione and Polixenes interact as Leontes narrates to playgoers his understanding of the exchanges. Most readings of the play understand Hermione to be falsely accused, and in this moment playgoers are offered an aside that misunderstands and misrepresents what we are seeing occur. As is usual with asides, we understand Leontes to be telling the truth as he sees it, yet we simultaneously are presented with the chance to do our own watching and interpreting. As Leontes becomes more enmeshed in his own thoughts, he uses language that connects him to the tragic modes at work in these early scenes of the play:

> Affection! thy intention stabs the centre.
> Thou dost make possible things not so held,
> Communicat'st with dreams (how can this be?),
> With what's unreal thou co-active art,
> And fellow'st nothing. (2.1.138–42)

This personified word "affection," at the time of *The Winter's Tale*, had meanings other than affectionate regard or liking; it still carried the now-obsolete meanings, "irrational behaviour, over-whelming passion, lust and animosity."[5] Here Leontes sees affection as an active participant in his confusions, a role he questions but cannot seem to overcome. As playgoers we must question what affects the character who can see what we see and interpret so differently. This scene mirrors in many ways the watching scene in *Othello*, except *The Winter's Tale* removes the Iago figure, leaving us as playgoers in a culpable position of not sorting out the error.

In some ways, this scene exemplifies the weight of interpretation that Shakespeare's later plays rest on the playgoer. The romances depend more on masques and modes of spectacular entertainment, yet these are elements of stagecraft that rely more on us as playgoers to maintain our end of the stage-illusion. We know that Leontes errs in his judgment of his wife, yet we also know that the stage machinery of tragedy requires the events occur. The later plays gamble on playgoers' willingness to participate even more actively in imaginatively developing stage illusion. *The Tempest*'s adherence to the unities of time, place, and action is undermined by those very unities; the narrative is not contained by the frame of the stage. The revenge tragedy plot began much earlier in a pre-play past elsewhere and has nearly exhausted itself by the time the shipwreck is complete. Ferdinand and Miranda's betrothal ensures we have moved into a realm other than tragedy, and the remainder of the play resolves these generic difficulties by integrating the different characters into society according to their roles as travelers. *The Winter's Tale* moves Leontes into the realms of romance through the play's comedic frames after the landing on Bohemia. The use of the comedic disguise forces Leontes to recognize truths other than his own solipsistic, tragic understanding of his own world. These patterns in the generic adjustments may help us understand how the plays manage to produce some of the effects which are so moving in our experience of them as theatrical vehicles.

I suggested in the Introduction that these elements of stagecraft were not apparent solely in Shakespeare's plays, but that some aspects were specifically connected to early modern theater. The particularities of the early modern theater and playing conditions gave rise to some conventions and innovations distinctly related to the spaces for which these plays were written. More importantly, these elements of stagecraft were a part of the fabric of the plays of the period, inflected by the modes of thinking, speaking, seeing, acting, and even being, which were available in the early modern era. A brief examination of Christopher Marlowe's *Tamburlaine, Part One* shows some of the ways similar stagecraft elements appear in other earlier plays of the early modern period.

Although dating to 1588, Marlowe's *Tamburlaine, Part One* remained an active part of the theater repertory.[6] The play has many elements that undoubtedly contributed to its popularity: descriptions of far-off places, exotic characters, appearances of many kings and leaders, spectacular stage imagery, and the rise of a character who articulates his ambitions in stirring verse. The play also demonstrates many stagecraft elements related to those I have discussed in relation to Shakespeare's plays. When Tamburlaine declares in 3.3 that he "Will first subdue the Turk, and then enlarge / Those Christian captives which you keep as slaves," he relies on the meaning of "enlarge" as "to release from confinement or bondage."[7] The concurrent meaning, "To render more spacious or extensive; to extend the limits of (a territory, enclosure, etc.); to widen (boundaries)," clearly resonates with the conquering attributes of the play.[8] Zabina in 4.4 also uses "enlarge" with both meanings intact: "Let us live in spite of them, / Looking some happy power will pity and enlarge us" (4.4.97–8). Many scholars have pointed out the importance of geographical and cartographical measurement in the play. Emrys Jones has explored some of the implications of terrestrial space in Marlowe's *Tamburlaine* plays, including the plays' structural divisions and the plays' connections to contemporaneous innovations in painting.[9] Garrett Sullivan has pointed out that "the measured language of Tamburlaine coincides with both the actor's measured strides and the character's measurement of the lands he conquers."[10]

The ceremonial aspects of the play rely on what Ruth Lunney terms, "ritualisation of stage action" (173).[11] Both *Tamburlaine* plays, she argues "draw upon the conventional signs of power and loss of power, along with the conventional spatial signals of elevation and abasement. Positioning and distances are ceremonially determined."[12] She argues that the "most innovative feature of spatial rhetoric in the *Tamburlaine* plays, however, lies in a shift towards a more 'rhetorical' organisation of space."[13] For example:

> This 'rhetorical' effect is seen especially in the escalating extravagance of vertical positioning [...]/ In Part One, when Tamburlaine ascends to his throne by means of his unfortunate footstool, the movement relies upon traditional spatial language, but its effect is to show Tamburlaine himself as master of ceremonies, appropriating the signs of power, able to redefine himself as 'the chiefest lamp of all the earth' [*Tamb* 4.2.36] and his opponent as 'base villan' [*Tamb* 19].[14]

However, we might more thoroughly account for the force of Marlowe's powerful narrative by examining the stagecraft elements of the play directly connected to the space of the stage itself. These devices can be divided into questions of spatial control and questions of temporal experience, the speed with which events occur. A comparison of 1.1 and 1.2 can clarify some of the ways characters' movements and the control of the stage space develop the playgoers' comprehension of the events portrayed. The first character entrance of the play establishes a courtly space while verbally undermining the power of the first speaker Mycetes: "Brother Cosroe, I find myself aggrieved, / Yet insufficient to express the same" (1.1.1–2). Despite the markers of control of stage space evidenced by Mycetes entering with his court, and although Mycetes speaks first, and in a declarative mode, he claims essentially his lack of speech. His attempt to wield power '"I might command you to be slain for this / [...] might I not?" is immediately undermined by Meander denying it: "Not for so small a fault, my sovereign lord" (1.1.25). Already, as playgoers, the spatial markers have been disrupted. Mycetes manages to control some of the movement of the play when he dismisses Theridamas, but this control is short lived. When he orders Menaphon to follow Theridamas, Mycetes is quickly undermined by Cosroe: "Nay, pray you, let him stay" (1.1.87). Cosroe's mockery quickly, within fifteen lines, drives Mycetes himself to depart: "Meander, come, I am abused, Meander" (1.1.106), leaving Cosroe and Menaphon holding the stage space and available when Ortygius and Ceneus arrive "*bearing a crown, with others*" (1.1.135 SD). Obviously Mycetes' power is undermined – visually, verbally, spatially – before we playgoers see Tamburlaine.

Comparatively, Tamburlaine's appearance in 1.2, establishes control of stage space in terms that support Tamburlaine's power. His entrance, "*leading Zenocrate*," with multiple "*other* Lords" and "soldiers *loaden with treasure*," establishes Tamburlaine's power, and the remainder of the scene supports and develops that control of power through the spatial control of the stage (1.2.sd). The entrance of a soldier with news of "A thousand Persian horsemen are at hand" leads Tamburlaine to claim – to the lords and to Zenocrate – "You must be forced from me ere you go" (1.2.120). When Techelles says, "Come, let us march," Tamburlaine refuses to move. Instead he requests, "Stay, Techelles, ask a parley first" and even more forcibly, "Keep all your standings, and not stir a foot. / Myself will bide the danger of the brunt" (1.2.150–1). The rhetorical imperatives and the stage spaces combine here to indicate and develop Tamburlaine's control over the space in which these characters exist.

In *Tamburlaine*, 1.2 also introduces another useful effect for the play, an effect of simultaneity developed through the use of asides. When Theridamas enters he, surprised by Tamburlaine's appearance, describes in an aside how his expectations of a "Scythian shepherd" did not prepare him for how

> His looks do menace heaven and dare the gods,
> His fiery eyes are fixed upon the earth,

As if he now devised some stratagem,
Or meant to pierce Avernus' darksome vaults
And pull the triple-headed dog from hell. (1.2.154–61)

We then immediately have an exchange between Tamburlaine and Techelles, speaking to one another, lines that clearly Theridamas cannot hear. Essentially Tamburlaine and Techelles' speeches (asides to one another) set one part of the stage as theirs and Theridamas' speech of wonder sets another part of the stage as his. These two sets of speech establish simultaneity in that, as playgoers, we understand them to be temporally simultaneous. The effect though is one of slowing the events. The similar nature of their responses to one another supports the similarity of the experiences for Theridamas and Tamburlaine. In disbelief Theridamas asks, "A Scythian shepherd, so embellished / With nature's pride and richest furniture?" (1.2.155–6). Astounded, Tamburlaine says "With what a majesty he rears his looks!" (1.2.165). Of course Theridamas is enfolded into Tamburlaine's plans. Spatially reinforcing that closing, the scene ends with all the characters leaving together.

The opening line of act two makes clear that our understanding of the stage space must be different than it was in the first act. Cosroe opens the act with "Thus far are we towards Theridamas," emphasizing the movement that is structurally supported by the brevity of the scene. The opening of 2.2 likewise emphasizes movement when Mycetes says: "Come, my Meander, let us to this gear." In 2.3 playgoers return to Cosroe and Tamburlaine, in a swift back and forth emphasizing the temporal speed of both the plot and the action, Cosroe: "Now, worthy Tamburlaine, have I reposed/ In thy approvèd fortunes all my hope." In the midst of this fast-paced act, 2.4 offers an unusually explicit stage direction: "*to the battle* and Mycetes *comes out alone with his crown in his hand, offering to hide it.*" The opening stage direction is usually expanded in modern editions to "*[Enter the armies] to the battle [and exeunt] and Mycetes comes out alone with his crown in his hand, offering to hide it.*" This opening ensures that playgoers are unusually aware of the important action taking place offstage, while we are suddenly – with Mycetes' entrance – left out of that action for the moment. When Tamburlaine enters at line 16, we are aware that he too has left the main action happening offstage. The events of the scene confirm the reversal of spatial experience.

Although Tamburlaine obviously holds the crown in his hands, (Mycetes says, "Come, give it me"), Tamburlaine *does* return it. In the reversed moments of the short forty-two-line scene, we playgoers are privy to a reversed situation where Tamburlaine does not act as he has and will throughout the rest of the play. Simultaneously other important events are occurring offstage while we experience events in some form of "backstage." I have already discussed in Chapter 4 how a similar technique in the dagger scene in *Macbeth* allows the establishment of activity elsewhere that adds privacy to the remaining moment on the stage. We are aware of the events occurring in the battle melee, yet we remain in this now more private space with Mycetes and Tamburlaine. We are allowed as witnesses to something doubly private.

Despite modern editors' quibbles with the placement of scene breaks in *Tamburlaine, Part One*, the shifts in locations and character changes show a clear pattern in the play. The first act and final act have longer stretches of scenes and the middle acts of the play depend on shorter, quicker scenes. The final act, if marked as one scene, is the longest scene of the play. These shifts in the numbers and lengths of the scenes clearly produce the changes in speed of the action. The shorter scenes quickly move the playgoers between locations and characters and increase the momentum. The long sustained final scene offers playgoers the spatially enclosed and geographically static cage that contains Bajazeth, a stage property that itself helps to maintain and develop the closure offered at the end of the play. Much of the power of the play depends on the concerted effects of control of stage space in combination with the rhetorical emphasis on movement and location.

The importance of control of stage space arose in playwrights before Shakespeare and continued in other later playwrights of the early modern period. A popular play both in its period and in production ever since, *The Duchess of Malfi* (1614) offers fascinating examples of stage space in a play that constantly toys with the notion that we, as playgoers, might be bafflingly tricked or completely aware. Or we might be both at the same moment: accepting a trickery of which we are fully aware. The showing of the wax figures to the Duchess in 4.1 is a much examined example of spectacular effects in the play. In her illuminating discussion of the difficulties of staging the play, Lois Potter has shown some ways that productions strive for a "successful fusion of the realistic and dreamlike qualities of the play."[15] These elements in the play, which have been seen as disparities or have caused difficulties for productions, frequently rely on differences established between the play and the effect on the playgoers. Ought we to recognize the figures as wax figures or as bodies? How do we reconcile the fact that the figures are probably embodied by the actors who were playing the roles in the play? Webster's play develops many of its effects through careful control of the stage space. An examination of the long scene 4.2, which includes the Duchess' death, reveals many of these stagecraft elements.

Given the length of the scene and its inclusion of complicated entrances and exits, it will be helpful to review the series of events and the order in which they are presented. The scene begins with the Duchess and Cariola. A servant enters with news of the madmen's imminent appearance; the madmen appear, perform, and depart. Bosola enters "*like an old man;*" the executioners enter about fifty lines later.[16] The executioners are on stage for about sixty-five lines before the Duchess says, "Come, violent death" (4.2.226). Then Cariola's strangling occurs within ten lines of the order to strangle her, immediately after which Ferdinand enters. He departs before Bosola recognizes, "She stirs! Here's life" (4.2.330), and the Duchess then dies (according to a stage direction) twelve lines later.

Part of the Duchess' power in the scene arises, despite her confinement, from her absolute control over and constant inhabitation of the stage space. Her discussion with Cariola emphasizes what they hear outside their space and muses on the prison, but uses visual description to escape the space in which they are confined: "Th' heaven o'er my head seems made of molten brass; / The earth of flaming sulphur" (4.2.24–5). With language relating to the stage space in which she finds herself, the Duchess comments to Bosola,

> I know death hath ten thousand several doors
> For men to take their exits; and 'tis found
> They go on strange geometrical hinges,
> You may open them both ways. (4.2.211–14)

She immediately continues the line to reconnect "way" to the means of exiting: "Any way, for heaven sake, / So I were out of your whispering" (4.2.214–15). Despite her desire and description of escape, the long scene and her presence on the stage emphasize her spatial confinement. The protracted engagement of the executioners develops the inexorability of the Duchess' death, while her own actions establish her physical position for her death: "they that enter there / Must go upon their knees" (4.2.225–6). The Duchess' movements in this scene determine much of the stage imagery presented to playgoers. In ways deeply connected to the control of the stage space, Webster's stagecraft develops the emotional tension of the scene.

Attention to these stagecraft elements, and the ways they work in concert with the language of movement and location, may improve our understanding of early modern plays by playwrights other than Shakespeare. When we go to the theater, we go with the anticipatory desire that the performance will provide us with enough stage-illusion to transport us. As playgoers engaged in the collaborative work of producing and understanding the stage-illusion, our own role cannot be underestimated.

Notes

1. Norman Rabkin, "Rabbits, Ducks, and *Henry V,*" *Shakespeare Quarterly* 28.3 (1977): 279–96.
2. Rabkin, "Rabbits, Ducks," 279–80.
3. More recently, Jeanette Dillon's work has examined how stagecraft elements inflect our readings of the history plays, particularly in relation to the source materials on which Shakespeare depended.
4. See particularly chapter five: "Theatre as a Spatial Art" (Henry S. Turner, *The English Renaissance Stage: Geometry, Poetics, and the Practical Spatial Arts 1580–1630* (Oxford: Oxford University Press, 2004): 154–85).
5. John Pitcher's excellent introduction in the Arden series edition of *The Winter's Tale* (London: Methuen, 2010) sets out the generic frames at work in the play; this quotation comes from page 39.
6. John D. Jump notes that, according to Philip Henslowe's diary, "between August 28, 1594, and November 13, 1595, the Lord Admiral's Men acted Part I fifteen times and Part II seven times." Christopher Marlowe, *Tamburlaine the Great, Parts I and II*, edited by John D. Jump (Lincoln: University of Nebraska Press, 1967).
7. Jump, ed. *Tamburlaine the Great, Parts I and II*: these quotations are from 3.3.46–7. Subsequent quotations have in-text citations. This definition appears in the *Oxford English Dictionary* at v.II.6a.
8. *Oxford English Dictionary*, v.II a.
9. Emrys Jones, "'A World of Ground': Terrestrial Space in Marlowe's *Tamburlaine* Plays," *Yearbook of English Studies* 38.1–2 (2008): 168–82.

10. Garret Sullivan, "Space, Measurement, and Stalking Tamburlaine," *Renaissance Drama* 28.1 (1997): 3–27, 23.
11. Ruth Lunney, *Marlowe and the Popular Tradition: Innovation in The English Drama Before 1595* (Manchester: Manchester University Press, 2002), 173.
12. Lunney, *Marlowe and the Popular Tradition*, 173.
13. Ibid., 174.
14. Ibid., 174–5.
15. Lois Potter, "Realism Versus Nightmare: Problems of Staging *The Duchess of Malfi*," in *The Triple Bond: Plays, Mainly Shakespearean, in Performance* (University Park: Pennsylvania State University Press, 1975): 170–89, 189.
16. Quotations are taken from Leah S. Marcus' Arden Early Modern Drama edition of *The Duchess of Malfi* by John Webster (London: Methuen, 2009). This stage direction appears at 4.2.113; all subsequent quotations have in-text citations.

Bibliography

Baldo, Jonathan, *Memory in Shakespeare's Histories: Stages of Forgetting in Early Modern England* (London: Routledge, 2012).
Banister, Richard, *Banister's Breviary of the Eyes*, in Jacques Gillemeau, *A treatise of one hundred and thirteene diseases of the eyes, and eye-liddes. The second time published, with some profitable additions of certaine principles and experiments, by Richard Banister* (London: Felix Kynston for Thomas Man, 1622); STC 12499.5, Folger Call Number STC1362.
Beale, Simon Russell, "Hamlet," in *Players of Shakespeare 5*, ed. Robert Smallwood (Cambridge: Cambridge University Press, 2003), 145–177.
Berry, Ralph, *Shakespeare's Comedies: Explorations in Form* (Princeton: Princeton University Press, 1972).
Booth, Stephen, "On the Value of *Hamlet*," in *Reinterpretations of Elizabethan Drama*, ed. Norman Rabkin (New York: Colombia University Press, 1969), 74–93. Reprinted in *Critical Essays on Shakespeare's* Hamlet, ed. David Scott Kastan (London: Prentice Hall, 1995), 19–42.
Bradbrook, Muriel, *Themes and Conventions of Elizabethan Tragedy* (Cambridge: Cambridge University Press, 1935).
Braunmuller, A.R., (ed.), *Macbeth*, by William Shakespeare (Cambridge: Cambridge University Press, 1997).
Brooks, Harold (ed.), *A Midsummer Night's Dream*, by William Shakespeare (London: Thomson Learning, 1974).
Brown, John Russell, "The Setting for Hamlet," in *Stratford Upon Avon Studies 5:* Hamlet, eds. John Russell Brown and Bernard Harris (London: Edward Arnold, 1963), 163–184.
———, *Shakespeare and the Theatrical Event* (Houndmills: Palgrave Macmillan, 2002).
———, *The Shakespeare Handbooks:* Hamlet (Basingstoke: Palgrave, 2006).
Carroll, William, (ed.), *Macbeth*, by William Shakespeare (Boston: Bedford, 1999).
Chapman, George, *Blind Beggar of Alexandria* (London: William Jones, 1598), STC 4965.
Clark, Stuart, *Vanities of the Eye: Vision in Early Modern European Culture* (Oxford: Oxford University Press, 2007).
Cohen, Brent M., "'What is it you would see?' Hamlet and the Conscience of the Theatre," *ELH* 44.2 (1977), 222–247.
Coleridge, Samuel Taylor, *Lectures and Notes on Shakespeare and Other English Poets*, T. Ashe, ed. (London: George Bell, 1897).
Cook, Albert, "Space and Culture," *New Literary History* 29.3 (1998), 551–572.
Coursen, H.R., "Shakespeare in the Sticks," *Shakespeare Quarterly* 36.5 (1985), 644–647.

Crooke, Helkiah, *Mikrokosmographia: A Description of the Body of Man. Together with the Controversies Thereto Belonging*, (London: William Jaggard, 1615), STC 6062.
Dallington, Robert, *A Method for Travell. Shewed by taking the view of France. As it stoode in the yeare of our Lord 1598*, (London: Thomas Creede, [1603]), STC 6203.
Dent, R.W. "Imagination in *A Midsummer Night's Dream*," *Shakespeare Quarterly* 15.2 (1964), 115–129.
Dessen, Alan, *Elizabethan Drama and the Viewer's Eye* (Chapel Hill: University of North Carolina Press, 1977).
Dessen, Alan, and Leslie Thomson, *A Dictionary of Stage Directions in English Drama 1580–1642* (Cambridge: Cambridge University Press, 2001).
Dillon, Janette, *Shakespeare and the Staging of English History* (Oxford: Oxford University Press, 2012).
Dobrée, Bonomy, "*The Tempest*," 1952, in *Twentieth Century Interpretations of The Tempest*, ed. Hallett Smith (Englewood Cliffs: Prentice-Hall, 1969), 47–59.
Duncan-Jones, Katherine, (ed.), *Sir Philip Sidney* (Oxford: Oxford University Press, 1989).
Edgerton, Samuel Y., *The Mirror, the Window, and the Telescope: How Renaissance Linear Perspective Changed Our Vision of the Universe* (New York: Cornell University Press, 2008).
Edwards, Philip, (ed.), *Hamlet*, by William Shakespeare (Cambridge: Cambridge University Press, 2003).
Egan, Gabriel, "Hearing or Seeing a Play?: Evidence of Early Modern Theatrical Terminology," *Ben Jonson Journal* 8 (2001), 327–347.
Evans, G. Blakemore (ed.), *The Riverside Shakespeare*, 2nd edn. (Boston: Houghton Mifflin, 1997).
Ewbank, Inga-Stina, "*Hamlet* and the Power of Words," *Shakespeare Survey* 30 (1977), 56–78.
Farabee, Darlene, "*Antony and Cleopatra* and *Romeo and Juliet*," *Shakespeare Bulletin* 29.2 (2011), 196–204.
———, "*A Midsummer Night's Dream* and *Othello*," *Shakespeare Bulletin* 30.2 (2012), 181–188.
Fitzpatrick, Tim, *Playwright, Space and Place in Early Modern Performance: Shakespeare and Company* (Aldershot: Ashgate, 2011).
Fletcher, Angus, *Time, Space, and Motion in the Age of Shakespeare* (Cambridge, MA: Harvard University Press, 2007).
Forker, Charles, (ed.), *Richard II*, by William Shakespeare (London: Thomson, 2002).
Foakes, R.A., (ed.), *A Midsummer Night's Dream*, by William Shakespeare (Cambridge: Cambridge University Press, 1984).
Frey, Charles, "*The Tempest* and the New World," *Shakespeare Quarterly* 30.1 (1979), 29–41.
Frye, Northrop, (ed.), *The Tempest*, by William Shakespeare (New York: Penguin, 1959).

Garber, Marjorie, *Shakespeare After All* (New York: Anchor, 2004).
Gillies, John, *Shakespeare and the Geography of Difference* (Cambridge: Cambridge University Press, 1994).
Gossett, Suzanne, (ed.), *Pericles*, by William Shakespeare and George Wilkins (London: Thomson, 2004).
Granville-Barker, Harley, *Preface to Hamlet* (New York: Hill and Wang, 1957).
Grene, Michael, *Shakespeare's Serial History Plays* (Cambridge: Cambridge University Press, 2002).
Gurr, Andrew, "*The Tempest*'s Tempest at Blackfriars," *Shakespeare Survey* 41 (1989), 91–102.
Hakluyt, Richard, *The Principall Navigations, Voiages and Discoueries of the English nation, made by Sea or ouer Land, to the most remote and farthest distant Quarters of the earth at any time within the compasse of these 1500 yeares: Deuided into three seuerall parts, according to the positions of the Regions whereunto they were directed* (London: George Bishop and Ralph Newberie, 1589), STC 12625.

———, *The principal navigations, voiages, traffiques and discoueries of the English nation, made by sea or ouer-land, to the remote and farthest distant quarters of the earth, at any time within the compasse of these 1500. yeeres: deuided into three seuerall volumes, according to the positions of the regions, whereunto they were directed. This first volume containing the woorthy discoueries, &c. of the English ... and the famous victorie atchieued at the citie of Cadiz, 1596. ... By Richard Hakluyt Master of Artes, and sometime student of Christ-Church in Oxford* (London: George Bishop, Ralph Newberie, and Robert Barker, 1598–1600), STC 12626.
Harbage, Alfred, *Annals of English Drama 975–1700*, revised S. Schoenbaum (Philadelphia: University of Pennsylvania Press, 1964).
Hartley, Andrew James, "A Dream of Campus," *Shakespeare Survey* 65 (2013), 194–210.
Higgins, Iain Macleod, *Writing East: The "Travels" of Sir John Mandeville* (Philadelphia: University of Pennsylvania Press, 1997).
Hillman, David, *Shakespeare's Entrails: Belief, Scepticism and the Interior of the Body* (Basingstoke: Palgrave, 2007).
Hinman, Charlton, (ed.), *Mr. William Shakespeares Comedies, Histories & Tragedies* (New York: Norton, 1968).
Hiscock, Andrew, *The Uses of this World: Thinking Space in Shakespeare, Marlowe, Cary and Jonson* (Cardiff: University of Wales Press, 2004).
Hodges, C. Walter, *Enter the Whole Army: A Pictorial Study of Shakespearean Staging: 1576–1616* (Cambridge: Cambridge University Press, 2004).
Holland, Peter, (ed.), *A Midsummer Night's Dream*, by William Shakespeare (Oxford: Oxford University Press, 1994).
Homan, Sidney, "*The Tempest* and Shakespeare's Last Plays: The Aesthetic Dimensions," *Shakespeare Quarterly*. 24. 1 (1973), 69–76.
Hulme, Peter, *Colonial Encounters: Europe and the Native Caribbean 1492–1797* (London: Routledge, 1992).

Hulme, Peter and William H. Sherman, (eds.), *The Tempest*, by William Shakespeare (New York: Norton, 2004).
Ichikawa, Mariko, *Shakespearean Entrances* (London: Palgrave Macmillan, 2002).
Jenkins, Harold, (ed.), *Hamlet* by William Shakespeare (London: Arden/Methuen, 1982).
Johnson, Samuel (ed.), *Macbeth* in *The plays of William Shakespeare in eight volumes, with the corrections and illustrations of various commentators; to which are added notes by Sam Johnson* (London: J and R Tonson, 1755), 367–484.
Jones, Emrys, *Scenic Form in Shakespeare*, 1971 (Oxford: Oxford University Press, 1985).
Jones, Emrys, "'A World of Ground': Terrestrial Space in Marlowe's *Tamburlaine* Plays," *Yearbook of English Studies* 38.1–2 (2008), 168–182.
Jonson, Ben, *Bartholomew Fair* in *Three Comedies*, ed. Michael Jamieson (New York: Penguin, 1966), 325–460.
Kermode, Frank, (ed.), *The Tempest*, by William Shakespeare (London: Methuen, 1954).
Kingsley-Smith, Jane, *Shakespeare's Drama of Exile* (Basingstoke: Palgrave, 2003).
Kinney, Arthur, "Macbeth's Knowledge," *Shakespeare Survey 57* no.1 (2004), 11–26.
Kittredge, George Lyman (ed.), *Macbeth* by William Shakespeare (Boston, MA: Ginn and Co, 1939).
Knight, G. Wilson, *The Shakespearian Tempest*, 1932 (London: Methuen, 1953).
Knights, L.C., "*The Tempest*" in *Shakespeare's Late Plays*, eds. Richard C. Tobias and Paul G. Zolbrod (Athens: Ohio University Press, 1974), 15–31.
Kranz, David, "The Sounds of Supernatural Soliciting in *Macbeth*," *Studies in Philology 100*, no.3 (2003), 346–383.
Langer, Susanne, *Feeling and Form* (Upper Saddle River, NJ: Prentice-Hall, 1977).
du Laurens, Andreas, *A Discourse of the Preservation of the Sight: of Melancholike Diseases; of Rheumes, and of Old Age*, trans. Richard Surphlet (London: Felix Kingston for Ralph Jacson, 1599) STC 7304.
Lefebvre, Henri, *The Production of Space*, trans. Donald Nicholson-Smith (Oxford: Blackwell, 1991).
Lindley, David, (ed.), *The Tempest*, by William Shakespeare (Cambridge: Cambridge University Press, 2002).
Loomba, Ania, *Colonialism/Postcolonialism: The New Critical Idiom* (London: Routledge, 1998).
Lopez, Jeremy, *Theatrical Convention and Audience Response in Early Modern Drama* (Cambridge: Cambridge University Press, 2003).
———, "Eating *Richard II*," *Shakespeare Studies* 36 (2008), 207–228.
———, *The Shakespeare Handbooks:* Richard II (Basingstoke: Palgrave Macmillan, 2009).
———, "*Dream*: The Performance History," in A Midsummer Night's Dream*: A Critical Guide*, ed. Regina Buccola (London: Continuum, 2010), 44–73.

Lucking, David, "Imperfect Speakers: Macbeth and the Name of King," *English Studies* 87.4 (2006), 415–425.
Lunney, Ruth, *Marlowe and the Popular Tradition: Innovation in The English Drama Before 1595* (Manchester: Manchester University Press, 2002).
Mack, Maynard, "The World of Hamlet," *Yale Review* 41.4 (1951–1952), 502–523.
Malone, Edmond, ed. *The plays and poems: of William Shakspeare, in ten volumes; collated verbatim with the most authentick copies, and revised: with the corrections and illustrations of various commentators.* London: J. Rivington and Sons, 1790.
Marlowe, Christopher, *Tamburlaine the Great, Parts I and II*, ed. John D. Jump (Lincoln: University of Nebraska Press, 1967).
Marlowe, Christopher, *Christopher Marlowe: The Complete Plays*, eds. Frank Romany and Robert Lindsey (New York: Penguin, 2003).
McCarthy, Mary, "General Macbeth," *Harper's Magazine* (June 1962), 35–39; reprinted in *Macbeth* ed. Sylvan Barnet, 2nd rev. edn. (New York: Signet, 1998), 157–167.
McDonald, Russ, *Shakespeare's Late Style* (Cambridge: Cambridge University Press, 2006).
McInnis, David, *Mind-Travelling and Voyage Drama in Early Modern England* (Basingstoke: Palgrave Macmillan, 2013).
McMillin, Scott, "Shakespeare's *Richard II*: Eyes of Sorrow, Eyes of Desire," *Shakespeare Quarterly* 35.1 (1984), 40–52.
McMullan, Gordon, "What is a 'late play'?" in *The Cambridge Companion to Shakespeare's Late Plays*, ed. Catherine M.S. Alexander (Cambridge: Cambridge University Press, 2009), 5–27.
McNeir, Waldo, "*The Tempest*; Space-Time and Spectacle-Theme," *The Arlington Quarterly* 2.4 (1970), 29–58.
Muir, Kenneth, (ed.), *Macbeth* by William Shakespeare (London: Thomson, 1962).
Norwood, Richard, *The Sea-Mans Practice, Contayning a Fvndamentall Probleme in Navigation, experimentally verified: namely, Touching the Compasse of the Earth and Sea, and the quantity of a Degree in our English measures. Also an exact method or forme of keeping a Reckoning at Sea, in any kinde or manner of sayling. With certayne Tables and other rules usefull in Navigation, As also in the Plotting and Surveying of places. The Latitude of the principall places in England. The finding of Currents at Sea; and what allowance is to bee given in respect of them* (London: George Hurlock, 1637), Wing N1360.
Orgel, Stephen, "Prospero's Wife," in *The Tempest*, by William Shakespeare, eds. Peter Hulme, and William H. Sherman (New York: Norton, 2004), 201–215.
Orgel, Stephen, (ed.), *The Tempest* by William Shakespeare (Oxford: Oxford University Press, 1987).
Palmer, D.J., "'A new Gorgon': Visual Effects in *Macbeth*," in *Focus on Macbeth*, ed. John Russell Brown (London: Routlege & Kegan Paul, 1982), 54–69.

Palmer, Sir Thomas, *An Essay of the Meanes how to make our Travailes, into forraine Countries, the more profitable and honourable* (London: Mathew Lownes, 1606), STC 19156.
Parker, Patricia, *Shakespeare from the Margins: Language, Culture, Context* (Chicago: University of Chicago Press, 1996).
Pennington, Michael, *Hamlet: A User's Guide* (New York/London: Limelight Editions/ Nick Hern Books, 1996).
Pitcher, John, (ed.), *The Winter's Tale* by William Shakespeare (London: Methuen, 2010).
Poole, Kristen, *Supernatural Environments in Shakespeare's England: Spaces of Demonism, Divinity, and Drama* (Cambridge: Cambridge University Press, 2011).
Potter, Lois, "Realism Versus Nightmare: Problems of Staging *The Duchess of Malfi*," in *The Triple Bond: Plays, Mainly Shakespearean, in Performance* (University Park: Pennsylvania State University Press, 1975).
———, "A Brave New *Tempest*," *Shakespeare Quarterly* 43.4 (1992), 450–455.
de Quincey, Thomas, "On the Knocking at the Gate in Macbeth," in *The London Magazine July to December 1823 Vol VIII* (London: Taylor and Hessey, 1823), 353–356.
Rabkin, Norman, "Rabbits, Ducks, and *Henry V*," *Shakespeare Quarterly* 28.3 (1977), 279–296.
Rackin, Phyllis, "The Role of the Audience in *Richard II*," *Shakespeare Quarterly* 36.3 (1985), 262–281.
Ralegh, Sir Walter, *The Discoverie of the Large, Rich and Bewtiful Empyre of Guiana*, 1596, ed. Neil L. Whitehead. (Norman: University of Oklahoma Press, 1997).
Reiman, Donald, "Appearance, Reality, and Moral Order in *Richard II*," *Modern Language Quarterly* 25.1 (1964), 34–45.
Rosenberg, Marvin, *The Masks of Hamlet* (Newark: University of Delaware Press, 1992).
———, *The Masks of Macbeth* (Newark: University of Delaware Press, 1978).
Scaliger, Julius Caesar, *Exotericarum Exercitationum Liber Qvintvs Decimvs, de Svbtilitate, ad Hieronymvm Cardanvm* (Lvtetiae [Paris]: Michaelis Vascosani, 1557).
Schell, E.T., "Who Said That—Hamlet or *Hamlet*?," *Shakespeare Quarterly* 24.2 (1973), 135–146.
Shakespeare, William, *The Riverside Shakespeare*, 2nd edn. ed. G. Blakemore Evans (Boston: Houghton Mifflin, 1997).
Sher, Antony, "Leontes and Macbeth," in *Players of Shakespeare 5*, ed. Robert Smallwood (Cambridge: Cambridge University Press, 2003), 91–112.
Shewring, Margaret, "Staging *Richard II* for a new millennium," in *Richard II: New Critical Essays*, ed. Jeremy Lopez (London: Routledge, 2012), 135–162.
Shickman, Allan, "The 'Perspective Glass' in Shakespeare's *Richard II*," *Studies in English Literature, 1500–1900* 18.2 (1978), 217–228.

Sidney, Sir Philip, *Profitable instructions;describing what speciall obseruations are to be taken by trauellers in all nations, states and countries; pleasant and profitable. By the three much admired, Robert, late Earle of Essex. Sir Philip Sidney. And, Secretary Davison 1613* (London: Benjamin Fisher, 1633), STC 6789.

———, *The Defence of Poesy*, in *The Oxford Authors: Sir Philip Sidney*, ed. Katherine Duncan-Jones (Oxford: Oxford University Press, 1989).

Smith, Emma, *Macbeth: Language and Writing* (London: Bloomsbury, 2013).

Smith, Bruce R., *The Acoustic World of Early Modern England: Attending to the O Factor* (Chicago: University of Chicago Press, 1999).

———, "Taking the Measure of Global Space," *Journal of Medieval and Early Modern Studies* 43.1 (2013), 26–48.

de Sousa, Geraldo, *At Home in Shakespeare's Tragedies* (Farnham: Ashgate, 2010).

Spurgeon, Caroline, *Shakespeare's Imagery and What It Tells Us* (Cambridge: Cambridge University Press, 1965).

Stewart, Alan, *Shakespeare's Letters* (Oxford: Oxford University Press, 2009).

Stoppard, Tom, *Rosencrantz and Guildenstern are Dead* (New York: Grove Weidenfeld, 1967).

Stradling, Sir John, *A Direction for Trauaillers. Taken out of Ivstvs Lipsius, and enlarged for the behoofe of the right honorable Lord, the yong Earle of Bedfored, being now ready to trauell* (London: Cutbert Burbie, 1592), STC 15696.

Styan, J.L., *Shakespeare's Stagecraft* (Cambridge: Cambridge University Press, 1971).

Sullivan, Garret A. Jr., "Space, Measurement, and Stalking Tamburlaine," *Renaissance Drama* 28.1 (1997), 3–27.

———, *Sleep, Romance and Human Embodiment* (Cambridge: Cambridge University Press, 2012).

Thompson, Ann and Neil Taylor, (eds.), *Hamlet* by William Shakespeare (London: Thomson, 2006).

Tillyard, E.M.W., *Shakespeare's History Plays* (London: Chatto & Windus, 1951).

Tompkis, Thomas, *Lingua, or The Combat of the Tongue and the Five Senses for Superiority* (London: N. Okes, [1607]).

Traversi, D.A., *An Approach to Shakespeare* (New York: Anchor, Doubleday, 1969).

Tribble, Evelyn, "'When Every Noise Appalls Me': Sound and Fear in *Macbeth* and Akira Kurosawa's *Throne of Blood*," *Shakespeare* 1.1–2 (2005), 75–90.

Turner, Henry S., *The English Renaissance Stage: Geometry, Poetics, and the Practical Spatial Arts 1580–1630* (Oxford: Oxford University Press, 2004).

Vaughan, Alden T., "William Strachey's 'True Reportory' and Shakespeare: A Closer Look at the Evidence," *Shakespeare Quarterly* 50.3 (2008), 245–273.

Vaughan, Virginia Mason and Alden T. Vaughan, (eds.), *The Tempest*, by William Shakespeare (London: Thomson Learning, 2001).

Vaughan, Virginia Mason, "*The Tempest* (Review)," *Shakespeare Bulletin* 27.3 (2009), 468–471.

Walsh, Brian, "The dramaturgy of discomfort," in *Richard II: New Critical Essays*, ed. Jeremy Lopez (London: Routledge, 2012), 181–201.

Warburton, William, (ed.), *Macbeth* by William Shakespeare in *The Works of Shakespear in Eight Volumes*, vol. 6 (London: J&P Napton, 1747).
Webster, John, *The Duchess of Malfi*, ed. Leah S. Marcus (London: Methuen, 2009).
Wells, Stanley, and Gary Taylor, (eds.), *William Shakespeare: The Complete Works* by William Shakespeare (Oxford: Oxford University Press, 1986).
Wilders, John, (ed.), *Antony and Cleopatra* by William Shakespeare (London: Arden/ Routledge, 1995).
Wood, Robert E., "Space and Scrutiny in *Hamlet*," *South Atlantic Review* 52.1 (1987), 25–42.
Woodruff, Paul, *The Necessity of Theater: The Art of Watching and Being Watched* (Oxford: Oxford University Press, 2008).

Theatre productions

A Midsummer Night's Dream, by William Shakespeare, directed by Charles McMahon, Lantern Theater, Philadelphia PA, March 10 – April 17, 2011.

A Midsummer Night's Dream, by William Shakespeare, directed by Mark Lord, Goodhart Theater, Bryn Mawr PA, November 10–18, 2006.

A Midsummer Night's Dream, by William Shakespeare, directed by Bob Hall, Flatwater Shakespeare at Lincoln Foundation Garden, Lincoln NE, June 15–26, 2011.

A Midsummer Night's Dream, by William Shakespeare, directed by the Repertory Company of the Actors' Renaissance Season, Blackfriars Playhouse, Staunton VA Jan–Mar 2009.

The Tempest, by William Shakespeare, directed by Jim Warren, Blackfriars, Staunton VA, June–December 2011.

Index

Note: "n" after a page reference denotes a note number on that page.

American Shakespeare Center *see* Blackfriars Playhouse
asides 3–4, 7, 29, 40n32, 67n1, 84, 147, 159–60, 163–4

Bacon, Francis, *Advancement of Learning* 38n14
Baldo, Jonathan 47, 67n8, 68n14
banishment *see* exile
Banister, Richard, *Breviary of the Eye* 16, 33, 38n2–3, 40n37
Beale, Simon Russell 95n26
Berry, Ralph 19, 35, 38n13, 40n33, 41n40
Blackfriars Playhouse 11, 36, 41n41, 133–4, 148, 151n18
Booth, Stephen 88, 89, 96n52, 96n53, 97n58
Bradbrook, Muriel 40n32
Braunmuller, A. R. 119, 122n5, 124n42, 125n45, 125n46
Brooks, Harold 37n1, 41n42
Brown, John Russell 76, 77, 85–6, 94n19, 94n20, 94n24, 95n26, 96n44

Carroll, William 122n5
Chapman, George, *Blind Beggar of Alexandria* 26, 39n23
Clark, Stuart 16, 38n7, 38n8
Cohen, Brent M. 17–18, 38n11
Coleridge, Samuel Taylor 3, 14n3
Cook, Albert 94n10
Coursen, H. R. 41n43
Crooke, Helkiah, *Mikrokosmographia* 19–20, 23, 33–4, 38n6, 39n15, 40n38, 123n16

Dallington, Robert, *A Method for Travell* 2, 14n2
Dent, R. W. 39n27
Dessen, Alan 40n29
Dillon, Janette 28, 40n30, 67n2, 68n15, 167n3
Dobrée, Bonomy 153n32
doubling roles 24–5, 63, 69n33

Edgerton, Samuel 16–17, 38n9
Edwards, Philip 77, 86, 94n21, 95n30, 95n34, 96n46
Egan, Gabriel 14n7
entrances and exits 5–7, 12, 17–18, 28–9, 32, 40n31, 45, 48, 66–7, 67n10, 74, 79–80, 85, 89–92, 94n11, 96n51, 96n54, 100, 109, 111, 116, 118–19, 140–1, 157, 159, 166–7
Etzold, Lee Ann 21–2, 39n17
Evans, G. Blakemore 18, 41n42, 90, 95n30, 95n34, 123n20, 145, 152n25, 153n35
Ewbank, Inga-Stina 87, 96n48
exile (or banishment) 50, 52–3, 56–9, 68n26, 69n26, 82–3, 95n36, 106, 133, 137, 139, 149
exits *see* entrances and exits

First Folio
  act and scene breaks 96n54, 150n10
  generic divisions 155
  line arrangement 61, 68n17, 94n25
  punctuation 140
  speech prefix 41n42
  stage direction 29, 32, 45, 48, 67n10, 75, 85, 94n12, 96n42, 100, 117, 120, 121, 124n37, 153n37
  word choice 123n9, 123n20

177

Fitzpatrick, Tim   40n29
Fletcher, Angus   102, 122n7
Foakes, R. A.
Forker, Charles   44, 60, 61, 65, 67n6, 67n10, 68n18, 68n19, 68n22, 68n24, 69n30, 69n31, 69n32, 69n34
Frey, Charles   149n1

Garber, Marjorie   153n36
genre   3, 13–14, 35, 40n40, 63–5, 70–1, 127, 145–9, 155–8, 160–1
ghost   70–5, 77–80, 88–90, 94n11, 95n27, 96n54, 102–3, 107, 111, 114–15, 120–1
Gillies, John   129, 150n6, 150n9, 154n43
Globe Theatre   11, 154n43
Gossett, Suzanne   14n5
Granville-Barker, Harley   72, 76, 93n4, 94n19, 95n30
Grene, Michael   59, 69n27, 69n28
Gurr, Andrew   150n10

Hakluyt, Richard, *Principall Navigations*   138, 152n24
Hall, Bob   25, 28, 36, 39n20
Harbage, Alfred   123n17
Hartley, Andrew James   12, 14n10
Higgins, Iain Macleod   152n23
Hillman, David   75, 94n14
Hiscock, Andrew   83, 95n37, 95n38
Hodges, C. Walter   89, 97n56
Holland, Peter   18, 26, 38n12, 39n22, 39n24, 39n25
Homan, Sidney   150n13
Hulme, Peter   128, 150n6, 150n8
Hulme, Peter and William H. Sherman   141, 152n29

Ichikawa, Mariko   40n31, 96n51, 96n54, 153n39

Jenkins, Harold   93n2, 94n11, 95n30, 95n31, 95n33, 95n34, 96n49
Johnson, Samuel   122n3

Jones, Emrys   40n36, 94n16, 119, 121, 124n34, 125n47, 130, 150n11, 162, 167n9
Jonson, Ben, *Bartholomew Fair*   128, 150n5
Jump, John D.   167n6, 167n7

Keegan, James   134
Kermode, Frank   140, 152n27, 153n41
Kingsley-Smith, Jane   58, 68n26
Kinney, Arthur   123n21
Kittredge, George Lyman   98, 101, 119, 122n2, 122n5, 124n41
Knight, G. Wilson   150n12
Knights, L. C.   153n36
Kranz, David   122n4

Langer, Susanne   116, 124n34
Lantern Theatre   21, 39n17
du Laurens, Andreas   16, 38n4, 38n5, 95n29
Lefebvre, Henri   110–11, 124n23
letters   95n39, 117, 118
Lindley, David   127–8, 150n4, 151n14, 153n35
location   1–5, 12–14, 17, 31–3, 44, 46–8, 54, 64, 70, 71–5, 79, 82–3, 86–93, 98–104, 107–8, 110–11, 116–17, 120–2, 129–30, 132–6, 138–9, 144, 157, 165
Loomba, Ania   128, 150n7, 150n8
Lord, Mark   39n19
Lopez, Jeremy   36–7, 40n32, 41n44, 43, 55–6, 60, 66, 67n5, 68n25, 69n29, 69n35, 132–3, 151n16
Lucking, David   123n14
Lunney, Ruth   162, 168n11–14

Mack, Maynard   70, 93n1
magic (as plot device)   20, 24, 31–2, 114–15, 145, 156
Mandeville, John, *Mandeville's Travels*   138, 152n23
Marcus, Leah S.   168n16
Marlowe, Christopher, *Tambourlaine, Part One*   161–5, 167n6

McCarthy, Mary   123n19
McDonald, Russ   148, 151n17, 153n38, 153n40
McInnis, David   8–9, 14n6
McMahon, Charles   39n17
McMillin, Scott   67n4
McMullen, Gordon   153n41
McNeir, Waldo   132, 150n13, 151n15
measurement of distance   52, 88, 105–6, 134–5, 146, 161–2
Muir, Kenneth   101, 122n6, 123n17, 124n22

normalizing character   30–1, 62–3, 64, 90, 120
Norwood, Richard, *The Sea-Man's Practice*   134, 151n20

offstage action   6, 50, 53–4, 56, 72, 96n51, 98, 100–1, 113, 164–5
Orgel, Stephen   140, 152n26, 153n33

Palmer, D. J.   118, 124n35, 124n40
Palmer, Sir Thomas, *An Essay of the Meanes*   142, 153n31
Parker, Patricia   39n18, 40n27, 95n36
Pennington, Michael   95n28
perspective   3, 5, 14, 19–22, 30, 34, 38n14, 43, 51, 65, 67n3, 92, 158
  linear perspective   16–17, 38n9, 112–13
Pitcher, John   167n5
play-within-the-play   27, 35–6, 82–3, 90
Poole, Kristen   38n9
Potter, Lois   149, 154n42, 165–6, 168n15

de Quincey, Thomas   112–13, 124n24–9

Rabkin, Norman   158, 167n1–2
Rackin, Phyllis   46, 68n13

Ralegh, Sir Walter, *Discoverie of Guiana*   138, 152n24
Reed, Parker   11
Reiman, Donald
Robbins, Sanford   149
Rosenberg, Marvin   76, 94n18, 96n40, 96n43, 103, 123n10, 123n11

Scaligar, Julius Ceasar   105, 123n16
Schell, E. T.   92, 97n62
Sea Venture   126
Shakespeare, William
  All's Well That Ends Well   39n26
  Antony and Cleopatra   90, 97n60, 97n61
  As You Like It   39n26, 40n28
  Cardinio   153n41
  Comedy of Errors   142, 156–7
  Cymbeline   32, 34, 143–4, 148, 153n41, 155
  Hamlet   13, 39n26, 40n32, 68n11, **70–93**, 98, 111, 114, 120, 158
  1 Henry IV   34
  2 Henry IV   34
  Henry V   1, 3, 5–6, 157–8
  1 Henry VI   6–7
  2 Henry VI   68n16, 68n23
  3 Henry VI   68n16
  Henry VIII   153n41
  King John   94n16
  King Lear   31, 39n26, 58, 158–9
  Love's Labors Lost   157
  Macbeth   9–10, 13, 46–7, **98–122**, 158, 165
  Measure for Measure   39n26
  The Merchant of Venice   157
  A Midsummer Night's Dream   12, **15–37**, 42–44, 45, 49, 62, 68n12, 70, 75, 78, 94n12, 94n23, 100, 114, 127, 155–7
  Much Ado About Nothing   39n26
  Othello   6, 138, 159, 160
  Pericles   3–4, 5, 14n5, 148, 153n41

Shakespeare, William – *continued*
  Richard II 13, 38n14, **42–67**,
    70–1, 76, 99, 104, 111, 136, 157
  Richard III 7–8
  Romeo and Juliet 11, 34, 39n26,
    44, 57–8
  The Taming of the Shrew 157
  The Tempest 12–14, 39n26, 122,
    126–49, 155, 160–1
  Troilus and Cressida 150n3
  Twelfth Night 2, 40n28, 139
  Two Gentlemen of Verona 29
  Two Noble Kinsmen 153n41
  The Winter's Tale 40n32, 114,
    139, 144, 148, 153n41, 159–61
Sher, Antony 114, 124n30–2
Shickman, Allan 67n3
Sidney, Sir Philip, *The Defence of
  Poesy* 17, 38n10, 71–2, 93n3
Sidney, Sir Philip, *Profitable
  Instructions* 138, 151n22
sightlines 11, 46, 49–50, 75, 77
Smith, Bruce R. 72–3, 93n8, 104,
  117, 123n12, 124n36, 126,
  150n2
Smith, Emma 119, 124n43
de Sousa, Geraldo 123n8
sleeping characters 24–5, 32–5,
  40n39, 106–7, 135–6
soliloquy 3–4, 7–9, 21–2, 29–30,
  40n32, 42–3, 46, 62, 67n2,
  96n40, 100–3, 111, 139, 157
Spurgeon, Caroline 106, 123n18
stagecraft 1, 3–6, 10, 12, 13–14, 33,
  64, 109, 155, 159–61, 166–7
Stewart, Alan 117, 124n38–9
Stoppard, Tom 97n57
Stradling, Sir John, *A Direction for
  Trauailers* 142, 152n30

Styan, J. L. 10, 14n8, 32, 40n35,
  40n36
Sullivan, Garrett 34, 40n39, 162,
  168n10
Suphlet, Richard 16
surveying 51–2

Thomson, Leslie 40n29
Thompson, Ann and Neil
  Taylor 77, 83, 94n19, 94n22,
  94n25, 95n30, 95n34, 95n35,
  96n49
Tillyard, E. M. W. 44–5, 67n9
Tomkis, Thomas, *Lingua* 105,
  123n17
Traversi, D. A. 73, 87, 93n9,
  94n15, 96n47
Tribble, Evelyn 104, 123n13
Turner, Henry S. 4–5, 14n4, 40n34,
  68n21, 158–9, 167n4

Vaughn, Alden T. 149n1
Vaughn, Virginia Mason and Alden
  T. Vaughn 141, 152n28,
  153n32, 153n36

Walsh, Brian 44, 67n7
Warburton, William 98, 122n1,
  122n3
Webster, John, *The Duchess of
  Malfi* 165–7, 168n16
Wells, Stanley and Gary
  Taylor 97n60
Wilders, John 97n60
Wilkins, George 153n41
Williams, George Walton 125n46
Wood, Robert E. 96n50
Woodruff, Paul 72, 93n5, 93n6,
  93n7, 119, 121, 125n44

The manufacturer's authorised representative in the EU is Springer Nature Customer Service Centre GmbH, Europaplatz 3, 69115 Heidelberg, Germany. If you have any concerns regarding our products, please contact ProductSafety@springernature.com

Printed and bound by CPI Group (UK) Ltd, Croydon, CR0 4YY
23/03/2026
02076673-0008